B2

12
8

The Healing Power
of Doing Good

The Healing Power of Doing Good

THE HEALTH AND SPIRITUAL BENEFITS OF HELPING OTHERS

Allan Luks

WITH PEGGY PAYNE

FAWCETT COLUMBINE · NEW YORK

A Fawcett Columbine Book
Published by Ballantine Books
Copyright © 1991 by Allan Luks and Peggy Payne

Grateful acknowledgment is made to The Fetzer Foundation and
Joan Borysenko for permission to reprint excerpts from "Healing
Motives: An Interview with David C. McClelland" by Joan
Borysenko from *Advances: The Journal of Mind-Body Health,* Spring,
1988.

Library of Congress Cataloging-in-Publication Data
Luks, Allan,
The healing power of doing good : the health and spiritual
benefits of helping others / Allan Luks with Peggy Payne. — 1st ed.
p.   cm.
Includes bibliographical references.
ISBN 0-449-90451-2
1. Altruism. 2. Volunteers—Psychology. 3. Voluntarism-
-Psychological aspects.   I. Payne, Peggy.   II. Title.
BF637.H4L85   1991
158'.3—dc20   91-37771
                                                 CIP

Text design by Debby Jay

Manufactured in the United States of America

First Edition: January 1992

10 9 8 7 6 5 4 3 2 1

Contents

Acknowledgments

Karen, Rachel, and David. My parents. David Kriser for his constant support. Gerry Goodman. The staff and board of trustees of the Institute for the Advancement of Health, especially the aid of T. George Harris, Neal Miller, Jim Autry, and Norman Cousins on this work. Howard Anderson. The staff and board of Big Brothers/Big Sisters of New York City. The more than three thousand volunteers and the wonderful organizations where they do their helping that participated in the survey on their health experiences. And Peggy Payne, who created this book's authoritative yet personal, caring narrative style.

—ALLAN LUKS

Thanks to all the people who were willing to tell their stories . . . and to the many others who helped in the research, including: Peter Bieler, Carol Bilbro, Bob Dick, Georgann Eubanks, Bill Finger, Patty Gibson, Ardis Hatch, Bob Lane, Lacy Maddox, Penelope Maunsell, Trudy Nelson, Suzanne Newton, Margaret Payne, Bob Phillips, Betsy Preston, Bink Prichard, Mahan Siler, Ann Smith, Nick Stratas, Brenda Summers, Harriett Taylor, Wayne Townsend, and Linda Williamson. And most of all thanks to Allan Luks, who has been so helpful and easy to work with that he must be on a constant helper's high.

—PEGGY PAYNE

The authors would also like to offer special thanks to Beth Rashbaum, Joëlle Delbourgo, and Barbara Lowenstein, who worked together to bring this book into being.

—ALLAN LUKS AND
PEGGY PAYNE

The Healing Power
of Doing Good

Introduction

THE search that has led me to understand how helping others can profoundly affect the health of the helper began as nothing more than a vague feeling.

Most of my career has been spent working with organizations that are engaged in efforts to make life better for other people. In addition I do volunteer work in New York City, where my family and I live. That is how I gradually came to recognize how often I experience sensations of pleasure and well-being while involved in helping.

A few years ago I began to suspect that I was not the only person who had stumbled upon these unexpected gains. The more I heard others talk, the more I wanted to understand this intriguing phenomenon that seemed to have almost magical effects. I had personal evidence that something beyond what was immediately apparent was going on because my own attraction to helping other people was so powerful and persistent. In fact I had shaped my adult life around finding opportunities to help people, from my first tentative efforts in the civil rights movement, to a stint in the Peace Corps in Venezuela, to a period of years in East Harlem as a community-action lawyer, followed by work heading an alcoholism agency that helped many thousands of individuals and families. In each situation I knew—I could feel it—that when I was doing for others, I was also doing for myself.

Then, in 1987, I took the position of executive director at the Institute for the Advancement of Health, an agency founded by physicians and scientists from leading medical schools and hospitals. The institute acted as a clearinghouse for information on mind-body interactions, the link between health and our emotions, stress, and behaviors. There I read about new research in several nations that showed how people involved with others were likely to be healthier than those who led isolated lives. Although these studies did not focus only on helping acts, they made me realize that there was some scientifically verifiable basis for what I had sensed about my own experiences of helping.

I had always thought that people who work in the human service fields have a tremendous opportunity to observe and make discoveries in the same manner as "hard" scientists. The ten years I spent teaching at the Fordham University Graduate School of Social Services showed me how often the world at large has served as a laboratory for human relations, revealing things about human nature that would never come out in an actual lab.

As I pursued the subject, I began to meet people whose experiences showed that helping could in fact be good for your health. One was Judy Weintraub, then secretary of a committee of organizations concerned with crime prevention, which met regularly at the United Nations. Judy, who has multiple sclerosis, had found that through helping other people she could actually diminish the effects of the disease and that her own strength and muscular control would increase for a short period of time.

A second person I talked with was a recovering alcoholic, who told me that when she had first become abstinent, she had volunteered to work on a telephone hot line. She was on the phone every day from two to five P.M. at the local office of Alcoholics Anonymous. Though she never met any of the people she helped, the effect on her personal well-being was dramatic. "I would come home and tell my husband I was euphoric from this phone work," she said. "It was like taking a drug. And believe me, I knew what a drug high was. Except this one lasted far longer."

A member of the board of trustees of the alcoholism agency and then of the Institute for the Advancement of Health, a man who had been my friend in addition to my colleague, David Kriser was another good example. At eighty-three years old, he was a very active helper as well as a philanthropist. He was also childless and living alone. I wondered if his helping might be part of what kept his health and spirits good. When I asked him about it, he told me that it was in fact critical. Indeed Kriser believed this so strongly that once my research into the subject began to take shape, he provided a grant to bring together some of the most prominent scientists in the mind–body field to discuss the health effects of helping.

In late 1987 I needed to move from the research clues and personal stories I had found to a wider sampling of people's actual experiences. *Better Homes and Gardens* published a small item on the research in the February 1988 issue calling for readers to write me at the institute about any health improvements they felt they had received from helping others.

The letters began to come in from all over the country, a first wave of about 250 responses. This is what researchers call an open-ended survey, a question with no specific boxes to check or sentences to complete. People are free to write whatever they want. The survey began immediately to show some clear results. When I performed a line-by-line analysis, circling the words that were repeated over and over in these often long and unstructured letters, a pattern began to emerge. Many people were reporting that as a result of their helping they were experiencing a rush of physical pleasure and well-being, increased energy, warmth, and actual relief from aches and pains. It was obvious that something very exciting was going on.

Many of those who wrote supervised volunteers and spoke not only of their own experience but of a larger picture:

- Belva Green, Allen County Cancer Society in Fort Wayne, Indiana: "We see it daily. We have several hundred volunteers who perform a great variety of services willingly and cheerfully. They seem to live longer and fuller lives than the folks occupied only with inner concerns."

- Dick Bullock, community educator, Carthage, Missouri: "Once volunteers feel the 'life enrichment' of helping, they get 'hooked.'"

- Yvonne Coakley, chairman of volunteers, American Red Cross, Pomona, California: "The relationship of altruism to health should be apparent to all thinking people."

The following month *American Health* published a piece I had written on the connections I had identified between health and helping. At the same time I began to work on confirming the findings by developing a survey that was more carefully controlled than the initial request for letters. This resulted in a seventeen-question survey document with forty-three possible answers. I designed this questionnaire with the help of Howard Andrews, Ph.D., a biopsychologist and senior research scientist with the New York State Psychiatric Institute. Andrews reviewed the questions to make sure we would get answers that were as clear and unbiased as possible. The confidential, anonymous questionnaire was distributed to 3,300 volunteers at more than twenty organizations throughout the nation that had contacted me about their interest in this work. It went to people with a broad range of experiences and backgrounds, including helpers of AIDS patients, homeless families, shut-ins, crime victims, runaway youths, and patients in giant urban hospitals. Volunteers in Appalachia, mental health aides in Illinois, people working in Colorado prisons, women executives who assist disabled children, and Florida workers with the elderly were among those who received the form. Then there was nothing to do about this part of the research but wait.

In the meantime a group of mind-body scientists came together in New York in June 1988, at a conference sponsored by David Kriser. At this meeting I presented the findings from the letters people wrote in response to the *Better Homes and Gardens* piece. The roster for this gathering was impressive, including Herbert Benson, the Harvard Medical School cardiologist and author of *The Relaxation Response*; Dean Ornish, the San Francisco physician and author of *Dr. Dean Ornish's Program for Reversing Heart Disease*, whose work has shown how decreasing feelings of hostility helps to reverse cholesterol buildup in the arteries; Neal Miller, Ph.D., who at Rockefeller University pioneered the development of biofeedback as a means of helping people gauge the effect of their emotions on their bodies; Suzanne Kobasa, Ph.D., of the City University of New York's Graduate Center, developer of the hardiness concept, which links several specific positive attitudes to better health; Kenneth Pelletier, Ph.D., at the University of California at San Francisco, who has studied the relationship between health and spirituality; Jaak Panksepp, Ph.D., at Bowling Green State University, who has performed leading research on the biochemistry of emotional bonding; and other researchers in the mind-body field. All of these scientists observed that there was indeed a significant phenomenon here, that it was "reasonable to advance the hypothesis" that altruistic behaviors enhance the helper's health, although there was probably no one single mechanism to explain this relationship.

Dr. Benson left that meeting with more than a hypothesis. He left with a new treatment technique that he was ready to put into action. At the New England Deaconess Hospital, part of Harvard Medical School, Benson directed one of the largest clinics focused on stress-linked problems. Among those treated were cardiac patients and people troubled by chronic pain, as well as others whose daily functioning was impaired because of high tension levels. Back in Boston, in addition to continuing to involve patients in exercise and meditative relaxation programs, Benson began prescribing volunteering to some as a vital step in achieving good health. And he began to get good results. In one stress-reduction class, for example, there was a woman in her mid-sixties who worked as a domestic. She had come because of severe angina pain, which had incapacitated her. In the program she learned relaxation techniques—breathing and concentration exercises. But what she found, Benson said to me, was that in order to really relax, she had to go out and teach the stress-reduction techniques to others. This teaching—as a volunteer in a school—enabled her to sustain her health. Though she continued to take her angina pills, the pain and incapacitation that she had previously suffered, despite the medication, went away.

During that same period *Reader's Digest* reprinted the article published earlier in *American Health*. And I appeared on the "Today" show to talk about what the stories in the letters could mean, both for individuals and for our whole society.

When the volunteer questionnaire responses came in,

they were astonishing. People's comments on not just the psychological benefits but also the physical effects added to the powerful testimonials about helping's healing potential that I had received in the letters. In the space at the end of the form people wrote additional notes about their experiences. For example,

"I got very excited for the individuals I helped. I felt very in control of myself and my body. I am a runner, and I felt I ran better than ever before. I felt very strong physically. Almost like nothing could conquer me. You want so much to help others, and when you do and see their reactions, you feel so good inside that it makes you explode with energy."

"Some months ago I was so stressed out that I could barely get four hours' sleep at night and I had all sorts of aches and pains. I had even tried antidepressant and anti-anxiety drugs, but to no avail. I then found out firsthand that it is love that truly heals. When I do nice things, I definitely feel a physical response. For me it is mostly a relaxation of muscles that I hadn't even realized had been tensed. . . . I can now sleep well at night, and most of my aches and pains have disappeared."

A total of 3,296 surveys were returned to me by volunteer organizations. After a computerized analysis of the survey by Howard Andrews, the man who helped me design the questionnaire, the cause-and-effect relationship between helping and good health became clear. Initial results from the first 1,500 surveys were published in *Psychology Today*, and the "Today" show called and said, "Come back on."

As my research became more widely publicized, it came to the attention of Nancy Jameson, director of the Retired Senior Volunteer Program (RSVP) in Carthage, Illinois. She sent me a copy of a 1976 federal study of the program, the results of which my survey was now helping to explain. At sites throughout the country the federally assisted RSVP encourages people over sixty to volunteer in hospitals, clinics, schools, and other service programs and institutions. The evaluators interviewed people at seventy sites, talking at each site with several senior volunteers as well as staff members, administrators, and advisory council members for the program. The study found that at 98 percent of these facilities the physical and mental health of the volunteers had improved significantly. But why? The report had only been able to guess.

Now, with the findings from my survey, it has become evident that the dramatic improvements in health produced by helping have specific, identifiable stages. They begin with a physical high, a rush of good feeling. What I now call helper's high involves physical sensations that strongly indicate a sharp reduction in stress and the release of the body's natural painkillers, the endorphins. This initial rush is then followed by a longer-lasting period of improved emotional well-being. In effect, helping produces within the helper a two-part response—the healthy helping syndrome.

My study also showed how to proceed in order to receive the most powerful health benefits out of our efforts to help others. A clear set of guidelines has emerged from the research that demonstrates how to maximize the health-enhancing effects. Helping others can truly be one of our most self-serving acts.

The research for this book provided further confirmation of the truth of my original findings. When my coauthor, Peggy Payne, set out to find volunteers to interview whose lives had been changed by their helping, there were two surprises still to come. One was how very easy these people were to find. There was no reason to limit our search simply to those who had responded to the magazine article or the questionnaire. Everywhere, it seemed, there were people with stories to tell. The second surprise was the nature of the stories themselves: So many of them asserted that the experience of helping had become the turning point in the person's life.

In the town of Woodsfield, Ohio; in New York City; in Los Angeles; and in several other cities, Peggy spent time with volunteers, sometimes watching them at work. She also did in-depth phone interviews with helpers in every region of the country. In a few instances names and identifying details have been changed because of the intimate nature of the experience described.

The stories Peggy and I heard and the findings from the surveys I've described combine to show helping's vast potential for the good of both the individual and the world we live in. Our study indicated that once people become involved in healthy helping acts, they experience strong benefits and therefore are motivated to help all the more. Their empathy for others, for strangers, grows, and their health improves. Unlike research into the health benefits of such other activities as exercise, the new knowledge about helping holds the power to affect not only the health of the individual but the health of our entire tension-ridden society.

—ALLAN LUKS

1

The Healthy Helping Phenomenon

ON a hot, muggy day in July at a racetrack in Virginia, a young woman in a wide-brimmed straw hat stood in the stands watching her boyfriend race his high-powered sports car around the long winding course of the track. It was the summer of 1967, and Randee Russell was twenty-one, a senior in college. She had seen several races in the four years she and "Michael" had been going together. But it was this race on this morning that would change her life, with ramifications that would propel her, some twenty years later, to a discovery of the healing power that can lie in helping another person. On this morning she stood in the bleachers with Michael's father, ignoring the heat, tracking with her eyes the familiar silver car as Michael rounded the course and roared past.

All around her, heads turned together, following the cars. She had him in sight as he went into the curve. She was still watching at the moment when his car lost traction, slid sideways, started to spin. For one second she stood motionless while the spinning car, with Michael in it, lifted completely off the ground. It was airborne and still turning, as if the propeller of a helicopter had come off and was whirling in slow motion. Then a heavy thud rang out across the field as the car smashed into a utility pole and there was a direct hit at the driver's seat. Randee threw off her hat and started to run, Michael's father ahead of her, the medics rushing from the side of the field.

The rescue team pulled Michael from the wreck. Except for a thin line of blood on his lips, he looked unhurt. He seemed to Randee to be sleeping. Then she heard his father say, "He's dead."

It didn't seem possible. She didn't believe it.

She watched as the race cars slowed to let the ambulance carrying Michael drive across the track on its way off the field. The cars slowed once again, minutes later, to let Randee and the others leave. On the way back to the hotel she saw the ambulance from the car window . . . stopped at a service station. The driver, unhurried, was standing out on the pavement feeding change into a soft-drink machine. She couldn't understand it: Why wasn't he rushing to take Michael to the hospital? The truth was still not real to her.

She never saw Michael again.

Almost twenty years passed before she fully came to terms with the reality of Michael's death and what it meant to her. "For a year afterward," she said, "I thought I would get a call saying that this was all an elaborate joke." Though she went on with her life, for years after that day, she was still intermittently preoccupied with death. For months at a time and longer she would think that she had fully recovered, until some trigger, perhaps the sight of a highway accident, would bring it all up again, and again her days would be interrupted by split-second fantasies of her own destruction, her nights haunted by dreams that Michael was still alive.

Finally, at the age of thirty-nine, she took the action that eventually freed her to face that death and end her fear. She became a volunteer.

"I was . . . looking for something to be devoted to," she said. She decided to become a volunteer for Hospice of Los Angeles, to spend time helping people who were dying. In choosing this kind of work Randee had begun to realize that trying to banish the images of death wasn't going to work, that instead she needed to look straight at it. "I mainly wanted to desensitize myself," she said. "I thought if I hung out with people who were dying, it wouldn't be such a bogeyman."

Her first patient was "Alice," a woman who was enraged by the fact of her illness and who would not accept that she was dying. Alice's demands began to wear on Randee. Nothing Randee could do seemed to satisfy her. She felt that she could not help Alice, and she eventually quit trying. But—most important—she did not give up on her effort to help. She pulled herself together to give it another try with a different patient. "If I had given up after Alice, I wouldn't have gotten Jane," she said. And it was helping "Jane" that so dramatically changed her life.

An elderly woman with terminal lung cancer, Jane had been told that she had three months to live. Randee was to help make those three months as comfortable as possible for her and her family. "It's a very one-sided story," Randee said later. "I got a lot from her." The two became very attached to each other, both of them sad that they had not met years earlier when Jane was well. When Jane went on living, it became easy for Randee to think that she wasn't going to die soon after all, even though Jane was rapidly deteriorating and no one could fail to notice the physical changes. And then for a few beguiling weeks she looked so beautiful, Randee said, "thin and radiant like a young Katharine Hepburn." This was the time when she began to say her good-byes.

"Then the day came." It was an afternoon Randee hadn't planned to visit, but with a bit of extra time on her hands she decided, on the spur of the moment, to drop by. The light was low in Jane's bedroom, the shades drawn. Beside the bed was Jane's husband of almost fifty years, one of their daughters, and a friend. Then she saw Jane. "I knew what I was witnessing was a death rattle, the whole body shutting down." Randee found that her training with Hospice had prepared her well for this moment. But no one in the room could bear to let Jane die. Jane's friends and family talked of getting her to the hospital.

Jane, however, had been very clear that she wanted to die at home, without heroic measures. Randee took each of Jane's loved ones aside and reminded them of that. And so together they all decided not to make the phone call for an ambulance.

In the dim light Randee watched as, one after another, each person resolved to let Jane go if the time had come. As that happened, and in the calm that ensued, the light seemed to rise in the room. It actually seemed to become brighter. And then, finally, the labored breathing stopped. "There was this absolutely silent, massive wind in the room . . . as if there was a tornado going through there that was totally quiet." Jane had died.

The family withdrew to another room then, and in a little while a nurse arrived. Together Randee and the nurse washed and straightened Jane's body, tucking the sheets around her, as if they were tucking a child into bed. It was an intimate and loving farewell. For Randee that farewell was a gift.

As she took care of Jane's body that afternoon, she felt a surge of physical life and strength.

By sunset it was time to leave Jane's apartment, and she hurried to the beach, to the park in Santa Monica that she and Jane both loved. She got there before the light was gone. "I saw everything there was to see in that sunset," she said. "It was a huge spiritual experience.

"Having been there, I felt as though I had been part of

a wonderful event." Randee had first set out to be "de-sensitized" to the fact that we die, but instead the reverse had happened. Being in that room brought death close in a way that made her more sensitive both to living and to dying. Death, which she had known only as a sudden, unbelievable nightmare, was now natural, powerful, and truly part of life. The difference in actually feeling it happen was "kind of like the difference between thinking about being pregnant and actually being pregnant . . . all the millions of little physical changes that happen."

The euphoric feeling that came over her that afternoon lasted for about ten days. For a month after that she found that she was untroubled by daily irritations or problems with her work. Almost three years later she still feels the effect of that day. The violent fantasies and nightmares have ended, and with a new sense of peace, at the age of forty-three, Randee became pregnant for the first time. By helping another person face death she helped herself most of all.

THE FINDINGS

Randee's story is a remarkable example of how in helping others we help ourselves. Her experience clearly shows what people have long known at the back of their minds: that doing good makes you feel good. This book will demonstrate, through medical and survey data as well as through the firsthand stories of individual helpers, that this health improvement is a real and reliable phenomenon and that it works to improve physical and psychological health, as well as enhancing feelings of spiritual well-being. My research has shown that it is the *process* of helping, without regard to its outcome, that is the healing factor.

This process can be effective to some degree for virtually every sort of human ill. Regular helping of others can diminish the effects of disabling chronic pain and lessen the symptoms of physical distress. And it can ease the tension of able-bodied people who are overworked and living in stressful times.

Specifically our national survey resulted in the following observations:

- *The healthy helping syndrome has different phases.* A total of 95 percent of the volunteers reported that personal helping on a regular basis gives them an immediate physical feel-good sensation, which I call helper's high. This is phase one of the healthy helping syndrome.

- *The "high" has clear and definite components.* Nine out of ten helpers experienced one or more of a characteristic set of physical and emotional sensations during this rush, involving sudden warmth and increased energy, as well as a sense of euphoria.

- *Phase two of the healthy helping syndrome brings a sense of calmness.* This second, longer-lasting phase involves feelings of increased self-worth, calm, and relaxation.

- *People who experience the healthy helping syndrome have better perceived health.* Volunteers who reported these specific sensations were more likely than other helpers to view their health as better than that of others their age. Survey respondents often dated their perception of being in superior health to the beginning of their helping efforts.

- *The health benefit returns whenever the helping act is remembered.* Nearly eight out of every ten volunteers said the good feelings of the healthy helping syndrome would return, though in diminished intensity, when the helping act was remembered.

- *The greater the frequency of volunteering, the greater the health benefits.* There was a ten times greater chance that volunteers who said they were healthier than others would be weekly rather than once-a-year helpers. Again, the helpers reported that the specific improvements they noticed in their health—ranging from less pain and fewer colds to overall well-being—coincided with their greater frequency of volunteering.

- *Personal contact with the people being helped is important.* Those who had personal contact with the people they helped were more likely to experience the feel-good sensation than those who did not have a one-to-one experience. And respondents with personal contact were more likely to become more frequent and therefore healthier helpers.

- *Helper's high results most from helping people we don't know.* Helping strangers, not just family and friends, was correlated with the greatest chance of experiencing helper's high. Those who only aided family and friends were the helpers least likely to report this arousal.

- *Certain experiences are particularly effective.* Volunteers credited societal influences—actual helping experiences and concern for the community—as a motivator in making them regular helpers slightly more often than they cited parental or religious teaching. When available, family and religion are of course powerful influences; however, today we see increasing family breakups and a decline in religious observance. This finding indicates that we can turn to public efforts to promote helping on a large scale.

- *Men and women have an equal opportunity to benefit from this high.* Men and women experienced this high in equal proportions—95 percent of each reported it.

THE JOY OF HELPING

Not long after the study was completed, I discussed these results at a meeting in San Francisco sponsored by the national organization Volunteer. Over one thousand representatives of private and government-sponsored volunteer organizations were present. The responses I received were virtually identical: "You're not telling us anything new. Of course there are health benefits!" But the value of the study is not so much in its novelty as in its explanation of *how* helping improves health and what *kinds* of volunteering produce the greatest benefits. With these data we now have material to motivate people to become regular helpers.

Without this knowledge the problem with volunteering for many people is that, from the outside, it may not look like a health-producing pursuit at all. Many of us share the same private reaction to requests for our assistance: "Me? A homeless shelter? Are you kidding?" Whether we admit it or not, the very thought of taking part in an activity that may involve going into rough neighborhoods or working closely with people who smell bad or look disreputable can be very off-putting. Further—in fact the obstacle most frequently cited—is finding the time. Most of us are already too busy. How can we find time to help? There is also the very real fear of being in emotionally overwhelming situations in which our stress level will increase rather than decrease. Then, too, there is the reluctance to get personally involved with strangers. And we are often uncomfortable starting a new and intimate activity on our own. As a result of these and other reasons many a volunteer has only gotten started by accident or by a weary sense of obligation. That's how I began.

I had grown up in the suburbs of New York, in Rock-

ville Centre on Long Island, a middle-class community
with few minorities. And though I was a very parochial
New Yorker—north meant the Catskill Mountains, and
south meant New Jersey—I was always interested in different cultures. So, as I reached college age, I decided to
major in international relations and to go to school in
another culture: the American South.

It was 1959 when I arrived in Chapel Hill, at the
University of North Carolina. The campus spilled into
the whole town. It was a village of huge shaded quadran-
gles, old brick sidewalks and classroom buildings, big oaks
and magnolias, and the white-columned Old Well that
was the symbol of the university.

The first thing I noticed was the heat. But I also took
note of something else that I wasn't at all prepared for in
those first days: segregation. I knew about it, I'd heard
about it, but I had never actually seen it the way I saw it
here. It opened my eyes. The school had one black student that I knew of, and there were fraternities that rewarded their pledges for eating in the restaurants that
maintained strict segregation. Everywhere I looked there
were public facilities posted with signs dividing them into
Colored and White sections.

I noticed this—and then I went on with my new life
as a college student. I jumped into the social life, joined
a fraternity, spent beach weekends at Myrtle Beach, took
the train down to New Orleans to Mardi Gras. At the
same time, by my sophomore year I couldn't help but see
that the world around me was starting to change rapidly.
With civil rights demonstrations becoming more frequent, the headlines were impossible to ignore. The civil
rights movement had begun. I wanted to do something to
help. Like many volunteers, I had grown up in a family
that encouraged a caring attitude toward all people.

There was also another reason for my interest in civil
rights. Starting at age fifteen I had worked as a busboy and

coat checker in a restaurant where my co-workers were mainly men who were black and poor. Sometimes after a night of clearing tables and hanging up wet fur coats, we used to go out together. In the course of those nights I came to what was at the time a startling realization—that these people were no different from me. So when, as a college student, I was faced with a legal system that argued that black people *were* somehow different, I wanted to do something on their behalf. But I didn't know what to do. I felt very hesitant, very uncertain and shy.

Finally I took one small action. A group called the Student Peace Union, which had formed to lobby for nuclear disarmament, had taken on the civil rights cause on campus. They were organizing a march against segregation by local businesses. I joined the march and walked down Franklin Street, the central street of this picturesque little town. It was a short walk, a few familiar blocks, and I was a sign holder, nothing more. I felt no connection through this act with the people I wanted to help. It seemed very remote. I felt as if my effort had failed; I returned to my regular routine.

But as it happened, the civil rights movement had not let go of me. After graduation from UNC I went to Georgetown Law School in Washington, D.C., where I was appointed in my third year to the job of editor of a student publication. By this time John F. Kennedy was president, peace signs were everywhere, and it was easier to find encouragement to work for social change. So I decided to redirect the focus of the magazine, making it a commentary on the human issues behind the legal ones, the fundamental realities behind the facts all of us were so busy memorizing.

The magazine was called *Res Ipsa Loquitur*, which means "the facts speak for themselves." Researching an article for this publication took me back to North Carolina—where I finally got involved.

Just before noon one Saturday in October 1966, four of us, all students, drove into Enfield, a small farming community in central North Carolina. More than half the town's three thousand residents were black, and in my reporter's capacity I intended to find out whether the Voting Rights Act was being enforced or whether blacks were still being denied the right to vote.

We were arriving at the close of a three-week voter registration drive. Evidence of tension was everywhere. Not far from the signs on the grocery window—Fatback 18¢ lb., Sausage 3 lbs. $1—were other signs that said, One Man—One Vote/For Freedom. People on the street caught sight of our racially mixed group, and their faces glowered with anger. Cars with Confederate flag insignia cruised slowly up and down the main street.

I was scared. I had never had any ambitions to be the hero type.

We turned off the main street onto a long, tree-shaded road, which led to the black side of town and to the home of Reed Johnson, funeral-home proprietor and leader of the Enfield branch of the Halifax County Voters Movement. Sitting in Johnson's living room, law students, white undergrads from Duke University, and local black high school students worked to plan a strategy for the day. In the midst of that session I kept noticing Reed Johnson, a man who was risking a great deal to help in this work.

Johnson was one of the many funeral parlor owners in the South who had become local black leaders of the civil rights movement. Since white mortuaries wouldn't handle the burials of black people, the black undertaker who became a rights advocate was free from economic retaliation from the white community. Yet none were free from the threat of other forms of retaliation.

Johnson didn't need recognition to advance himself financially; he was leading a comfortable life. I remember having iced tea and sandwiches in his large, well-furnished home. The night before, by contrast, we had slept in a wood shack on a country road, a house that was cold, lit only by a few hanging bulbs, and owned by a black family who wanted to be involved in the movement. Unlike the owners of this house, Johnson was a black man who was already leading a life of relative freedom and comfort. He decided to put himself on the line to help other black people. What was most striking about him was his ease, his confidence, his apparent sense of trust in himself. It didn't occur to me at the time that this might be because of and not in spite of the efforts he was making.

After our meeting at Johnson's house we went back to the main street with a plan. The younger students were to try to get blacks to come into the courthouse and register, and the law students were to monitor the registration procedures used.

The courthouse was flanked on one side by the police station and on the other by a large gray-cement "sportsman's hall." Men with rifles on their shoulders were walking past the courthouse where people had to enter to register. I noticed that these men kept going out and coming in again. If these were deer hunters, they were making very short hunting trips. They seemed to be doing nothing but patrolling the courthouse area. I asked a young black, who elaborated: "That's the Klan, man."

We found no irregularities in the voter registration that day. Everything was legal; everyone who sat down at the desk was registered. The problem was, not surprisingly, that there was a very low black voter turnout.

By the end of that day I had also made a discovery about myself. Without noticing what I was doing, I had put aside my notebook and become involved, gently talking to and reassuring the potential voters arriving at the courthouse. The excitement and the sense of satisfaction that came from that involvement, that effort to help, have guided the way I have lived my life ever since.

More than twenty years later I am now understanding what happened to me that day and why.

THE BIRTH OF THE CONCEPT OF STRESS AND THE MIND-BODY FIELD

The new information about the health benefits of helping is yet another page in the evolution of our understanding of how our behaviors, thoughts, and emotions can affect our well-being. The medical knowledge that lets us begin to understand helping's impact on the helper is based on scientific work, much of which burst forth in the 1970s, on how the mind interacts with the body, and on the much-misunderstood concept of stress and its effects.

The discovery of stress as a physiological state actually goes back to Hans Selye. More than fifty years ago, as a young Hungarian medical student studying in Prague, he observed an odd characteristic of many hospital patients. Many of them, regardless of the different natures of their various diseases, were suffering from the same constellation of symptoms—fatigue, weight loss, joint pains.

Some years later an accidental discovery in the laboratory brought these observations into sharper focus. His findings are related in his 1956 classic, *The Stress of Life*. In the 1930s, while at the Department of Biochemistry of McGill University in Montreal, he was engaged in research on sex hormones. He injected rats with various ovarian and placental extracts. With the first ovarian extracts he noticed an enlargement in the adrenal cortex and a reduction in the immune system's lymphocytes, as well as stomach ulcers. Selye became excited, concluding that his extracts must contain some new ovarian hormone. "You can well imagine my happiness! At the age of twenty-eight I already seemed to be on the track of a new hormone."

However, Selye went on to find that not only ovarian but also placental extracts produced these reactions—and then that extracts of the kidney, spleen, and other organs produced the same changes. His research continued until he finally began to understand what was happening: This negative body arousal was caused simply by the rat's experience of "getting a shot"; the content of the injections was not important.

With further sets of investigations he established that external experiences and traumas could indeed trigger a physiological response. He named this response *stress*, by which he meant the response of the body to any demand on it. This work led to the publication in the British journal *Nature*, July 4, 1936, of Selye's first paper explaining how the stress syndrome could be studied.[1]

Selye found that there could be good stress, which he called *eustress*, such as falling in love, as well as bad stress, or *distress*, such as the threat of an injury. Both initially arouse the body and produce similar physiological responses, including a racing heart and increased breathing rate, but the arousal caused by distress feels bad, is sustained longer, and goes on to damage our health.

The fight-or-flight response, an inherited survival instinct, illustrates the findings. The challenge that prompts this response, whether it is emotional or physical, good or bad, stimulates the sympathetic nervous system. This in turn sparks the adrenal glands to pump adrenaline into our bloodstream, giving us extra strength. In addition corticosteroids, which are powerful hormones, and adrenaline work together to release fatty acids into the bloodstream where they become energy for our muscles.

This arousal, if it is prolonged, as happens with distress, shifts from a source of strength and energy into a cause of deterioration. For example, corticosteroids, which are designed to reduce inflammation and tissue injury to help us fight, will also, over a prolonged period, suppress immune-system functioning. Increased adrenaline and corticosteroids, which in combination work to interfere with the action of insulin and thereby boost the amount of blood sugar available for immediate energy needs, can aggravate diabetes. And as the adrenaline-produced fatty acids needed for energy stay in the blood, the liver converts them into cholesterol, which can lead to arteriosclerosis. The speeded-up heart rate required for circulating body chemicals and oxygen for quick response to a threat will, if prolonged, increase the risk of high blood pressure, stroke, and heart disease.

The critical life goal, said Selye, is to find behaviors and techniques that interrupt and relieve the physical state of distress brought on by daily tensions. These could include religious services, hot baths, saunas, and meditation. But he emphasized that to diminish tension in our daily lives successfully, the new behavior would probably be one that requires some effort. Selye based his comment on the observations that both animal and man need to *act* in order to obtain benefits for themselves.

Selye developed a theory that he called altruistic egoism. This describes a way of life that would (in addition to many other benefits) help us to quiet our bodies' daily distress responses. It would require, he said, that we adopt behaviors that involve "the creation of feelings of accomplishment and security [in ourselves] through the inspiration in others of love, good will and gratitude for what we have done or are likely to do in the future." We experience these good feelings through helping others, he said, and the body will then shift out of its unhealthy arousal state into a more natural equilibrium.

FORTY YEARS OF MIND-BODY RESEARCH

It began to be clear from the work of Selye and other researchers that external events that do not actually touch the body can drastically affect our health because of the physiological responses evoked by our attitudes and emotions toward such events. Research on this phenomenon, much of it begun in the late fifties and early sixties, began to produce results in the early seventies, creating what seemed to be a sudden outpouring of new information.

Scientists at Johns Hopkins Medical School in Baltimore discovered that our brain produces its own morphinelike substances, such as endorphins, which not only kill pain but also produce powerful good feelings, even euphoria.

Swiss researcher Hugo Besedovsky found dramatic rises in the electrical activity in animal brains when the immune system goes into action; neuroscientist Karen Bulloch located the neurological communication pathways between the brain and the immune system; and J. Edwin Blalock discovered that immune cells produce the same chemical hormones previously thought to be only in the brain. What all of these findings tell us is that when an experience registers in the brain, it triggers electrical and chemical messages that may also travel to and affect the immune system, the body's first line of defense against infections.

Attitudes toward life, and how they stimulate the body, now became a fruitful subject of study. Evidence emerged that feelings of hopelessness and helplessness can be a significant health risk, while joy, optimism, and a sense of commitment seem to be good for physical and emotional health.

During the 1970s physicians Meyer Friedman and Ray

Rosenman, at the Mount Zion Medical Center in San Francisco, reported on some landmark work on healthy-versus-unhealthy attitudes. They showed that hostile, "Type A" people, who responded to life's tensions with aggression and anger, were more likely to experience higher cholesterol, triglyceride, and catecholamine levels—all known to be triggered by prolonged stress—which lead to increased risk of coronary problems. In fact the greater the hostility, the greater the amount of cholesterol clogging the arteries, the worse the angina symptoms, and the more frequent and severe the heart attacks. Their work confirmed a clinical suspicion dating back to the nineteenth century and released a wave of new investigations that quickly produced new conclusions regarding healthy-versus-unhealthy responses to external stressors.

The "negative," or unhealthy, responses to stressful events were found to include not only hostility but also feelings of helplessness, hopelessness, and isolation. University of Pennsylvania psychologist Martin Seligman has done work focusing on the damaging effects of feelings of helplessness. People who feel depressed and unable to take charge of improving their own lives experience weight loss, reduced appetite, ulcers, and other signs of stress. For example, a study of U.S. soldiers with the flu found that those who had previously been classified with a helpless-depressed personality trait took by far the longest time to recover.

Feelings of helplessness seem to make people more vulnerable to pathogens, Seligman says, a factor that can affect incidence of disease, recovery time, and even rate of death. "A variety of species," he writes, "from cockroaches to wild rats, from chickens to chimpanzees, from infant to aged human—seem to show death from helplessness." The immediate physical cause of death can come from a wide variety of causes: from infection to heart attack to malnutrition. Though no one physical common denominator has been isolated, a slowing of the heart is among the possibilities suggested. "The absence of physical uniformity, however, should not blind us to the reality of the phenomenon or to its regular psychological cause, the only single cause we can specify at this stage of our knowledge: helplessness, the perception of uncontrollability. . . . Death from helplessness is real enough."[2]

Continuing explorations of the unity of body and mind have shown that we can make conscious changes in our mental and emotional states that can be used to produce positive physical states. Herbert Benson, a Harvard Medical School cardiologist, found that in contrast to the condition of chronic tension into which so many of us fall, we can learn to produce what he calls the relaxation response. This is the physical state—hypometabolism, or slowed metabolism—that results when the body shifts out of a distress into a eustress response. The slower heart rate, decreased breathing rate and oxygen consumption, lower blood pressure, and reduced metabolism of this state have the potential to counteract the harmful effects and uncomfortable feelings created by persistent readiness for emergency action.

In *The Relaxation Response* Benson and coauthor Miriam Klipper described the evolution of this discovery, going back to the famous behavioral work of B. F. Skinner. Skinner's work illuminated the extent to which external environment determines behavior. In studies involving training pigeons to peck at a key for food pellets, Skinner succeeded in using external rewards to shape the animal's voluntary muscular behavior.

Then came the pioneering work on biofeedback of Neal Miller, Ph.D., of Rockefeller University. Miller showed that control of *involuntary* bodily processes was also possible. Operating on the idea that mental acknowledgment of a biological function allows one to take control of that function—for example, learning to ring a bell when you experience a certain feeling—Miller used rewards and punishments to train rats to control internal involuntary functions, such as blood pressure.

Results of this sort focused new attention on claims that had been made for centuries in the East. Practitioners of yoga and Buddhism had long been saying that they could control physiological function by meditation, which involves focusing on something other than their own thoughts—concentrating on their breathing or on a sound—and thus blocking out the causes of stress.

In 1968, according to Benson, practitioners of Transcendental Meditation came to Benson's laboratory at the Harvard Medical School, where he was studying the relation between a monkey's behavior and blood pressure. The TM practitioners asked to be studied; they felt that their meditation techniques allowed them to lower their own blood pressure. The test results were powerful: These people, during their practice of meditation, showed a significant decrease in oxygen consumption, in other words, a slowing of the metabolism. Therefore the body's resources during meditation were under less pressure. In addition alpha waves, slow brain waves that are generally present in people who are relaxed, increased in frequency and intensity.

A view of the physiological mechanisms at work came from the studies of Swiss Nobel Prize–winning physiologist Walter Hess, M.D. In experiments with cats Hess produced the changes associated with both states—hypermetabolic emergency readiness and hypometabolic deep relaxation—by stimulating different parts of the animal's hypothalamus. The slowed or hypometabolic processes that Hess described in the cat are what Benson calls, in humans, the relaxation response.[3] The work with the meditators was further proof that we do have the ability to affect our so-called involuntary bodily responses through our emotions, actions, and thoughts.

Out of the rapidly expanding field of mind-body research has also come the discovery that not only our individual emotions but our emotional ties to each other affect our physical well-being. Research into social relationships—why more isolated persons suffer increased risk of death—gained a new prominence in the mid-1970s. Studies revealed a dramatic decrease in health problems and death rates for people who are socially involved, compared with those who are isolated. A paper in the July 29, 1988, issue of the highly respected journal *Science* found that the data from such studies suggested that the lack of social relationships constitutes a major risk factor for health that rivals in importance the effects of such well-established health factors as cigarette smoking, blood pressure, blood lipids, exercise, and obesity.[4]

There is evidence that social support can protect people from diseases that range from arthritis to tuberculosis, as well as psychiatric illnesses.[5] In 1979 an important study by epidemiologists Lisa Berkman and Leonard Syme, of the University of California at Berkeley, examined the mortality of seven thousand randomly chosen residents of Alameda County, California, over a nine-year period. An index of social ties was assembled based on marital status, number of close friends and relatives, frequency of contact with these people, church attendance, and involvement in other groups. This well-known study found that the people with few social ties had mortality rates two to five times higher than those with more ties.[6]

In 1982 James House, chairman of the sociology department at the University of Michigan, found in a study of men in rural Georgia that during this time period those with multiple social ties were two to three times less likely to die than men without them. This was true for men of widely varying ages, backgrounds, and health conditions. It was becoming more clear that solitary leisure—watching TV, listening to the radio, and reading—does not provide the kind of relaxation that helps us to resist the ravages of daily stress.

The findings continued to emerge. In 1987 in Sweden, in the first study to look at a representative sample of an entire nation's population, Kristine Orth-Gomer, of the National Institute for Psychosocial Factors and Health, examined the lives of over 17,000 people during a six-year period. She discovered a dramatically lower risk of death in those socially involved. During the period of the study, for every 3.7 socially isolated people who died, only one socially involved person died.

Theories about the reasons for this linkage have generally fallen into two categories, both of which may play a part in any one helping situation: Human relationships (a) buffer the effects of stress; and (b) provide a more direct benefit by acting not as damage controllers but as actual health enhancers. The buffering hypothesis argues that by having friends, we feel less alone in our suffering, so the stress-causing events are not felt as deeply and the body's arousal is reduced. The direct or "main effects" hypothesis is based on the idea that social support in itself triggers positive, health-producing bodily reactions.

Then came research by Dr. Dean Ornish, of the University of California at San Francisco Medical School, resulting in information about how actually to repair some of the damages of heart disease. This important work combines improved eating habits with stress-reduction techniques designed to counteract the impulse toward hostility. In 1990 his studies received prominent attention as he showed that this regimen not only lowered levels of cholesterol but actually reduced the amount of fatty buildup already in the arteries. Ornish has also concerned himself with the emotional ramifications of hostility, claiming that it creates an exaggerated focus on the self that can intensify feelings of isolation and separateness, which, in their turn, invite increased stress and further physical damage. To counteract this, Ornish actually had patients who did not like each other clean each other's laundry. "This is real open heart surgery," he said. He found that this experience succeeded in lowering the levels of hostility and the amount of chest pain in the individuals involved.

Although research has established the links between our minds and our bodies, and the effect our ties with others have on our health, few of us have adopted the kinds of behaviors that build on this knowledge or that give us the healthful break from tension that we need. Most of us live with a great deal of stress, showing up as tension, tight muscles, back pain, and diverse other symptoms. The effect seems almost universal. Forty-three percent of Americans now say that stress has actually made them ill in some way. This is because we have not learned techniques to counteract our bodies' reflexive response to stress. Not counting the occasional emergencies that occur, each of us in the course of a day may have as many as twenty to fifty small emotional arousals involving stressful incidents, says Keith Sedlacek, M.D., medical director of the Stress Regulation Institute in New York. These arousals, which can occur even during sleep, lead to a slight increase in heart rate, blood pressure, and tightening of muscles. While this kind of physical readiness may be helpful in an emergency, it is of little or no practical value for dealing with a moment of tension in traffic or an argument at the office. These continued little arousals can have a cumulative effect, leading to such stress-linked ills as high blood pressure, headaches, backaches, sleep disturbances, eating disorders, colitis, diarrhea, and constipation, to name just a few examples.[7]

This is why, as stress pioneer Hans Selye predicted, we need a stress-reduction technique that involves our *daily* way of looking at and interacting with others—the source of most of our emotional stress. In *The Stress of Life* Selye argued for the development of altruistic egoism. Its fundamental principle is to do good for the self by making the effort to do good for others, to *"earn* thy neighbor's love." This philosophy advocates the creation of feelings of satisfaction and security through the inspiration of love and gratitude in others.

My findings show that regular helping of others is a practical prescription that can accomplish this, as well as the remarkable physical and emotional benefits the helper can experience as a result.

"BABY MAGIC"

Randee's story of facing death is about how helping others helped her to recover fully from a major life crisis. More typical are the tales of people who lead high-stress lives and who find that regular helping takes away the tightness in their shoulders or backs, for example, replacing feelings of chronic discomfort with a sense of well-being.

With heavy professional responsibilities on top of all the usual demands of being a wife and mother, "Lynn" was living a life both full and stressful. As the director of a private preschool she worried about competing for students, pleasing worried parents, and placating her school's supervisors. At home she had two teenage children of her own. It didn't seem possible to add one more regular commitment to her schedule. But she made that commitment. Once a week after work she took the fifteen-minute walk to a nearby urban medical center, Long Island College Hospital, where she put on gloves and a bright yellow sterile gown. Then she would go into the glass-walled space that she had once overheard someone call the dumping room, where new babies with medical complications were kept for observation. Her job there was to hold, feed, and diaper the babies; there didn't seem to be enough parents or nurses to handle the job alone.

Twelve years ago Lynn had been in a hospital herself. She was having constant back pain, severe enough that a doctor put her in traction and said that surgery was necessary. But she did not want to have the operation. Instead she took part in a program at the Rusk Institute for Rehabilitation Medicine of New York University Medical School, which taught her that coping with stress could control most back problems. Relaxation techniques helped, but the periodic flare-ups continued—until she began to help with the babies. She chose this work after seeing an article I had written on the benefits of volunteering.

On a recent hospital day she arrived to find ten babies in the room, four being fed and most of the rest crying. They were so small that their crying sounded like the mewing of kittens.

Some of the babies who pass through this room have been abandoned, often by parents who are drug addicts, and some of them show postnatal signs of drug withdrawal. Many of them have been born to mothers who could not afford medical care during their pregnancies and did not go to a hospital to deliver. Here they sleep in tiny beds, each crib tagged with a sticker giving the baby's last name and a few relevant statistics.

Lynn leaned down to a waist-high crib to pick up her first baby of the day, a week-old boy, who, like the others, was dark-skinned and very small. These babies, with all their problems, seemed uncommonly beautiful, their dark eyes huge, their bodies so impossibly small. This boy was named "Madison." Born outside of a hospital, he was awaiting the results of a drug test and then placement with foster parents. "It's scary to hold some of them," Lynn said, settling Madison in her arms. "You can feel all their bones right in your hand."

Madison latched onto a bottle with surprising vigor. Lynn rocked back and forth, feeding him.

Then, without fanfare, a new baby was brought in, half an hour old, big and pink and howling. He was brought here for monitoring of his glucose because of his unusually large size. This little linebacker looked so startlingly healthy that the others suddenly seemed even smaller. By severe contrast the baby nearest him, "Sanchez," who was born with heart and liver problems, was in an incubator. At birth Sanchez weighed a little over two pounds.

While a nurse was taking care of the newest arrival, Lynn had finished feeding Madison and had patted him to sleep on her shoulder. "On to the next one," she said, putting Madison in his bed, then leaning over again to scoop up "Dupree." She made no effort to protect her back, which had been, she said, a little stiff when she arrived.

Dupree had curly black hair and features that looked almost grown-up. He was two weeks old, and he was trembling, sometimes faintly, sometimes in shudders that moved through his whole body. "I'm sorry, I'm sorry," Lynn said to him, as she held and rocked him.

Lynn spent her entire two hours in the nursery lifting and lowering babies, feeding and diapering. At the end of that time her back pain had vanished. Getting her coat on, leaving the hospital, she noticed something else: Her hands still had the smell of babies. "Baby Magic," she said, taking a sniff. Baby Magic is a brand of baby oil—and an apt description of what had taken place in Lynn's life.

HEALTHY EMOTIONS

Lynn's helping efforts provided both a break from the pressures of her regular responsibilities and a way to experience the emotions that are particularly conducive to good health. Although Lynn's work in the hospital nursery brought her face-to-face with problems too large for any one person to solve—the effects of drug abuse and poverty—she still felt that she was bringing comfort to one baby after another.

Just as hostility and other attitudes can lead to ill health, there are also emotions that can enhance health and lower the risk of disease by counteracting the effects of stress and creating positive bodily reactions. Among these good-health emotions are trust; feelings of self-worth, self-control, or self-determination; a sense of challenge and commitment; optimism; and joyfulness. Making the kind of effort that Lynn does stirs in us a sense that we can make a difference, that we can exert some control over our own lives and be of use to others as well, despite our knowing that some of these children may not survive and that many will go on to lead troubled lives.

In work that draws together a number of these health-enhancing emotional factors, Suzanne Kobasa, Ph.D., a psychologist at the Graduate School of the City University of New York, developed the concept of hardiness. After studying executives at Illinois Bell during the stressful three and a half years when it was being separated from AT&T, she found that executives who met that period's stresses with a combination of the following three attitudes were the least likely to become ill. These were the people who (a) felt the greatest degree of control over their own fate; (b) viewed the tasks they faced as challenges; and (c) felt a strong sense of commitment to some overriding purpose. Kobasa called the three ingredients hardiness and concluded that this quality "is three times as powerful as social support and exercise put together in determining who gets sick in a period of high stress." A key to achieving hardiness, she notes, is being able to "spend some time on another part of one's life where one can get positive feedback."[8] Other studies demonstrate the similar healing power of trust, optimism, and happiness.

All of these "positive" attitudes and emotions are available through the act of helping. Though there can be frustrations, difficulties, and outright bad experiences involved in helping other people, our survey respondents overwhelmingly report that helping can be highly effective at improving feelings of self-determination, at providing healthy challenges and rewarding feedback, and at reinforcing feelings of commitment to something worthwhile, thus producing moments of joy and a lasting sense of optimism.

An incident that occurred a few years back bore powerful testimony to the almost magical effects I've enjoyed from my own helping activities—and the strength of the attraction that this work holds. It is testimony all the more powerful for having been filtered through the eyes of another person who was galvanized by it. It happened during my time as a community-action lawyer in East Harlem, at the close of a project that had been difficult but successful. I was working with the residents of two decaying tenement buildings abandoned by the landlord. These people were living in apartments that had no heat and no hot water. You could stand in a bathroom in one apartment and look up through holes in the ceiling to the bathroom in the apartment above. The narrow stairways were covered with graffiti, the doors were loaded with innumerable locks that tenants had put on in a vain attempt to secure themselves against break-ins. It was the early seventies, in the midst of a wave of heroin use.

I was working with the tenants to organize a repair effort. After many meetings, problems, and false starts, most of the people in the building agreed to pool their money to start to improve the building. At first no one wanted to contribute because, after all, how did they know the other people would? Suppose one person put in money and the others didn't? We began by building up the feeling that together we could and would accomplish this.

The group did become organized, pool their limited supplies of cash, and open a bank account. But each new step forward was plagued by more problems. Some of the repairs we made were quickly ripped to pieces again by vandals. Our building superintendent, a young boy, was shot. Heroin addicts stole our supplies. The problems seemed insurmountable. But finally we did it. We had the boiler working, most of the leaks fixed, and the window-panes replaced. I couldn't believe it had happened. We planned a party to celebrate.

On the afternoon before the party several of the men who lived in the building and I went out to the patch of ground behind the building to take care of one more problem. There was a large buildup of "airmail garbage," trash that had been thrown out of the windows. It had been piling up and decomposing in that yard for a long time. So we spent the afternoon digging out the trash, getting down to real East Harlem dirt. We got a tree from a man who gave away pine trees, a sort of Johnny Appleseed of New York, and we planted it. Then we went, still dirty from the work, to the party.

It was held at the local center of the Children's Aid Society. Residents of the building had brought potluck dishes. Spanish music was playing, people were dancing. It was great. Everybody was happy; we had done what we set out to do. My wife, Karen, had come, bringing with her a friend, Jerome Ruderman, who was new to this whole enterprise. Like me Jerome was a lawyer. He had a senior position handling contracts for a major motion picture company. Jerome and Karen arrived at the party in time to see the presentation of a gift to me—a complete surprise. The residents had chipped in and bought me an attaché case, so big that I doubt an airline would let it pass for a carry-on. Jerome stood and watched all this happening, watched my reaction, and said to Karen, "I can't believe what Allan is getting out of this." Jerome was right; it was a great night for me. And it wasn't the attaché case that warmed my heart.

Something had, though. And Jerome, who had arrived at this party unsuspecting, saw it and was so powerfully impressed by it that he couldn't get it out of his mind. He had not been satisfied with his corporate position, but wasn't sure what work would be more fulfilling. Now he had an idea. So he quit his job, went back to school, and became a guidance counselor. He's now well into a new career working with youth. What he saw happening to me that night—the effect of the powerful positive emotions on my own sense of well-being—he wanted for himself.

THE MAKINGS OF A PEACEFUL REVOLUTION

Exercise and good nutrition, for all their power to keep us healthy, are not enough. The next revolution in health care must be to bring to our awareness the health potential of helping others. The present headlined health revolution will not be completed until people realize that no matter how much they concentrate on themselves, they cannot achieve optimal health. They have to relate to others. This new information is something that all of us, at least at the back of our minds, already somehow know: that doing good *feels* good. But with the rising levels of crime and fear in our communities and the increasing busyness of our lives, it is easy to forget, to believe mistakenly that we are protecting ourselves by avoiding others. In fact the opposite is true.

"Altruism is like a muscle," Norman Cousins told me, reflecting on our new data on volunteering and health. Author of *Anatomy of an Illness*, Cousins—who died at the end of 1990 while teaching at the medical school of the University of California at Los Angeles—was a leading proponent of the healing power of mind–body interactions. This altruism muscle "must be used," he said, "or it atrophies. People, especially in urban areas, now appear locked into inertia because they are overloaded. There is only one way to break it: Reach out and help the person nearest you. You'll feel the good feeling, the shock of recognition—and as you help, the helping will spread."

This change can only begin with each of us individually. Let's take a closer look at how helping works within the body—at the intoxicating rush of good feeling called helper's high and its subsequent calming effects on body and mind, which together make up the healthy helping syndrome.

2

Helper's High:

THE FIRST PHASE

NAT BLEVINS was standing out in the middle of the highway stopping traffic. A tall, handsome man, forty years old, bearded, wearing a baggy sweater that made his long arms look like flags waving, he was good at the job. The traffic stopped while a bus turned slowly off the road into the long driveway of a group home for people with AIDS.

Then Nat got out of the road and, like a tour guide, shepherded the busload of people into the house for lunch, a meal hosted by the people with AIDS who lived here. The guests he brought in that Thursday afternoon were dancers and singers, the cast of *Heart Strings*, the national touring musical production that was raising money for patient care and AIDS education. It was the day before the *Heart Strings* performance in Durham, North Carolina, and he was one of three local coleaders.

He came into the house as if he were bounding onto a stage himself, full of energy and excitement. Standing in the living room, doing a little dance of his own, he talked with another volunteer about feeling "juiced." His schedule was crowded with meetings, phone calls, and events such as this lunch. He sat down for a moment at one end of the living room, talked a few minutes with two of the home's residents, both of them women, one of them very thin. And then he was off to the kitchen, grabbing a cookie off the buffet table while waiting for the line to move through; greeting more people; moving from person to person, room to room; making sure everything was going well.

The party lasted an hour and a half—a house full of young, healthy dancers and singers, a few volunteers, a few people with AIDS. After lunch the performers stood around the piano in the den and sang some of the songs from the musical. And then they were out the door again, Nat again in the lead.

On Friday night the show opened to a full house—not one empty seat. A sell-out ten days before the performance, it was the culmination of many months of work. When the lights went down, first the mayors from cities and towns in the area were introduced, one after another, then other public figures who were involved in the benefit.

Finally Nat stepped into the spotlight at the corner of the stage. Before he could say a word, the crowd rose to its feet. He waited, through wave after wave of applause. When quiet finally settled over the room, he introduced himself. "I'm Nat Blevins," he said, to the raptly attentive hall. "Tonight I speak from the bottom of my heart. I speak . . . as a person who is thriving with HIV disease."

He stood before a crowd that seemed festive, excited, and, if you looked quickly, as healthy as the dancers. "Tonight," he said, "a quarter of the people here either have the human immunodeficiency virus that causes AIDS or have a family member who is infected. When the bad times come again," Nat said, speaking out across this room filled with warmth, high energy, and purpose, "when the bad times return, from the disease, the discrimination, or the financial pressures, come back to this moment, this evening, take the strength. You can get through it. You've got friends.''

The performance that followed was a musical telling the story of a town beset by a terrible cloud—the story of AIDS and the human community. The show that night raised $100,000 in cash and in-kind contributions for the housing of people with AIDS. Nat Blevins's part in that effort, the days and months of advance work he did, in addition to helping other people, also helped to keep him alive.

"It's probably the only reason I'm alive today," he said, speaking not merely of that project but of all his efforts to help people with AIDS.

In the seven years since he first fell ill, Nat has learned how to create the moments, the "highs," that help him keep going. He "absolutely" feels again and again a strong physical sensation arising from his helping efforts. It is a sensation that empowers him. "It's something that happens when somebody smiles back or you touch somebody soul to soul," he said.

What Nat was talking about is *helper's high*, the powerful physical reaction that begins with a burst of energy and good feelings and is a sign that unhealthy, fatiguing stress has decreased in our bodies.

Nat Blevins has needed the help of that health-giving burst of strength. Two and a half years before the night of the *Heart Strings* performance, he became part of an HIV support group with a membership of eighteen. In a little over two years the other seventeen people have died.

"Five of my closest buds got sick," he said, "and within a year and a half they were dead."

On this day in February 1990 Nat had symptoms of his own. The disease had first begun to show in him in 1983. A staph infection in his elbow was not responding to medication. At that time AIDS was not well known.

When he finally took the test in 1984, he tested HIV positive.

"You walk out," he said, "with a diagnosis of a nasty, socially unacceptable, gruesome disease that is quote one hundred percent fatal, and the best thing they can say is 'keep a positive attitude.'" Under the circumstances it was hard to do. Still coping with the demands of graduate school, he watched the deaths of friends and the spread of the disease in the community around him as he tried to face his own future.

In September 1987 he was feeling run-down, chronically exhausted. "I felt like a car battery with some of the cells dead. I was sleeping twelve or fourteen hours a day. I could not get juiced, period." He went into a clinic for tests. "Every lab test that came back was textbook perfect"—with one exception. The T-4 cells, helper immune cells that work against the virus, should have been in the 800 to 1,000 range. But his test result was only at about the 100 level—"the disaster zone," he said.

"That's the point at which we clinically defined what was going on." He began taking AZT, joined the support group, and continued to see his friends and now his fellow support group members die from the effects of this disease that was beginning to take a serious toll on him as well.

The turning point for him, the change in his own state of mind, came in a psychotherapy session. "There was a moment in therapy when I turned to the therapist and said, 'I have to do something. I can either let this eat me up or I can go to work.'"

His new work began with taking care of those friends. "It started when these guys started getting sick. I made a real commitment to every one of them that I was there, period, whatever it meant. I ended up doing a lot of direct care—hands-on, straight-up physical stuff." When all of those friends were gone, he said, "I gave myself time to scream and yell, and then said, 'Now it's time to look outside the house, outside of me.' I offered my services to the AIDS service project for grant writing and envelope stuffing." From there he moved to work for the AIDS Community Residence Association (ACRA), which now pays him to work part-time and gets his full-time efforts, often day and night.

The conventional medical advice to people with AIDS is to take it easy, rest, get lots of sleep, and eat a well-balanced diet. Nat often gets four to six hours of sleep a night. The chocolate chip cookie he ate in the early afternoon at the AIDS group home was the first thing he had eaten that day. He was too busy to stop. He had broken all the rules but one: Keep a positive attitude. That one he had kept through his efforts to help. Much of the time now he is fired-up with energy, active, vigorous, engagingly cheerful, in circumstances that often seem impossible.

Looking back, Nat has known more than one person who attempted suicide on receiving the HIV-positive diagnosis and at least one who succeeded. "I had one friend who went home, wrote his will, paid his bills, and blew his brains out."

Not long ago Nat attended three memorial services in five days. That same week he drove the twenty minutes to an appointment to talk to a corporate head about making a contribution. He cried as he drove, cried the whole way. Later he joked about having made good use of his time: That was all the time he had to cry, and he had taken full advantage of it. It often feels "impossible to walk into CEO offices and maintain a rational exterior," he says. Yet he continues to find the strength to do so.

To look at him at lunch with the troupe of dancers and singers, one would see no sign of ill health. Forty years old, he still looked ready to race down the court for a lay-up shot, though, as he put it, "I am not without medical manifestation." He had had a few bad months in 1989, "lost about fifty pounds, had some intestinal problems." In early 1990 he was back up to a hundred and eighty-five pounds, at six feet three inches. But he was having other problems. Huge warts on the bottoms of his feet seem to be "unfixable. I'm beginning to show nerve damage." He was having, simultaneously, chronic pain in his feet and also loss of sensation there.

"There's no question in my mind," he said, "that I'm dealing with an active process." Yet through it all he is continuing to be vigorous and active, a full-time, indefatigable helper and community leader. He could tell an audience that he was thriving, and they could see that it was the truth. And the reason it was true, he believed, was that, day after day, through his many forms of helping, he was experiencing powerful moments of connection with other people. The losses have been nearly unbearable. And yet "the love and connections never go away, that energy never goes away." What he saw when he was at the turning point that led him to embrace helping was that "this I can run on. The other I can die on."

THE NATURE OF THE HIGH

The kind of moments that Nat Blevins was describing— the powerful physical sensations that helping produces— are the first stage of the healthy helping phenomenon. The impact begins with a characteristic experience that many regular volunteers will immediately recognize. In my survey I found that an overwhelming number of volunteers confirmed this observation. A full 95 percent reported a physical "feel-good" reaction. To understand how this sensation signals body changes linked to health benefits, let's take a look at what this initial experience is, how it feels, and what causes it.

I have heard people compare the physical sensation of the healthy helping syndrome to intoxication, to an energy bolt, to the sustained high that runners get from their exercise, to an orgasm, to the serenity induced by yoga. While some of these reactions may at first seem contradictory, their diversity is easily accounted for by the two-part nature of the helping syndrome.

The experience begins with a burst of energy and feelings of physical exhilaration—helper's high. This "rush" is then followed by a longer-lasting, heightened sense of calm and emotional well-being, a sort of high plateau, which we discuss in the next chapter. Some helpers have more to say about the initial rush, while others focus on the calm that follows.

Of the helpers surveyed, however, nine out of ten reported *specific* sensations experienced as an initial result of helping. To recap those findings, 54 percent mentioned warmth, 29 percent cited increased energy, 21 percent felt a druglike euphoria. More than half listed additional positive physical and emotional responses.

"It was a tremendous rush, like I could run for a hundred miles," said Tammy Foley, a twenty-four-year-old kindergarten teacher in Othello, Washington, of her own experiences with helper's high. "I felt like I had been zapped by an energy bolt. It was very euphoric. My whole body, especially my hands, really tingled. I felt very light and happy and content. My stomach tingled like 'butterflies' and I felt like I bounced while I walked."

Tammy taught at a school with many students from low-income families, and she "sort of adopted them." Some days she would take students home with her and make cookies.

"I have known for a long time," Tammy said, "that, for me at least, when I'm helping someone, I feel the best. As soon as I finish up one project, I want to start right away on another. When I was in college, I would get really stressed out and get bad headaches. As soon as I would volunteer somewhere, my headaches would stop, my energy would improve. I would do fantastically on my tests, and I enjoyed even dreary tasks more. Sometimes I was elated and had such a rush, I couldn't settle down for hours. I kept charging all over the house, smiling and hugging everyone, singing. It was wonderful. And then, when I calmed down, I was so relaxed."

The sensations of helper's high are indicative of a sudden sharp reduction in the effects of bad stress, or distress, on the body. And at the same time the high is a sign of a state of "good stress," or eustress. Recent research has distinguished between those changes in the body that occur to facilitate a good, short-lived but intense effort—such as that of exercise or helping, which can be health-enhancing—and those evoked in response to a prolonged strain, such as being in an ongoing state of emotional stress, which can damage the body. In a review of these studies Dr. Keith Sedlacek, medical director of the Stress Regulation Institute in New York, cites the role of the stress-related catecholamines and cortisol secretions. When we stress ourselves briefly, the catecholamines increase but not the cortisol, this latter being the most potent and most potentially damaging of the hormones produced by the adrenal cortex. But the cortisol level rises when our arousal becomes prolonged, and then distress occurs. "The negative stress response seems to lock the muscles and blood pressure into a more tense situation that can create serious mental and physical problems," notes Sedlacek.

The helping act is one way of escaping the state of stress resulting from daily demands that have no easy solution. The feeling of helper's high, or exhilaration, which so many volunteers have described is the first step in that escape.

Helper's high is a signal that the body's distress reaction

is abating. Volunteers report sensations of warmth and greater energy. The surface warmth of the limbs is the result of a reversing of the stress-caused flow of blood to the arm and leg muscles and a simultaneous opening up of the peripheral blood vessels. This peripheral blood flow causes a warming of the body's surface. For example, when you're under stress, your hands are cold. When the stress drops and the body relaxes, your hands will be warm.[1] Increased energy is reported because the drained feeling, from being in a continued stressed, hypermetabolic state has gone; the body's consumption of oxygen, the heart rate, blood pressure, and muscle tension all drop.

Helper's high is also most likely a sign of endorphins being released into the bloodstream. Endorphins are naturally occurring opiates in our bodies that seem both to relieve pain and to promote a sense of well-being, even euphoria. The initial high that exercisers feel is also thought to be the work of the endorphins.

I will never forget my own first experiences of helper's high, back when I was in the Peace Corps in Venezuela. I was living in a little cement-block house in an urban slum, working during the day as a lawyer, mainly on a project to inform the poor of their legal rights regarding everything from child support to getting legal title to their land. It was tough going for me for a while. For one thing I was speaking Spanish, and that was work. For the first six months I was translating all day in my head, from English to Spanish, from Spanish to English. I would come home exhausted—and hot. The first thing I'd do when I got home was sweep the cement floors of the house with water, to try to cool the place down.

It was about that time of day when the neighborhood children would start to appear. The house I was living in had a broken wooden door, which wouldn't lock well. At least a couple of times a week at dusk I could count on seeing the bright-eyed face of a small boy appear in that doorway, calling out *"Musiu."* That's what they called me, a slang word that meant, good-naturedly, "foreigner." Behind that one boy there would be half a dozen more, barefoot, shirtless, ranging in age from eight or nine to about eighteen. They would sit around in my big, all-purpose room, and we'd talk. Sometimes our conversations were all for fun, and sometimes I'd work in a little advice about going to school or improving their hygiene. I didn't know if I was really helping, but I was feeling, night after night, a burst of energy that was new to me. It was like a half-dozen cups of coffee, but better. I would come home tired, and then, after talking with the kids collected around me, I'd be on top of the world. On the nights when I came home and didn't hear anybody yelling *"Musiu,"* I'd feel let down. It would seem that something was missing. When they did come, I'd feel a "buzz" for hours after they left. Sometimes it was hard to go to sleep. This was the high, and in the morning I would have the benefit of the calm, acting as a buffer against any feelings of sleep deprivation and as a guard against the regular frustrations of the day.

ENDORPHINS: A KEY TO THE BIOCHEMISTRY OF HELPING

Endorphins are one of our body's many kinds of neurotransmitters—messenger molecules that carry a signal (such as Danger! Pain! Get ready! or Feel good!) to our brains. Endogenous (within the body) morphinelike substances that are naturally occurring, they are powerful enough to create a narcoticlike high in us when released.

To understand the endorphin reaction, it is important to know something about how our brain cells communicate with each other. Each cell is situated at a minutely small distance from the next cell. Messages of all kinds are carried across these gaps by various chemicals—the above-mentioned neurotransmitters. Pain messages are transmitted by a chemical known as Substance P, which attaches to neurons sensitive to it. Endorphins can interfere with the release of Substance P and thus inhibit the transmission of pain information—hence, no pain. Narcotic drugs are thought to work to reduce pain because they are similar in chemical composition to these naturally occurring substances and can mimic the signals the endorphins send.[2]

The role of endorphins in our bodies has now been linked not only with the muffling of pain but with sensations as familiar and cheerful as the feeling of a "thrill" or as dramatic as a druglike high. Today we know that we can create such sensations within ourselves by our own activities. We can trigger such brain messages by creating circumstances that are conducive to the release of this naturally occurring chemical substance. Helping others seems to be one such means of stimulating endorphin release.

The presence of endorphins in helper's high is indicated by two different kinds of research. One has to do with the much-acclaimed findings from the laboratory of Jaak Panksepp, Ph.D., who has discovered the part these substances play in our tendencies to form emotional bonds. The other concerns what we now know about runner's high and similar sensations.

Plasma tests have demonstrated beyond a doubt that the strain—the good stress, called eustress—of exercise causes the pituitary gland to step up its production of endorphins in the blood. This is the leading research explanation for the sensation called runner's high. Scientists have measured a rise as great as 200 percent in runner's endorphin levels after a 28.5-mile race. Researchers speculate that vigorous exercise may open up the blood-brain barrier, allowing endorphins in the blood to enter the brain and produce their effects.

We now have massive amounts of anecdotal evidence in the form of reports from volunteers concerning the physical rush produced by helping. While helpers compare it to everything from sex to too much coffee, they most often compare it to an exercise high, and the results they describe are indeed very similar to the endorphin-linked burst-and-calm effect produced by exercise. Runners have reported that their high is a feeling of terrific physical well-being, absence or decrease of pain, heightened self-esteem, and a subsequent calm. Volunteers say the same.

"I'm a regular person," said Jini Foster, age forty-six, of Norwell, Massachusetts, "not a superwoman like you read about." But her volunteer efforts—reading to first- and second-graders and sorting and packing food for the needy at a distribution center—seem to revitalize and restore her rather than deplete her, just as the effort involved in exercise does. "It's kind of like a high—runner's high," she said. She finds that tiredness leaves her, and "a euphoric feeling" comes over her instead.

A New Canaan, Connecticut, woman who has volunteered one afternoon a week at a nursing home for eleven years made a similar comparison. Her job is to help get the wheelchair patients into the dining room and to help them with their trays. "I go home tired, but with a new spurt of energy such as one feels after a really good game of tennis."

"Rikki" feels, as a result of helping, a powerful rush, followed by a sense of being refreshed. She has been relying on this sensation all her life. As a four-year-old, she already knew that helping other people felt good. She needed some feel-good sensations because she was a child who was abused and neglected. She remembered being a preschool child and "making things for a neighbor, a person who liked me a lot." She made cards, pictures.

"My natural parents were very cruel people, and I think that I had such a strong desire to be loved that I sought out affection from outsiders. I would do the most thoughtful things for people just to hear kind words. Those words gave me that good feeling."

As a twenty-eight-year-old with a husband and a small child, she is still helping and giving at every opportunity. The feeling she has when she does this, she said, is not quite like any other, but she uses sexual imagery to describe it. "I'm not sure I can explain what the 'feel-good' sensations are like. In one word I'd say orgasmic! I tend to get light-headed, quite mellow, and my body becomes very relaxed. The orgasmic feeling in my head is tingly, and I do have waves or rushes of good feeling. It kind of rushes upward, maybe from my chest area, almost like a numbing sensation, but it feels really good. I feel very refreshed and happy."

There is laboratory research that shows that the brain opioids, which include the endorphins, are involved when animals exhibit friendly and playful interactions with each other. Though the neurobiology of bonding and helping behaviors is not yet well understood, Jaak Panksepp, a psychology professor at Bowling Green State University, has found that the mechanism consists, in part, of processes involving the brain opioids and that these are actuated in moments of parental involvement and play and during comforting social interactions, such as grooming.

One set of experiments he's done to link bonding behaviors with endorphins and other morphinelike substances involved giving dogs naloxone, a drug that blocks endorphins from attaching to brain cells. Dogs dosed with naloxone exhibited a striking increase in tail wagging, a signal that the dogs were endorphin-deprived and thus wanted to be petted. Alternately, when the dogs received low doses of morphine, the drug equivalent of a naturally occurring endorphin reaction, the tail wagging decreased. The dogs were now satisfied; they had no need to seek the contact that could stimulate endorphins since they already had the chemical reaction they wanted. All very interesting, you may think—but why would there be a brain biochemistry conducive to the formation of social ties?

Panksepp has analyzed the place that altruism (and other forms of social bonding) fit into our survival-of-the-fittest biological evolution, and he emerges with a view of helping as consistent with the best hopes of the species: Helping is ultimately a self-serving behavior, since it may be biologically necessary for reproduction and survival of certain species. He further suggests that in the evolution of the human species the chances of survival may have been improved by cooperative efforts in such otherwise primitive and self-serving enterprises as hunting. The need to build on and maintain these forms of cooperation may have been a key factor in the expansion and development of the human brain. In short, as *Homo sapiens* evolved and brain size increased, parts of the brain contributing to the capacity to cooperate might have developed to a greater degree than others. Intrinsic helping tendencies may thus, like dominance urges, be embedded in the human brain structure, may even be part of what we think of as human nature itself.

The feel-good endorphin-activated bonding may be a positive biological adaptation that has assisted in the survival of the human species and the individual. And certainly the sense of bondedness is at the heart of helping. It can be both the inspiration for altruism and the result of the altruistic act.[3]

My survey found that personal contact greatly enhances the chances of experiencing helper's high. One volunteer, Stephanie Bass, a free-lance writer and political consultant, has felt a high that is "like flipping on lights." She is a very active volunteer in grass-roots political organizing. For the high to hit her, she needs two elements to be present: to be working for a cause she is passionate about and to have close contact with people. Much of her work involves making direct efforts to enlist other people to work for the cause.

Recently she was the speaker at a series of "house parties" aimed at gathering support for a new North Carolina group called Women-Elect. While political work can often mean envelope stuffing, Stephanie's role was different. At these parties, each held at a private home, ten or twelve women gathered to hear what she had to say about the new organization's purpose. The group size was "small enough to be comfortable," she said. "You had a sense of knowing who you were with." With only a dozen women present "you can look in the face of everybody there, you can touch them, you can hug them good-bye."

First she speaks to the group, explaining why she feels that their help is needed. "What I get excited about is the interpersonal stuff. I say something. Then they say, 'Yeah!' and get excited." She likes "to see the people's eyes light up." Then she asks them for time and money. When she asks for their help and then sees people get out their checkbooks and write the checks, it's a very satisfying moment. "It's the same thing I feel when I see Carolina hit a tough shot in a basketball game."

When the meeting is over, "I come away feeling very energized." In fact after an evening party she has a hard time going to sleep. But this is different from the effect of a cup of coffee—"that's more of a jag." This is a feeling of happiness that "borders on euphoria."

Like eight out of ten volunteers in our survey, Stephanie noted a recurrence of the feel-good sensation when she remembered the helping acts. She found that the physical reaction often goes well beyond the day of the effort. As we talked, she was still feeling "pumped up" from a meeting that had happened eleven days earlier. "It's energizing," she said, "it also feels rejuvenating. It feels like it nurtures something in me."

She laughed. "I think I'm an adrenaline junkie," she said. "I'd rather be pumped up than laid-back." In an average week she was working a minimum of eight to ten hours on this project. "I must like it," she said, "because I complain, but I keep putting in the hours."

Like Stephanie, I keep putting in the hours too. I'm still getting that high I felt on those nights twenty years ago in Venezuela. And for me, like so many others, the establishment of a personal bond, however temporary, is at the heart of the process.

One of my recent volunteer activities reminded me of the time I used to spend with the Venezuelan boys. Lately I've been spending an occasional overnight in a church basement that is serving as a one-night home for homeless men. I do this through a consortium of churches and synagogues in New York that is providing space for the homeless. What the evening usually turns into is a bunch of guys sitting around talking, and talking in a situation of safety that they probably don't regularly find on the streets.

On my nights to help I go home after work, change into sweats or jeans, then head over to Saint Agnes Church, a big Catholic church in downtown Brooklyn. The program is sponsored jointly with a nearby synagogue, Congregation Baith Israel Anshei Emes. The basement where we stay is a large, open area with a small kitchen off to the side. Working with one other volunteer, we set up cots and start warming up the dinner. By 8:20 the ten homeless men have arrived.

These are men whose common problem is the lack of housing. But several have other problems too. A large number have foot injuries and have trouble walking. I've seen a lot of ulcerated sores on these people. While this program does not generally cater to men who have severe mental problems, it still brings in some who seem to have trouble making their thoughts connect clearly. It takes them time to think.

Even so, at dinner, we have good talks. We'll eat the food that members of the two congregations have contributed. It can range from canned soup to the leftovers from a lavish catered affair. One night the synagogue sent over dishes that weren't regular fare for any of us, from a wedding dinner with a Middle Eastern menu. The men kept saying, "What is this?" when we put out the different kinds of stuffed grape leaves, eggplant dip, and honey and nut pastries. But they loved it.

We sit around after dinner over coffee and talk about politics and life on the streets and how the world is now. We talk about jobs, families. It's a nice feeling of connection. It's like any conversation in a pub or coffeehouse.

Then at 10:30 the lights go out. We sleep on cots, a dozen of them, spaced six feet or so apart in the big room. We'll each usually wear underwear or long johns. It's not really comfortable, and I don't sleep well there. It's cold in the room, and all night the boiler keeps banging. At the back of my mind I have some fears, too, though I've relaxed a lot since the first night I spent here. I do fear that one of the men might become violent or deranged. But nothing like that has happened. Instead they have all been easy to deal with and have seemed incredibly grateful for our efforts.

In the morning we're up at 5:30. Breakfast is usually frozen French toast and, for some reason, an ever-abundant supply of Oreo cookies. We shake hands as they leave. By this time I know their first names. As we're parting, I have a strong feeling of the connection we've made, temporary though it is. I tell myself that they don't feel quite so unattached when they go back out there.

Then I go back out onto the street myself. And that's when the helper's high hits me. I'm not usually a runner. And I might not have gotten into this habit had I not found the subway badly delayed one morning. That day I started to run, with an eye out for a stray cab. But I discovered, as I covered block after block, that I didn't need a cab. I was so full of energy, I could have run all day. Now I jog the two or three miles home on most of these mornings, sometimes as the sun is just coming up. I have the feeling when I come out of that church basement that I could jump over tall buildings. I feel that energy for the rest of the day.

The energy that goes along with helper's high is powerful and can keep you going back for more. But more important are the long-term effects. The feelings of warmth and tingling, the "rush," add up finally to more than a momentary phenomenon. Because these sensations are signs of a sharp reduction in stress, they also signal a respite in the process of wear and tear on the body's systems. Helper's high welcomes us to the first phase of the healthy helping syndrome, which signals better physical and emotional health for the helper.

3

The Calm That Follows:

THE SECOND PHASE

AS powerful as any immediate physical effect that helping produces is the often-astonishing improvement in the emotional well-being of the helper, the feeling of calmness and serenity that follows the brief initial burst of the helper's high. Together these two phases contain within them all the physical and emotional sensations that volunteers described and that I now call the healthy helping syndrome.

Looking at the components of this longer-lasting heightened sense of emotional well-being, we see that 57 percent of the volunteers mentioned an increased sense of self-worth, and 53 percent noted such gains as greater happiness and optimism as well as a decrease in feelings of helplessness and depression. Experiencing the full healthy helping syndrome provides a powerful antidote to life's daily stresses.

That helping others has this calming and soothing power is paradoxical, because we all know that coming to someone's aid can bring us face-to-face with tragedy as well. And yet, in spite of the terrible troubles that helpers encounter, in spite of our inadequacy to solve the massive problems of the people we deal with, in spite of the fact that sometimes we help someone who disappoints us badly, helping can make us happy.

The emotional calmness that follows the brief physical feelings of exhilaration is very similar to what people involved in strenuous exercise frequently report: a relatively long-lasting sense of emotional well-being that follows the initial, very pleasurable physical arousal.

Eight out of ten volunteers report that this sense of well-being can recur—for hours or even days—when they remember the actual helping act. Helping's emotional benefits are more lasting and so may be more beneficial than those of physical activity. In fact a national Gallup survey of exercisers found that only 44 percent of exercisers reported gains in self-worth, one of the important emotional benefits of both helping and exercise. By comparison, 57 percent of the volunteers in our survey cited this benefit.

Consider the story of David Kriser, a man who has used the recurring emotional benefits of helping to maintain daily health for a very long and active life. At eighty-three years of age, David is a multimillionaire, traveling yearly to fish for salmon in Alaska and to shoot ducks in Mexico. With his brothers, he developed a business that handles auctions for large manufacturers. In addition he has devoted himself to helping other people—because it makes him feel good.

"Don't get the idea I'm a wildly practicing philanthropist," he said, playing down his efforts. But his contributions have made him one of the better-known health donors in New York City. New York University Dental School has been named after him, as have the lung cancer clinic at Beth Israel Hospital and chairs in the NYU department of anthropology. A recent project he found "very exciting" was making a contribution to Beth Israel to double the size of the emergency room and establish a specialty training program for emergency room medicine. And of course it was David who gave me the grant to convene my mind-body conference in 1988.

In addition to these gifts David performs another kind of helping act, a daily effort that brings him into close contact with people. Enter his small midtown office or his home, and you will see him meeting or on the phone with friends, friends of friends, or strangers referred to him about a health problem or some other difficulty. He first counsels, then tries to arrange the help that's needed. Sometimes he will arrange an appointment with the right medical specialist. Comparing his large philanthropic gifts to his daily personal helping, he is very clear about what helps him most: "Check writing means nothing. What has been invaluable to my health and functioning is person-to-person contact.

"I live alone, and there are many days I feel lousy. It becomes hard to function. Then I'll get a call, see someone who needs help. I'll spend time and effort helping him. I can't tell you how good the feeling is that I receive out of this. The depression leaves, at least for that period of time. I function better."

He made this discovery through experience and through one of his typical early-morning debates with himself many years ago. "In the mornings, about five or six o'clock, I have had sufficient sleep, and I lie in bed and philosophize. I have a debate with myself." His typical topics for his morning thinking sessions revolve around "the problems of staying alive, of living with people, of handling life's problems. Sometimes you try to clarify your life and your lifestyle and to understand situations a little better." There was no special catalyst that he knows of to turn his thoughts on that particular day in the direction they took. "This one morning at about quarter to six my question was, What gives you a good feeling in your gut? What makes you feel good? Is it making a deal for a million or a half a million? Is it catching a tarpon? The answer was: When I helped somebody." From that morning on, he decided to look for more ways to help people.

THE PHYSICAL BASIS FOR THE CALM

Imagine the undoing of the stress reaction. Start with the anatomy of a very tense person. The muscles in the walls of the peripheral blood vessels are contracted in an effort to pump more blood to the organs and muscles that are prepared for battle. The person is breathing fast to get oxygen as quickly as possible. This kind of breathing causes additional tension in the muscles that are involved. The taxed muscles then need more oxygen, which calls for quicker delivery of blood. Pulse rate and blood pressure are elevated to meet the need.

When the calming, or the undoing of the stress reaction occurs, the body's oxygen consumption starts to drop. The oxygen that cells were using to burn nutrients at a stepped-up pace is no longer needed in such quantities. This slowdown takes the pressure off the overworked circulatory system, which is responsible for pumping oxygen-rich blood to needy cells. The fast breathing that occurs when the body is trying to race more oxygen to the cells can then slow down. And that eases the muscles of the chest and shoulders. All the indicators of a racing, oxygen-hungry metabolism fall. The body has entered a state of ease.

This feeling of calm that is available to each of us can be discovered through a number of different techniques, some of which have probably always been part of human behavior. Whatever breaks the cycle of mounting tension in which most of us live will do it, whether it's meditation or prayer or yoga. Helping others is one such cycle breaker. In addition, the process of helping not only averts negative preoccupations, it replaces them with recurring positive feelings which further help to keep the body relaxed.

THE MEDITATION CONNECTION

While many helpers compare the initial high to the runner's high, they compare the second phase, the calm, to the effects of meditation. Dr. Benson, the scientist who has probably done the most to explain and popularize the body's ability to oppose stress, particularly via meditation, calls helping a form of meditation.

The key, in helping as in meditation, whether you're repeating a mantra or teaching an illiterate adult to read, is that you're concentrating on a point outside yourself. What happens physically is that the out-of-self focus breaks into the person's usual tension-producing thought patterns, decreasing the activity of the sympathetic nervous system and thereby countermanding the body's stress reactions.

"These good feelings were like losing all sense of self except those capabilities I had to help the other person," reported a fifty-year-old in Fairfax, Michigan. "Tension seemed to leave my body. A relaxed feeling took its place. Even my mind seemed to be quicker and clearer."

A volunteer in Pittsburgh found that this feeling made helping worthwhile, in spite of the many difficulties and obstacles. "Sometimes helping others is not convenient, plain hard work, depressing (seeing how others live while delivering Meals on Wheels), or not appreciated. But concentrating on others makes us forget our own problems and troubles and lifts us out of ourselves."

During a recent conversation I had with Herbert Benson he recalled an encounter some years ago with the Dalai Lama, the most revered monk of Tibetan Buddhism. During this visit he heard one of his Harvard colleagues asking that spiritual leader about meditation and its effectiveness as a health measure. The man from Harvard was saying that although he thought meditation worked well during the time it was practiced, for most people there came a time each day when it was necessary to stop meditating and go "back out into the slings and arrows of regular life. How do you deal with that?" he asked. The Dalai Lama replied simply, "Look at what's in front of you."

In the intervening years Benson reflected on that answer. "For a while I wasn't sure what that meant," he said. "Then I realized that by looking in front of you, you attach your thoughts to other persons. That breaks the message of stress. And I now see that a way to make that really happen for a lengthy period is through helping."

For many people helping produces more powerful experiences than meditation, since it can often be easier to get outside yourself and so break the usual chain of the stress reaction by coming to another person's aid than by sitting motionless in a quiet, darkened room silently repeating a phrase to yourself. Yet, helping does duplicate meditation's complete shift of attention outside of one's daily focus. Helping is both a form of single-focus meditation, in which you concentrate on others instead of a sound or phrase, and a variation on what is known as "mindfulness," a state of heightened awareness of *all* the emotions, thoughts, and sensations that come to you.

Arline Keeling, age fifty, of Kaysville, Utah, found the calming sensation she got from helping others similar to what she felt when doing yoga, which she uses to control arthritis pain, tension, and anxiety. She had first turned to yoga when she stopped taking the antidepressants she'd been given for both depression and arthritis pain. "When I went off the antidepressants, it was very painful. I'm fairly healthy. Depression, I'm sure, has caused or was one of the causes of the arthritis." Yoga is an Eastern remedy that turned out to work well on both the psychological and the physical components of her suffering. "It's quite strenuous and very effective on arthritis. The punch line is I can now control my arthritis pain and tension or anxiety with one and a half hours of yoga. I get a very strong feeling of well-being because of the way yoga incorporates exercise plus relaxation."

She made a similar discovery about helping. "I had spent a day helping my daughter, who had had foot surgery, and driving home I noticed such a rush and an overall sense of well-being. It lasted all that day.

"It has always made me feel good doing things for other people, friends or family. I guess I've never really thought much about why. I've learned to control my body and mind to quite an extent, and I know for a fact that our minds and bodies work together.

"To go in there and help her, it gives you that same kind of a good-all-over feeling, kind of a lift." Suddenly you feel that "it's a beautiful day," she said. "You're so glad to be alive."

For her the result was less pain, less tension, more "good belly laughs" in a day. She sees the effects of both yoga and helping as "connected, all pretty well the same response," and she's adding helping to her list of things she can do to feel good.

Like Keeling and like Benson, people from both the lay and the scientific fields are coming to understand the links between mind and body, and beyond that the link to spirit as well. When I convened the conference of mind-body experts in New York, Benson, to prepare for the meeting, began to study the work of Pitirim Sorokin, a sociologist who had studied the lives of people who were "good neighbors," including people who had become saints, to see how altruism had developed. Sorokin founded the Harvard Department of Sociology in 1930 and in 1949 established the Harvard Research Center for Creative Altruism, which he directed for ten years. He saw helping as a form of meditation and meditation as a step on the path toward a more altruistic humankind. "The techniques of Yoga, Buddhism, Zen Buddhism, Sufism," he wrote, "together with the technique of prayer, serve as examples of the methods of altruization and spiritualization based upon complete transcendence of one's ego and on effective control of the unconscious drives and ego-centered conscious mind."[1] He defined a spiritual person as one who succeeds in identifying his "true being not only and not so much with his organism and his unconscious and conscious ego-centered 'mind,' but with the supraconscious Infinite Manifold (God, Nirvana, the Cosmic Mind, Atman, Tao, the Absolute . . .), transcending man's ego, indescribable by any words and undefinable by any concepts."[2]

Simply put, the spiritual goal of meditation is self-forgetfulness in the interest of identification with something larger than the self. And the goal of helping is also to go beyond the self, to identify with something larger. By helping another person we bring to consciousness the connection we each have with all other people. Those moments of connection with others, in the genuine desire to be of assistance, are a powerful reminder of our membership in some larger body, whether you call that larger being God, the Absolute, or the Family of Man.

SELF-WORTH/SELF-FORGETTING

As the helper forgets herself and feels less body distress, she naturally feels better about herself generally. Big increases in self-esteem are a basic component of the calm that follows. In my own survey more than half the people—a total of 57 percent—experienced a feeling of greatly enhanced self-worth because they had helped someone. Helping's ability to give a powerful boost to self-esteem also arises from the impact of truly feeling needed and of gaining a sense of being accepted in a partnership with other people.

For most of us it's too easy to allow daily problems and failures, large and small, to erode our sense of self-worth continually. Helping someone makes our bodies feel good and gives us back the healthier view of ourselves as good and valuable people. It is a buffer against the daily irritations that are so damaging to health and to self-image.

Another researcher puts it very well. Lowell Levin, professor of public health at Yale University, says that "when you're a helper, your self-concept improves. You are somebody. You are worthwhile. And there's nothing more exhilarating than that."

At a recent conference at Valparaiso University, sponsored by the Carillon Foundation, an Indiana mental health organization, one speaker was Harry Porterfield. He is a Chicago TV newscaster who over many years has specialized in interviewing people involved in their community, especially low-income residents. Asked what he believed to be the greatest benefit these volunteers received, he stopped to think, and then said, "It's a self-esteem feeling. I probably put that in importance ahead of most everything else."

He told the story of one volunteer who is spastic and has cerebral palsy and needs help for everything. He can only use one toe, but with that he is able to work as a statistician for the Weather Bureau. He told Porterfield that he "had to" volunteer because of how good it makes him feel, so he types out a column for the handicapped using his one big toe.

While it often happens that helpers get discouraged, those who are helping freely—rather than out of a sense of family or civic obligation—and who also have personal contact with the one who is helped are more likely to gain rather than lose self-esteem.

One personal experience of this calm, and of its impact on self-esteem, began on those evenings in the Peace Corps in Venezuela when the boys would come to my door. I would spend hours talking to them or their parents, and then later I would feel the helper's high so powerfully that sometimes it was hard for me to go to sleep. But on the following days what would occur for me was the calming sensation. And that would take place in spite of lots of obstacles.

My days during those two years would typically begin with some of the many little stresses that Peace Corps trainers had warned us sometimes erode the commitment of volunteers. For example, Maracay, the city I was living in, was extremely hot, even early in the morning. Though I worked in the little municipal building downtown, I was living in a slum where most of the houses were made out of cinder blocks and discarded tin signs. By the time I began to walk to the bus stop, dust and heat had already settled over everything. And then the bus itself would be a metal roasting pan.

I also quickly discovered that not everyone was friendly to my presence in the country. Because of my blond hair I was sometimes shouted at threateningly by someone passing on the street: *"Alemán,"* which means German, or *"Americano."*

All these incidents were annoying. But I found that on the mornings after I had spent a night connecting with the neighborhood families, neither the heat nor the name-calling was really very disturbing. Instead I felt a calm that seemed to shut out these irritations. I would think about the talk we'd had the night before—or maybe I'd shown a film outdoors for all the people who lived around me—and I would feel such a sense of well-being and, frankly, so good about myself that it acted as a sort of protection against the minor problems of the day.

I also had a regular daily test of this peaceful cast of mind. There was a man named Jaime who worked in City Hall with me, a planner, who stopped by my office almost every day for two years. Though he became my good friend, he also presented quite a daily challenge to my optimism. Every afternoon, when we returned from our siesta break, he would knock on my door, stick his head in, and say, "Allan, what's the answer?" What he meant was, What's the answer to poverty, suffering, and all the problems of the world? He believed it was hopeless, that there was no answer. I believed, and still do, that we can make a dent in the problems, that we can do some good.

But I was frustrated, because Jaime would never wait for me to answer. Every day before I could say anything, he would shut the door and head on down the hall. He was a dauntingly intelligent man—and he was embittered and cynical.

Fortunately that daily question was not our only contact. Some nights after work we would stop to have coffee in a café and we'd sit and argue. He was evangelical about his bitterness; he wanted me to be cynical too. And he was right about many of his points. In fact I could not prove that I was helping those kids and their families through my after-work conversations and advice. Yet, on the basis of my time spent with them, my efforts to help, and the sense of connection with them, I had a strong feeling of optimism, of self-worth—proof of the value, at least to me, of making the effort.

The feeling I had could evaporate, though. Easily.

When I would take a vacation, go to Caracas, go to discotheques with other Peace Corps volunteers, I'd be truly enjoying myself. But the self-doubts of how much we as volunteers could accomplish would start to grow. Yet ironically when I came back to my modest helping efforts in my neighborhood, my sense of well-being, confidence, and self-esteem would return.

In the survey I directed, volunteers reported that helping can lead us to a stronger sense of our ties with other people, as well as to feelings of mastery, challenge, optimism, joy, and self-control (in the sense of having some control over one's own fate). What follows is an example of the power it has both to calm our tensions and to raise our self-esteem by giving us the sense of connecting with others.

The story involves two men, both working as volunteers at the same public radio station, both suffering from feelings of depression. In one case the depression was very severe; in the other it was merely a case of the blues brought about by the sudden isolation of retirement and a move to the country.

Fred King, prior to his retirement, had been living in Hong Kong, working as manager-director of a men's clothing company. He had handled quality control at sites including Sri Lanka and the Philippines, as well as managing advertising and sales. When he was ready to retire, he and his wife came back to the United States and moved into a country home they had bought two years earlier. "It was quite a comedown from managing director of a corporation in Hong King to the backwoods," he said. "It took some getting used to."

He was retired for a year before he decided to volunteer at the radio station. "Another year would have had me in the funny farm," he said in a joking tone. To stop feeling so isolated, he drove to the nearest town and started giving away some of his expertise. In the six years since then he has spent twenty hours a week at the radio station, working as volunteer coordinator, handling incoming funds, doing some of the station's computer work. "It's a change to drop from a vice presidency to opening mail in the morning," he said, "but it doesn't matter."

What made the difference for him was not the routine chores but the feeling of being linked to others, "the association with people. There's a nice group over here at the station, and they couldn't show their appreciation more."

King's colleague at the station, Rafe Paull, had had a serious battle with depression. But he had a start in life that would almost seem to presage his eventual recovery. He was born in Jerusalem, at a weight of less than four pounds. Both he and his mother were in danger at his birth. His father went to a nearby temple to pray. After a time his prayers were interrupted by the arrival of the doctor who had delivered the child and who had also come there to pray. The doctor told the father that his wife and son were well and that he had named the boy himself: Raphael, for "the archangel of cure."

Decades later, Rafe Paull fell into what he described as over six years of "deep, deep clinical depression." In that period of time drugs had failed to help him; a hospitalization and a series of shock treatments had also failed. Then he took yet another drug, Prozac, a new compound on the market that was quickly becoming the nation's most frequently prescribed antidepressant. This time the drug worked. But once the process of recovery had begun, it was volunteering that, in combination with the drug, allowed him to sustain his recovery and continue to feel good.

Rafe had been, over the years, successful in sales, consulting, and public health organizational work—all because of his very easygoing, outgoing personality. "I've never known a stranger," he said. But when depression overwhelmed him, he completely retreated into himself. At the time he fell ill, he had a card and gift shop. He withdrew from the business. "I retired because I was depressed," he said. "I was incompetent."

"He used to sit in a chair and fall asleep all day, like somebody dead in the chair," said his wife, Shirley. During much of the time he was depressed, the Paulls were living out in the country, with no close neighbors. When Shirley would come home from work at night, she said, "I didn't know when I walked in the house whether he would be dead or alive." When he started to feel better, he recovered rapidly. "He became a whole lot more like he used to be, more garrulous, more outgoing, more self-assured."

As a pharmacist, Shirley had professional knowledge, which gave her an unusual vantage point from which to look at the effect on her husband of both the drug and the volunteering. Of his initial recovery she said, "We have to attribute it to the drug. Prozac made him able to go out and do the stuff he wanted to do." The volunteering has worked to reinforce the medication. "For him it has been a wonderful combination." She saw the positive results of his volunteer efforts helping him in two ways, through the ties he made with the people around him and through his return to a situation "where what he did or said or thought had some impact."

He is "an extremely intelligent, bright, funny man. He lost it for a while. The people who work down there have been good to him and good for him."

While he was still depressed, Rafe had gone with his wife, as the two of them had done for years, to volunteer once a year for the station's fund-raising marathon, by answering phones and running errands. When he started to feel better, it was the radio station that came to mind as a way of getting back out into the world again. Yet it was the feeling of being part of the team at the station, more than any particular pride in having helped in the broadcast of the music, that made the difference for him. "I delighted in the company," he said.

Social involvement, as we discussed earlier, appears to ward off the kind of feelings that actually increase stress and damage health. It can counteract loneliness, depression, hostility, and a sense of helplessness. The health-giving effect is magnified in situations where people believe they are making a social investment as well. Many volunteers share this belief. For example, someone who works with the elderly may have in the back of his mind that because he has offered help, he will therefore receive help himself when he is old.

To the cynical this may seem like a foolishly "magical" idea, but it can be a powerful one. Many volunteers told me that they thought that doing good now would some-how make society more responsive to their personal or family needs in the future. If many of us expect that helping others will lead to our receiving some form of aid in our turn in the future, this further diminishes the amount of stress in our bodies. We expect to feel better because of helping, and we do.

This is comparable to the so-called placebo or belief response. People who take an inert pill, believing that it contains medicine, typically show about a 30 percent improvement in a range of conditions, from seasickness to chronic pain. It works the same way with behavior that it does with pills. Belief that something good is going to happen because of a helping act further diminishes the negative impact of stress.

Many of the participants in the AT&T volunteer program, for example, made comments such as "I feel what comes around, goes around. If you help someone, I feel you will receive help when you need it for yourself." And from another: "I feel that I may someday need help and if I help someone, it will be returned to me in one way or another—spiritual as well as physical."

A practical use of this thinking is found in a new kind of volunteer program at work in half a dozen cities. The principle, developed by Edgar Cahn of the District of Columbia School of Law, is that elderly helpers will get credits for the help they give, which they can "cash in" later when they themselves are in need. One startling result generally true of these programs so far has been that while volunteers have been turning out in good numbers to help, they have been very slow to "spend" any of their credits. At this point only 1.1 percent of the 80,800 credits earned in the Miami program have been cashed in. Some observers think that this is because the volunteers are drawn to work because of the promise of the credit but then continue because it makes them feel so good.[3] It may also be the case that these helpers, as a result of their work, actually need less help.

Even though helping is not usually rewarded with actual credits, the helper is likely to emerge with a greater sense that people will be willing to help when his own time of need comes. This sort of social security can become a significant contributor to a more peaceful and less stressful view of life.

A TRANSCENDENT CALM

While many volunteers report the calmness and increased self-worth that follows the helper's high, only a few say they have tried to analyze why it happens. As a lifelong volunteer, "Mary" is one of the ones who has taken the time to question why. Why, with a job as a school administrator and two daughters, was she spending so much time working in the community? she wondered.

Her habit of helping began for her with the example set

by her father. Helping was a way of life in her family. "It's all I've ever known," she said. "My father was a Presbyterian minister. I saw that that was what he did, and I liked what I saw happen. One thing was that people liked him. He was about to do something for them, and in return he was well received. It was very satisfying to him." She believed that helping produced benefits.

Over the years she herself has done many kinds of volunteering, including most recently the teaching of writing in a men's prison. To walk into a prison for any reason is sobering. The guard behind the window at the gate, the security identification for visitors, the sudden awareness of high fences and walls, the prisoners themselves watching from their cells or from a distance out in the yard—*everything* is, at first, a reminder of where you are, of the crimes committed and the claustrophobic terrors that imprisonment can surely provoke.

But at the Creative Writing Club that Mary leads in a medium-custody prison, the awareness of these surroundings begins to fade. Mary and three men are listening to another of the club members read his poem. It's about being in a dark room with stars on the walls. Though the poet never explicitly says so, it is about looking out a prison window at night. It's a good poem. The poet, "Richard," a wiry young black man, is a constant talker, restless and opinionated. Mary, who obviously likes this man, is delighted with his new effort.

From the readings of poems and essays, the agenda moves to specific instruction. Mary talks about grammar. "Everybody _____ problems," she writes on the board. Is the correct verb form *has* or *have*? This is a group where some are educated and some are struggling with the basics.

But part of the way in which she helps these men is beyond grammar and poetry; it's in the relationship that she develops with them through the class. A few weeks earlier she had loaned Richard her copy of a biography of Gandhi, knowing that he was continuously stirring up trouble with the prison guards. He took the book from Mary and started reading it, slowly. By the time of the class meeting he had only read about fourteen pages, he said, but he had gotten the idea. He was acting like Gandhi, right here in this prison. He hadn't been in lockup for the past three weeks, which was a long time for him to stay out of trouble. Gandhi had controlled the world with only his words.

With the loan of that book, Mary had realized what the effort to help Richard had done for her. "It takes me outside of myself," she said. And at the same time she understood that she had something the prisoners needed; it was hers to give.

She also felt her volunteering was a form of that spiritual barter I've been talking about. "It's truly superstitious on my part," she said, but her feeling had always been "if you do this, it's like warding off evil." And it's like paying something back for the good you have already received. "I have been extremely lucky." She described her years so far as "a spared life," because she had had good fortune in many ways. "I feel like I owe something."

On a recent night, driving away from the prison parking lot, she listened to a piece of music by Mozart on the radio and realized that the work she had done with imprisoned people and with others who needed help was her own piece of original music, lifting her own spirits. "It's for me a creative work. It's a concert." She could never be a preacher, she said, and she doesn't write as well as she'd like. But she knows how much she can help people, and that feels like a good talent to have.

The benefits of helping go beyond basic self-esteem and a sense of security—to feelings of creative fulfillment like Mary's, to optimism about life, to real joy. When a small act that a helper can do with ease makes someone else's life better, then the one who helps is sometimes overwhelmed with feelings of joy and with a sense of the goodness of life.

Another helper who has tried to analyze why he experiences an emotional calming is "Steve," a man I have known since the 1970s. A law school graduate, he talks about how daily life stress can still unnerve him despite his many years of sobriety and his active role in Alcoholics Anonymous. "It's like noise, like having earphones always in your ears, always turned on," he said. "Sometimes it's worse, like those big blaster radios kids carry around. You want to run away. But you can't. It keeps coming into your ears."

To forget stressful thoughts, he said, "I first tried alcohol to mask it, make the world outside go away. But alcohol was the way to die. I learned that the healthy way to turn off the noise of stress is to go out of myself. At AA meetings people talk about themselves, their concerns. And we recovering alcoholics like to talk. So you focus on this person, and as you do that, it starts to turn off the noise. You can go to AA meetings every day. You also become part of a family. And remember that most of us, while we were drinking, felt so lonely, isolated, part of nothing," he said of the group's social support. "You are immediately connecting. That greatly reduces the 'radio noise.'"

As Steve demonstrates, the personal benefits of helping—the healthy helping syndrome, which begins with the high and then flowers into the sense of calmness and self-worth—can ease the bad effects of stress even in the most "emotionally raw" individuals.

Or consider the experiences of people who literally give a part of their bodies to help someone else. The *Annals of the New York Academy of Sciences* described what happens to the lives of kidney donors: "The act of making such a gift becomes a transcendent one. . . . Many donors testify that giving an organ was the most important, meaningful and satisfying act of their lives, one that increased their self-knowledge, enhanced their feelings of self-worth, gave them a sense of 'totality,' belief and commitment, and increased their sense of unity with the recipient, people in general and with humanity."[4]

It is not necessary to wait until you have an opportunity to donate a kidney or save the whole world to enjoy this good feeling of calm and human kinship. A small effort to help one person can create these same feelings and attitudes, emotions that, if they occur regularly in our stressful world, can lead to better physical health, better mental health, and overall happiness. More than simply leading to a healthier view of life, they are in themselves a healthier way of life.

4

How Our Health
Improves

JUDY WEINTRAUB has multiple sclerosis. In her apartment in New York's Greenwich Village are four telephones; she always has one close by because it's hard for her to move from one room to another to answer. She needs telephones, both for her work as a consultant to youth organizations and for her personal helping efforts. In her volunteering Judy does from home the bureaucratic legwork that uneducated people can't do to get the help they need. Sitting at her dining room table, she makes calls and takes calls. Her high-ceilinged living room, dimly lit on this particular morning, could easily seem far from the noise of life, could even seem lonely. And yet Judy, who is able to get out on crutches with assistance, is very much "plugged-in" to what's going on out there. She has a computer, a copier, and the scattered telephones. Her next acquisition will be a fax machine. With these tools at hand, she said, "I can make the revolution."

She is one of the many people who are making significant improvements in their own health through their helping of others. Her telephone work has helped to diminish the effects of as serious a disease as multiple sclerosis while she assists others in making big changes in their lives too.

One person she helped was a young single mother having problems with her teenage daughter. "Ellen" came to Judy's apartment, and the two of them talked. It was quickly clear to Judy that the trouble lay with the mother: "This woman was falling apart." As the story unfolded, Judy said, she learned that Ellen worked in a restaurant kitchen and had recently threatened to stab someone there with a knife. "Fortunately she had grabbed the sharpening steel instead of a knife." Ellen had been given an appointment with a psychotherapist, but this was still six weeks away.

So Judy got busy on the phone. "I used the right words, that I was afraid she was going to 'hurt herself or others.' " As a result Ellen was seen immediately. She is still in treatment, Judy said, "she has stopped trying to stab people," and her daughter is doing much better.

When helping others, Judy often feels a rush of strength that enables her to do things she can't usually do. On many nights she does not have the strength to heat her dinner or to lift a bottle of apple juice. On the night after seeing Ellen, however, she was able to do both those things—which, insignificant as they may seem to the able-bodied, can make the difference to someone who's not. As she said, "I had a lovely evening—when I could do what I needed to do."

THE SURVEY RESULTS

My survey found that out of the 95 percent of respondents who reported the sensations of helper's high, nine out of ten rated their health as better than others their age. This feeling of well-being is critically important. Studies have documented the fact that raising a person's perceived health status leads to reductions in stress that create actual health improvements. Most important for the purposes of this study, respondents to the helping survey frequently dated the perceived improvement in their health to the beginning of their helping efforts.

Frequency of helping was found to be crucial. There was a *ten times greater* chance that volunteers who saw themselves as healthier than others would be weekly rather than once-a-year helpers.

Or look at the helpers who said they were in bad health. The most frequently involved volunteers were also the least likely to report poor health. A slim 4 percent of the weekly helpers rated their health as poor for their age; in contrast, poor health was reported by 12 percent of those who help only once a year on their own, and by 20 percent of those who help once a year through a group—a difference of up to five times.

I received reports from people who can specifically relate their helping activities to a wide range of health gains, such as fewer colds, diminished pain from lupus, fewer episodes of flu, lessened tendency toward overeating, quicker recovery from surgery, help with insomnia, fewer migraines, and a cure for stomachaches. The list could go on and on.

What appears to be at work here is a combination of factors, varying in weight and frequency of occurrence, which include:

- The possibility of strengthening immune-system activity

- Decrease of both the intensity and the awareness of physical pain

- Activation of the emotions that are vital to maintenance of good health

- Reduction of the incidence of attitudes, such as chronic hostility, that negatively arouse and damage the body

- The multiple benefits to the body's systems provided by stress relief

The results of these factors are health benefits to the helper that can be astonishing in their impact. Helping contributes to the maintenance of good health, and it can diminish the effect of diseases and disorders both serious and minor, psychological and physical.

IMMUNITY AND THE MOTHER TERESA EFFECT

The body's immune system is a complex network of glands, organs, and cells that go into action when necessary to fight off invaders. The front line of the system is formed by the lymphocytes, or white blood cells, which patrol the bloodstream and fight invading substances. The system also includes other kinds of cells with assigned tasks, including the destruction of viruses and healing of tissue, and all aspects of this bodywide system are linked to each other in an information network—which in turn seems to communicate with the brain. It now appears that the brain speaks to the immune system through neurotransmitters and that the immune system produces similar transmitter compounds that send information back to the brain. In short, what we know about the physiology of immunity seems to be compatible with the notion that our immune system "knows" how we think and feel and is affected by our general mental state—and, in circular fashion, can affect it as well.

Many studies now tend to confirm that there may be a correlation between our state of mind, the state of our immune system, and the incidence of illness.[1] The higher rates of illness among people who have recently lost a spouse indicate, for example, that the stress of loss affects the mourner's immunity. As discussed earlier, there is extensive documentation of the shorter lifespan of people who feel socially isolated. Also at health risk, according to various studies, are institutionalized patients who have no sense of control over their lives, breast cancer patients who are pessimistic about their chances for recovery, and people who feel trapped in the wars of bad marriages.[2] Conversely we now have studies that suggest the healthful effects of happier states of mind. Case in point: Charles Carver, of the University of Miami, and Michael Scheier, of Carnegie-Mellon University, studied men about to undergo bypass surgery. They found that those who had revealed more optimistic attitudes on tests recovered faster from the operation than did those with gloomier states of mind.[3]

While there is certainly much controversy within and surrounding the relatively new field of psychoneuroim-munology (PNI)—the study of mind, brain, and immunity—there is a substantial body of clinical evidence showing that stress reduces immunity. The dispute lies in whether this reduction is sufficient to make a difference in a disease's outcome. Some say that it is not. Without question it is cruelly misleading to give people the idea that experiencing the "wrong" feelings will make them sick or having "right" ones will make them well, when in fact serious diseases are usually influenced by a complex multitude of factors, which we are far from being able to understand. However, animal studies have clearly shown that a creature weakened by stress has a higher likelihood of developing such serious diseases as cancer.[4]

In fact, the idea of a state-of-mind/state-of-immunity connection, though currently a hot topic, is not new. It recurs throughout medical history. Hippocrates, for example, observed that stress played a role in the occurrence of asthma. During the early 1900s, a time of high incidence of tuberculosis, the eminent Canadian physician Sir William Osler observed that the treatment of the disease was often more importantly involved with what the patient had going on in his head than what was occurring in his chest. Current research is now able to take advantage of advances in technology to begin to pin down the physiology of the connections between mind, mood, and immunity.

The fact that immune system suppression can be conditioned—which suggests that it can be controlled—was one of the breakthrough discoveries in this field. Psychologist Robert Ader at the University of Rochester, New York, as part of his researches in behavioral conditioning, performed an experiment similar to the famous one by Ivan Pavlov in which dogs are conditioned to salivate at the sound of a bell that they have originally associated with the arrival of food. In an effort to create negative conditioning and get rats to develop an aversion to saccharine, Ader injected them with a nausea-causing drug before they drank sweetened water. The conditioning worked, and usually after only one such injection the rats would get nauseated from the sweetened water without further injections of the drug. But there was a surprise: The rats died shortly afterward. This unexpected kink in the experiment arose from the fact that the nausea-causing drug was also a strong immunosuppressant. In effect, after their one injection the rats had not only conditioned themselves to feel nausea at the taste of the sweet water, as Ader had intended, but they had also induced in themselves the immunity-suppression effect that the drug had been causing. Their resulting vulnerability to diseases led to their deaths. Ader demonstrated that rats could suppress their own immune-system functions, which of course suggests that we, too, can suppress—and presumably enhance—our own immune systems.[5]

Later colleagues of Ader's, David and Suzanne Felten, did some of the work that illustrated how brain cells might communicate with immune-system cells. Through an electron microscope the Feltens actually photographed the connections between nerve endings and white blood cells that fight off infection. This was another landmark in the effort to prove that the mind and the immune system are able to talk to each other. Summing up the state of the art in a whimsical way in the journal *Equinox*, neuroscientist David Felten offered this limerick:

> We now have a clear-cut impression
> that bereavement or even depression
> can leave our secretions
> with serious depletions
> resulting in immune suppression.[6]

A growing number of researchers now believe that these communications can be positive as well as negative, that such states of mind as joy, optimism, and feelings of kinship with others can work to enhance our immune systems, even in the presence of the usual stresses of life. The *Journal of the American Medical Association*, for example, has reported that persons who were "good copers" with stress had significantly higher natural killer-cell activity (an indicator of immune function) than "poor copers."[7] A person who copes well with stress is one who, when confronted with an emotionally demanding situation, experiences the least amount of negative stress arousal of the body's systems. An optimistic, joyful attitude can act as a buffer against damaging arousal because the joyful person does not perceive every stressful situation as a threat.

The impact of the helper's cast of mind on immune function has been shown in a dramatic laboratory demonstration performed by David McClelland, an eminent professor of psychology formerly at Harvard and now at Boston University, who has done leading work for over forty years on human motivation and health. A Quaker, McClelland is also concerned about social problems. He and his colleagues had 132 students at Harvard watch a powerful fifty-minute film of Nobel Laureate Mother Teresa aiding the sick and dying of Calcutta. After the film he tested a sample of saliva from each of the students for the level of immunoglobulin A (S-IgA), a vital defense against the cold virus. He found that the students who had seen the film, regardless of whether or not they claimed to admire Mother Teresa's work, showed marked increases in this measure of immune-system function. In contrast, the showing of a pro-Nazi film *Triumph of the Axis*, about the Nazi destruction of Europe, produced no effect on the students' S-IgA. The "Mother Teresa effect" occurred even though the students were merely watching a movie.[8]

McClelland and his fellow researchers concluded that once we establish "an affiliative connection" with someone—a relationship of friendship, love, or some sort of positive bonding—we feel emotions that can affect the immune system. Further studies by others at Harvard seemed to confirm this conclusion: The students who showed more affiliative trust had greater helper-to-suppressor T-cell ratios, another immunity parameter that indicates our ability to resist disease.[9] "Finally," McClelland said in a letter to me, "we have preliminary evidence in a longitudinal study that people who are high in Affiliative Trust show fewer instances of major illnesses nine years after the assessment . . . was made." Helping others is a good way to build this sense of trust and connection and to add to our protection against disease.

SOME OF THE ILLS THAT
HELPING HELPS

You've already heard the story of Lynn and her "baby magic." Lynn's formerly severe back trouble is no longer a problem for her. And Tammy, the kindergarten teacher, found in her college years that volunteering made her headaches go away. *Headaches and backaches* together account for a large amount of our everyday "feeling bad." Lower back pain alone will affect nearly 80 percent of adults at some time in their lives.

Again and again I hear reports of how helping helps with these problems. Among the personal reports received in the volunteer survey were: a sixty-six-year-old Portland, Maine, resident who discussed the disappearance of lower back pain since involvement in the Infant Hearing Screening Program; a twenty-eight-year-old Girl Scout leader from Goleta, California, who noted, "There have been days when I have had a headache, gone to Scouts, and had it disappear"; and a forty-seven-year-old lay minister from Matthews, North Carolina, who explained how her constant headaches disappear during the service and for several hours after.

The multiple factors involved in the healthy helping syndrome are effective against both major and minor physical problems. Some helpers report that their efforts for others are useful in *weight control*. Food is one of the comforts that many of us turn to automatically in times of prolonged stress. If stress arousal doesn't let us relax, it seems to be a common impulse to try to counteract it through the solace of eating.

Sleeplessness, like overeating, is another response to continuing stress. The arousal of the body through stress reactions can overcome the body's need to sleep, to our detriment. When a helping act breaks the stress reaction, then the natural sequence of tiredness, relaxation, and sleep can occur.

McClelland's Mother Teresa research showed the effect of trust on immunoglobulin A, the body's defense against respiratory infections. In addition to this data on one possible emotion-immunity connection, we also have research demonstrating a direct link between stress and *infections.* Psychologist Sandra Levy, at the University of Pittsburgh School of Medicine, studied 106 healthy volunteers between the ages of eighteen and forty-five to learn about the activity of natural killer (NK) cells, a type of cell believed to play a role in the defense against infections and malignancy. As she reported at the 1989 annual meeting of the American Psychological Association, Levy found that the most cases of infectious illness during a six-month period were in the individuals with low NK activity and with particularly intense reactions to daily life stresses. One-third of those studied fell into this category, suffering from a higher incidence of illnesses that included colds, pneumonia, cold sores, fever, and sore throat.[10]

Acid stomach is another stress-related condition that can be diminished by helping acts. The shelves of antacid pills, tablets, and liquids in the drugstores of this country are evidence of the widespread occurrence of this complaint. When excess stomach acid stays at a high level, problems begin. Ulcers may result. Researchers report that depression and poor social support predispose us to painful stomach ulcers, as does an overly aggressive, hostile personality. These personal and social conditions make life's daily demands more threatening and thus stress-arousing, with results including excessive stomach acid secretions. Helping others can counteract this acid problem by starting to reverse feelings of depression, supplying social contact, and decreasing the feelings of hostility and isolation.

A forty-year-old Schaumburg, Illinois, resident talked

about taking on the volunteer role of a daily "listening post" at work. "I feel good to send people back to their desks after five minutes at mine with a smile, and I find my stomach stops hurting and my back doesn't ache after those minutes."

A widespread illness that can be very debilitating is *arthritis*, affecting one out of every seven Americans. Usually involving an inflammation or disease of the joints, treating it may require drugs, exercise, or even surgery. Helping—with its potentially meditative focus away from oneself—can provide very real assistance in minimizing the pain. Genevieve Plumb, seventy-seven years old, does volunteer work at both her winter residence in Florida and her home in Minnesota. She has tutored elementary school students in math and has also trained to be a reading tutor. Working with the children "felt so good, and was so demanding at the time that I forgot all about the aches and pains of the bit of arthritis which troubles me."

New medical research at the Stanford University Arthritis Center and the Veterans Hospital in Columbus, Missouri, has found that rheumatoid arthritis patients who decreased their depression and increased their sense of personal effectiveness were far better at pain control. Volunteering can have a powerful positive effect on both depression and the sense of personal mastery.

Lupus is an illness that involves pain in the joints; it, too, may be relieved by active involvement with others. A forty-two-year-old woman from Stroudsburg, Pennsylvania, who suffers from lupus has been a volunteer coach every summer teaching seventy girls cheerleading and in the process becoming known as the Spirit Lady. She reported to me that she came out of the hospital after being treated for lupus and felt very weak but still went to see the girls: "Although not physically up to going, I did anyway, and it was like a shot of vitamins to me." Her lupus has not gone away—but her life is transformed:

"The four weeks in the summer when I do Spirit Lady is a super time for me. I seem to be very happy during that time, and my illness seems to be or is in control."

Symptoms of *asthma* are also sometimes relieved by the stress-reducing effect of helper's high, because a drop in stress may, for some people, decrease the constriction within the lungs that leads to asthma attacks. A few years ago Jean Cantner, sixty years old, of Culpepper, Virginia, saw a notice in her local paper advertising a class in a nearby town for people wanting to be clowns. She enrolled and became a clown, going to visit nursing homes in a big baggy suit and a bright red wig, big shoes, and an oversize tie. The feeling she gets from her clowning is "almost light-headed and giddy—a natural high." She believes that it has helped her asthma. "When I feel good and I'm happy, it doesn't bother me as much."

Some helpers report that their helping of others has hastened their *recovery from surgery*. Again, the breaking of the stress cycle seems to be at the bottom of the improvement. Recent research at the VA Medical Center in Miami found that patients who were especially vulnerable to life stress prior to a hernia operation were far more sensitive to pain following surgery, used three times more narcotics, had more complications, and stayed in the hospital longer than those who were low reactors to stress. The subjects were twenty-four men, with a mean age of fifty-nine, who were facing surgery for the first time and were free of any other illness. These men were evaluated prior to the operation to assess the amount of recent stress in their lives and to find out how they responded to a stress test. The results showed that those with high recent levels of stress and high reactivity to the test were the ones who, after the surgery, experienced the more difficult recovery.[11]

Probably the hottest topic in the discussion about how emotions affect immunity focuses on *cancer*. The issue is whether the "right" feelings can help prevent the occurrence or at least recurrence of cancer. All we know at this point is that different states of mind do affect the immune system, which is responsible for resisting the growth of a tumor. But there is no proven relationship of these attitudes to either getting cancer or being able to fight it.

On the other hand, some initial research reveals a possible link. Helping behaviors produce the kinds of emotions and the stress reduction that might, according to these studies, slow the progress of cancer. Case in point: Research by psychologist Sandra Levy found that joyfulness—defined as emotional resilience and vigor—was the second most important predictor of survival time for a group of women with recurring breast cancer.[12] Helping can enhance our feelings of joyfulness and reduce the unhealthy sense of isolation.

Loneliness itself is beginning to appear to be a serious health risk. Research has shown that natural killer cells, lymphocytes that attack tumor cells or cells infected by viruses, declined in strength in medical students under the stress of taking an exam. But they were lowest in those students who were lonelier than their fellow students.[13] Helping others increases our sense of social support.

Research discussed at the annual meeting of the American Psychiatric Association and published in the medical periodical *Lancet* found that there was a relation between states of mind and lifespan of patients. David Spiegel, an associate professor of psychiatry and behavioral sciences at Stanford Medical School, reported that women with metastatic breast cancer who received, in addition to standard medical treatment, a year of weekly group therapy and instruction in relaxation techniques lived almost twice as long as those who received only the medical care. The women receiving medical care only lived 18.9 months, compared with an average of 36.6 months for those who took part in the mutual helping of a therapy group, as well as doing some relaxing exercises. In addition to the longer survival, the women taking part in group therapy had the added benefit of fewer mood swings and less phobia and pain. Regular helping is another way that we can create the feelings of social support and relaxation that this regimen of therapy apparently stimulated.

While neither researchers nor patients themselves know for sure what emotional well-being will do to prevent, cure, or slow this illness—the second most common cause of death—we do know that it can reduce a cancer patient's pain and at least open the possibility of longer survival.

Our number-one killer is *coronary artery disease*. In a single year about three million Americans will have this condition and about three-quarters of them will eventually die at an age considered to be premature, that is, before age sixty-five. For almost forty years scientists have been on the trail of a link between the emotions—specifically feelings of hostility and drivenness—and incidence of heart disease. Of particular importance was an epidemiological study by San Francisco physicians Meyer Friedman and Ray Rosenman. Begun in 1960, this study of 3,500 men lasted twelve years. The subjects were categorized as Type A's—driven, competitive, hostile—or as the more easygoing Type B's. The study revealed that the Type A men were two to three times more prone to heart attacks. Publication in 1974 of the book *Type A Behavior and Your Heart*, by Rosenman and Friedman, made the link between Type A behavior and heart disease public knowledge.[14]

In *The Trusting Heart: Great News About Type A Behavior*, Dr. Redford Williams at Duke University has outlined the damage that hostility does to the circulatory system and how a softening of that angry, cynical view of the world can reduce the risk of heart disease.

Williams and his colleagues took a look at the life

patterns of 118 lawyers who had undergone psychological testing twenty-five years earlier. Those who had scored high in hostility as students had a mortality rate that was over four times higher than that of their calmer colleagues. Those who rated highest on cynicism and anger fared the worst, with a death rate five and half times that of the more trusting and easygoing subjects.[15]

Hostility—"the frequent experience of negative emotions when dealing with others," as Williams defines it— is now recognized as an especially powerful trigger of the damaging stress. Stress chemicals—norepinephrine, epinephrine, and cortisol—contribute to higher blood pressure, raised cholesterol levels, and faster blood flow around the branch points of arteries. All of these conditions are believed to play a role in injuring the arterial inner lining. When this damage occurs, cholesterol accumulates at that spot, forming blockages, and the blood's platelets further stimulate the growth of the artery's muscular wall there. Further, the walls of arteries generally thicken from frequent rises in blood pressure.[16] These blocked arteries—arteriosclerosis—lead to heart disease.

A colleague, Dr. Hirokazu Monou, suggested to Williams that a Type A person may also suffer physical damage because of a weakened parasympathetic nervous system, whose job it is to calm the body when the fight-or-flight response is no longer needed. To test this idea, the researchers gave a stimulant to both Type A and Type B men (the opposite of Type A's) to stir up equal levels of accelerated heart activity. Results of EKG tests on these men showed that the hearts of the Type B men recovered much faster than those of the Type A's. The scientists concluded that Type A's might be getting less effective stress protection from their own nervous systems. The nervous system receptors that produce the calming reaction had been "down-regulated," worn out, by their constant stimulation in countering stressful situations.[17]

Research now shows that curbing hostility reduces the chances of having another heart attack and produces even more benefits for those who do not yet have heart damage. "It is far easier to patch a small hole in the dike than it is to stem the flood once a breach occurs."[18]

Additional work by psychologist Matthew Burg and others at Duke has found that the degree of social support that the Type A person has can mitigate this hostility. The Type A patient with more good friends had wider, less constricted coronary arteries than did the Type A who was more typically alone.[19]

In fact there is still other research that indicates that self-centeredness may be a key factor in coronary heart disease. A team from the University of California at San Francisco Medical School that included Larry Scherwitz and Dean Ornish counted the number of times that test subjects used such words as *I* and *me* and then correlated these with measures of intensity of anger and blood pressure level. "We found that the Type A students used twice as many self-references as the Type B students, and that self-references were highly correlated with both anger intensity and blood pressure levels." An even stronger correlation was found when the test was repeated with middle-age men who had been referred by cardiologists for an exercise stress test. The men whose stress tests came out abnormal were also likely to rate very high on their *I/me* usage. In addition the most self-involved patients tended to have a more severe case of coronary artery disease, as well as greater likelihood of depression and anxiety.[20]

Redford Williams, the Duke University physician who leads the medical school's Behavioral Medicine Research Center, has developed some suggestions for counteracting the psychosocial risk factors to heart disease. He suggests such behaviors as learning to relax, forcing yourself to stop cynical thinking whenever it begins, and learning to laugh at yourself. What they have in common is the capacity to break the cycle of the stress reaction. Williams also suggests that you "put yourself in the other person's shoes." The pioneers of Type A researchers, Friedman and Rosenman, found that when heart attack patients adopted lifestyles that reduced hostility, the repeat rate of attacks was cut in half. The kind of behaviors that could do this, they commented, involved "consideration for and . . . love for others."

In 1990 Dean Ornish, director of the Preventive Medicine Research Institute, outlined a method for reversing heart disease in a book by that title. Until recently it was generally believed that the fatty-plaque buildup in the arteries could only be reversed with powerful drugs, which had many side effects. Ornish's work combines a low-fat diet with stress-reduction exercises that address the emotional components of the problem. The results he has achieved show that lifestyle changes can begin to reverse even severe cases of coronary artery disease after only a year, without the use of cholesterol-lowering drugs.

Though no studies have yet measured the effect of helping alone on heart attack risk, doing for others is a highly effective stress-reduction technique. It performs several functions linked with reduced risk of coronary disease: It encourages empathy with others and enlarges the helper's social network, therefore breaking the cycle of stress and bringing on a sense of calm.

THE PATHS TO PAIN RELIEF

In addition to the effects of stress on specific diseases, medical investigations have also uncovered powerful connections between high levels of stress and increased pain, whether it comes from an injury or a chronic condition.

In essence stress seems to make us hurt more. Concomitantly, breaking the stress cycle appears to lower our pain sensations. Two factors appear to be involved in this: the work of endorphins in actually muffling the pain messages and the distraction of the sufferer from his own pain.

To understand how endorphins work on pain, it's important first to realize that we do not "hurt" until a pain message reaches the brain. The nerve endings that sense pain are called pain receptors. A painful area, such as an inflamed joint or torn muscle, will produce prostaglandins, natural substances that irritate and stimulate the pain receptors. On the way to the brain the messages of the pain receptors go to a part of the spinal cord called the dorsal horn. From these, many scientists believe, the signal is carried by a neuropeptide known as Substance P, which is a specialized transmitter of pain messages from the receptors to the central nervous system.

Parallel to this system of pain communication is a system of pain suppression, which is also activated by naturally occurring substances produced by our bodies—the endorphins we discussed earlier. These are the body chemicals that drugs like morphine imitate. Endorphin-bearing neurons located in the dorsal horn area abut the Substance P–transmitting neurons. If, as a result of exercise, meditation, helping acts, or other mental or physical transactions, the endorphins are released, they bind to the pain-signaling neuron, thus inhibiting the release of Substance P. As a result the brain gets less information that tells it to "feel pain."[21]

A second factor at work in helping's pain-relieving effect is, as mentioned above, the simple fact of being distracted from the source of the pain. Typically, when we don't think about it, it doesn't hurt as much. It seems to be possible to keep the nervous system too busy transmitting other messages to allow the pain messages to get to the brain.[22]

Being "preoccupied" with something other than the pain can be a very effective painkiller. For example, a ballerina may perform with injuries that "should" be very painful. But while she is onstage and performing, she is completely focused on the dance. In the same way a powerful focus on another person can keep the pain messages from getting through. A forty-eight-year-old volunteer from Utica, Michigan, who tutors in a literacy program, wrote me, "If you have any aches and pains, they are quickly forgotten. When I am involved with helping others, my own stress level is reduced. I don't get keyed up as easily. My whole body is revitalized." Another volunteer, twenty-four years old, from Selden, New York, discussed suffering from painful gynecological conditions and needing four operations in the last four and a half years—but recounted that as a medical assistant "I often call patients 'just to check on them' without the doctor's knowledge," and doing this extra "something nice for someone, it makes my pain more bearable." The federal government study of the Retired Senior Volunteer Program reported that "a common statement heard from numerous volunteers was, 'Serving helps take my mind off my aches and pains.' "

ALLEVIATING PSYCHOLOGICAL ILLS

Because of the effects on mood and emotion—the calming, the rise in self-esteem, the stirring of optimism and joy—helping others can make significant and sometimes dramatic improvements in psychological problems.

In a psychiatric hospital in a suburb of Chicago, "Elizabeth" discovered her first pervasive sense of the goodness of life, not as a patient but as a volunteer. Ironically she went to work as a helper in the same hospital where her psychiatrist had earlier urged that she spend some time as a patient. Instead of becoming a patient she continued to see her therapist and she became a volunteer. After a couple of years the work she has done at the hospital has helped to heal her to the point that not only is she no longer a candidate for hospitalization, she is beginning truly to enjoy her life.

Her problems were tough ones. She had been verbally and physically abused as a child, and as a woman of forty-two with teenage children these experiences had come back to haunt her. As a result she was badly depressed, she had gained weight because of eating binges, she had a distorted view of the world around her, and she tended unexpectedly to dissociate, to "fog out" of what was going on around her. Some days, she said, she would hear someone speaking English to her and it didn't make sense, "it would sound like a foreign language." At the same time there was one message, ringing in her ears since childhood, that was only too clear. Over and over she had been told in one way or another that people were not really interested in her, that she was not important, that people would simply use her and not respect her.

"It was hard to come here," she said. "I didn't want to come here. I was almost hospitalized here two or three times. I didn't like myself. I didn't like people."

She decided to do some kind of volunteer work as a result of a suggestion from her therapist; he wanted her to get out of her own narrow world and make some connections with other people. She remembered his saying, ". . . There's good out there in the world. You go out and look for it." This was a different message than she had heard before. And it came at a time when she had already begun to look outside of herself.

She saw a listing in a church newsletter of organizations that needed volunteers. There on the list was that same hospital, that familiar name. She had a gut sense that she would tackle her own fear of the world by coming to work at this hospital. "I came here to face up to it and get over it."

She wanted to help the people who were helping the patients, as a courier, a mail sorter, a secretary. Her work began with much fear. "I kept coming out here, forcing myself through it." One of her fears was that she would be perceived as someone who should be "on the other side of the fence," who should be a patient instead of a worker. Instead she found that she was treated as a "member of the team," that her efforts were valued. She also discovered that the "fence" itself was not the divider that she had once thought; she found that "the doctors are just folks, they're not gods on pedestals." As for the patients, she could indeed identify only too easily with them, and seeing others in the same position she had been in was scary. Yet, at the same time, seeing how far she had come gave her hope.

In recent days she has felt so much improved that sometimes she wants to tell all the patients how much better life can be. "I want to shout at them: Accept yourself and others. You *can* get a grip on yourself." Feeling helpful and valued by others "has helped give me some self-respect, some self-worth, some confidence." As she gradually discovered that doctors and patients are all people with human problems, she has widened her focus from her old obsessions about herself and what people would think of her. At the same time she's gotten her weight under control and English no longer sounds foreign. Though she does sometimes still hear the old messages about herself and how little she matters to other people, she's learned to "slam the door. Those messages don't come through as loud anymore."

Elizabeth donates her time, and yet, she says, "I feel selfish, like I'm here for myself." The work at the hospital "is helping teach me how to go about the business of living." She has come to think of herself as a person "joyously busy with living."

The power of altruism to affect mental health is widely recognized by mental health professionals. Irvin Yalom, M.D., author of *The Theory and Practice of Group Psychotherapy*, often considered to be the definitive book on the subject, listed altruism as one of the important healing factors at work in a successful therapy group. He has found that patients can be enormously helpful to each other, by offering insights and suggestions, reassurance, support, and the sharing of similar problems. At first many people resist the notion that they can be helped by someone as bad off as they are. "Generally, a patient who deplores the prospect of getting help from other patients is really saying, 'I have nothing of value to offer anyone.' "

"Psychiatric patients beginning therapy are demoralized and possess a deep sense of having nothing of value to offer others. They have long considered themselves as burdens, and the experience of finding that they can be of importance to others is refreshing and boosts self-esteem."[23]

Almost any volunteer will tell you that helping somebody else is good for curing a case of the blues. More than that, for many people helping others has been the agent that has made it possible to get through major life crises, to end bouts of depression that grow out of tremendous losses. Some argue that a couple of hours at work as a helper are as good as a strong antidepressant.

"Stuart," a high-level executive for a corporation in Boston, found at the time of his retirement that he was badly depressed. Depression runs in his family, he said. His brother had committed suicide.

When Stuart began to have thoughts of suicide himself, he got two kinds of help. One was pharmacological—a prescription for an antidepressant. The other was a chance to help others.

After fifty years of not going to church, Stuart happened one Sunday morning to be walking past a church that was performing Vivaldi loud enough to be heard out on the sidewalk. He went inside. Later, talking with the minister, he said he was depressed, that he was struggling through the transitional period before his new drug would fully take effect. Stuart told the minister he "would do anything" to keep busy. The minister put him to work. Stuart now teaches reading to illiterate adults, and he helps out at the church's soup kitchen.

As a man who has studied cooking with famous chefs, he is greatly overqualified for setting tables and handing out the plates of beef and macaroni stew. Yet he cheerfully does this or similar tasks, week after week. On this particular morning the homeless people had begun to line up on the sidewalk outside the church two hours before the doors were to open. At noon they poured in: people carrying shopping bags; one with a gray sack stuffed with an afghan; a man whose arms were covered with tattoos and who wore a ring in his nose; a young man on crutches, his foot in a cast; an old woman in filthy running shoes and the remains of a black Persian lamb coat. They moved quickly and quietly, and the chairs at the big round tables in the assembly room were soon filled.

Stuart, in the course of the lunch, had very little contact with these people. There were no heart-to-heart conversations, just the passing of plates and the offering of a few pleasantries. Stuart has found that these conversational overtures are not always well received. He remembered one lunch when he tried to help an old woman by carrying one of her shopping bags. "Get your goddamned hands off," the woman said to him.

And yet, working here, handing around the plates, has been a part of the mix of medicine and volunteer work that has restored Stuart to good mental health. He is highly energetic, he feels good, he isn't depressed any longer. He is giving.

Similarly, my national survey of volunteers received many stories from people who had found that only by helping others regularly could they maintain emotional health. A fifty-three-year-old Centerville, Iowa, native said, "I do volunteer visiting in a nursing home. Helping others, for me, is a necessity of life. My mental health would be hopeless without it." In fact, one volunteer, fifty-five years old, from Binghamton, New York, discussed what happened when her helping activity—caring for children—was taken away. "I watched children for about six months and then was informed they wouldn't be coming any more. . . . So now I am very depressed, sleeping a lot more, sitting around more. Just don't really care about anything anymore. . . ."

HELPING—AND BEING HELPED

A transformation in some ways similar to Stuart's took place at another soup kitchen in another town, hundreds of miles away, when a woman, depressed as a result of her husband's death, also asked a minister for help. Once again there was a minister who suggested a few hours a week at a soup kitchen. (Ministers must know from personal experience about the benefits of helping.)

"I was still in a daze," said Anna Eubanks, of that first day when she showed up to work at lunch in a downtown church soup kitchen in Raleigh, North Carolina. "The feeling I had when I lost my husband . . . I felt like I didn't have a friend in the world. You lose your best friend, what have you got?" When she arrived in the church hall that day, she didn't want to talk to anyone, and she didn't want anybody to talk to her. She was there to do what the minister had suggested, and that was to serve lunch.

At this church a free meal is served every weekday. An average of 110 people show up, sometimes over 200. Here the people come through a cafeteria-style line to get the food that is distributed by the volunteers. When the doors were finally thrown open in late morning, the crowd surged through, bearing down on the food line. They were mostly men, many of them black, a lot of them with injuries. Perhaps a dozen of them on this particular day had a hand wrapped in some type of bandage. In spite of those who were silent, toothless, glassy-eyed, it was a crowd that gave off a sense of raw physical power, as well as urgent need. It was a crowd that could easily be intimidating.

These were the people who greeted Mrs. Eubanks on that first day. "The first time, I didn't know what I was getting into," she said. "I looked out and saw all these people who were worse off than I was. I didn't see how I could possibly help."

She went home even more depressed.

But she decided to go back again. At first it was a matter of grit and determination. "I made up my mind I wasn't going to let a bunch of street people get me down. I accepted it. I made up my mind I was going to do it."

So, on the following Wednesday, she was back at her station again, handing out the cheese toast. The line of people passed in front of her again—some cocky; some sullen with downcast eyes, muttering; some exaggeratedly polite.

"I began to see their problems," she said. And as they passed down the line, specifying one piece of cheese toast or two, "I began to see they were accepting me, and thanking me." The transformation was accomplished in about four weeks: "I began to say, 'This is worthwhile.'"

"It was a hard pull at first." But she began to look around her once again, for the first time since her husband's death. She began to talk to her fellow volunteers, to the people who came through the line. Her grieving had not ended, but she had begun to take part in life again.

Four years later she still works the Wednesday lunch. Many of the people coming through the line exchange a few words with her, a jumble of greetings as they quickly pass.

"How do, ma'am."

"Good morning, good morning. I smell it a mile away."

"You're going to live to ninety-nine, you're so nice."

"Ain't you something? You something else."

Anna Eubanks looks forward to her one lunch a week in the soup kitchen now. "I have come down here at times I didn't think I was going to make it. I could tell that I was going to have a cold or the flu. But I'd get here, and then I'd forget myself."

On the days that she has been forced to miss, she said, a few of the regulars have asked about her. "Where is she?" they'll ask, "the lady with the cheese."

Experiences like Anna's were reported over and over in my volunteer survey.

THE POWER OF PERCEPTION

Good mental health raises our assessment of how good we feel physically. And that improvement in *perceived* health can be a very strong determinant of actual health.

My survey showed, as mentioned earlier, that people who volunteered once a week were ten times more likely to rate themselves as healthier than other people their age than were people who volunteered only once a year. Simply raising a person's perceived health status leads to positive emotions and traits that reduce stress and create additional real health improvements.[24] Research documents this effect. For example, a six-year Canadian study of three thousand people found the individual's *view* of his own health at the study's start to be a more powerful predictor of death than his initial physical health status, as measured by medical reports and number of visits to doctors and clinics. The people who viewed their health as poor at the start of the study were three times more likely to die than those reporting good health. In addition, data from the Alameda studies on the relation between good health and amount of social support showed that men seeing themselves as unhealthy had a mortality rate twice as great as those who saw their health as excellent. For women the risk was five times greater. What we *think* about our physical health can create stress or positive emotions which in turn affect our real physical condition.[25]

Compounding this is the fact that people who feel healthy and who feel good about themselves tend to live more healthfully. Researchers at the Social Science Research Institute in Illinois studied two thousand people, ranging from members of fitness programs to heart attack patients. They found that the individual's perceived health and feelings of personal control were critical factors in the question of whether he or she would adopt a healthy way of life. People who feel a greater sense of control over their own lives and health are more likely to eat a nutritious diet, make sure to get exercise, and refrain from smoking or abuse of alcohol.

A DAILY PRESCRIPTION

The health benefits produced by helping others compare well with many of the best results obtained by a variety of other healing agents: from painkilling or mood-elevating medication to regular exercise. But helping has some unique advantages that, taken together, go far beyond what many of our other health regimens can offer.

For example, helping is a practice that can easily be woven into daily life. It does not require a radical restructuring of our lives. To be helpful to others does not necessarily mean a change of careers or a move to the inner city. What it does mean is a change in perspective. Becoming part of an organized volunteer effort that offers a regular opportunity to help strangers, in a way that allows personal contact, will give you the greatest effect. But even the smallest actions—holding a door open for a stranger who is carrying a big box, or anything else you can do to make someone else's life a little bit easier—can contribute to your sense of calm and self-esteem, especially if you make it a point to keep your eyes open for such opportunities and perform such acts regularly.

At the age of eighty-three Blanche Goebel of Louisville, Ohio, considers her health to be "excellent, no high blood pressure, no medication. Most of my friends in my age group are on medication, one badly crippled with arthritis. Years ago I tried to follow the Boy Scout idea of a good deed every day, but I don't always make it. Now it's just when the opportunity arises."

She continues to visit people at the nursing home where her husband was a patient before his death. "After helping with Bingo, we play cards with some of the patients who love their game of euchre." She also writes letters to people who are going through very troubled times. "I think this might be a good project for those of us who don't have much energy."

"Depression goes along with old age, but even earlier on, when I was really down, I could snap out of it by doing something nice for someone. It leaves a glow that will see me through the bad period. I heard of one old gentleman who parks on the edge of the lot so that busier people can park closer. It makes him feel good, even though it's a small thing. I notice when others shyly tell me of their little helpful acts that they are always smiling and pleased with themselves. I've noticed that the unhappy and unhealthy ones are the selfish ones, the ones too concerned about self."

Helping others is a crucial part of what may be the most powerful cure yet discovered for those who are suffering from addictions. It is one of the fundamental principles of Alcoholics Anonymous and of the many self-help organizations that have grown up in its wake. In my years as executive director of the Alcoholism Council of Greater New York, part of the National Council on Alcoholism, I saw the kind of damage that addiction can do. AA and the other "Twelve Step" organizations teach that the healing process culminates in what is called the Twelfth Step, the helping of others who are struggling with the same problems they themselves have faced. It is a critical part of the new daily lifestyle that the former drinker must create.

"By helping others stay sober," said recovering alcoholic "Carol," "we stay sober ourselves." It was the helping of other alcoholics through AA that allowed Carol to break free of the damage that alcohol was doing to her life. And it was Carol's story of the euphoria she felt after volunteering on a telephone hot line that was one of the triggers for the research that led to this book.

"I celebrated twenty years of sobriety this spring," she said. "I'm now officially an old-timer." Addiction to alcohol has in one way or another influenced her life since she was six years old. She was the daughter of an alcoholic and had her first drink at age seventeen, which was the beginning of her own drinking problems. "I never had a social drink," she said. "The first time I drank, I blacked out and had a personality change." A sister and a brother became alcoholics as well. Her father died of problems related to drinking. She herself, in her seventeen years of drinking, was involved in several serious alcohol-related accidents and spent some time in a mental hospital after a suicide attempt. Now she can even talk about it with some lightheartedness. "Our family crest," she says, "is crossed bottles on a field of green."

"I wanted to stop drinking," she said of her early adult years. "I tried a lot of different things, but none of them worked: I got married, I had a baby, I got divorced, I was a disciple of a Sikh master, I was in psychoanalysis.

"I knew that there was something terribly wrong with me. I had some vague notion that there was a spiritual component." Each change that she made in her life would "work" for a year or so, then she would drink again. "AA was my last stop, really. It worked." But for the first five years she got only a precarious hold on sobriety; she had not yet moved to the philosophy of helping that seems to keep drinkers dry for the long haul.

Then, in 1975, her husband—she had remarried—took a job in the Midwest, necessitating a move. "It was a terrible time for me." She sold a business and moved a great distance from her son from her first marriage. She wasn't happy in the new location. She was still hanging on to her sobriety, she said, "but I was going down the tubes emotionally." A "sponsor"—an AA mentor—from home visited her and asked how often she was attending AA meetings. Carol said, "I hate AA here." The sponsor said, "Nobody asked you to like the meetings, just put your ass in a chair."

Carol took that pithy advice and started going to the meetings again. "I began to share how I was feeling, and people began to reach out to me." In addition, people there wanted *her* help. "A woman with six or seven years of sobriety was a rare commodity. Young women latched on to me. Of course I was a wreck. I said, 'I don't know that I have a lot to give you, but maybe we can help each other.' "

That was the turning point. These days she is a sponsor to recovering alcoholics all over the country. She and her family have moved several times, so there are people in several cities with whom she has this close tie. She is very active in helping in any way she can. "I put myself in the way of people who are struggling." These days, she said, "I have a perfectly wonderful life."

However, all the troubles of life did not end when she discovered the power of the Twelfth Step, of helping others. Three years after the turning point she experienced in AA, she and her family moved from the Midwest back home. She decided to get an MBA. As a forty-year-old former English major, she was fighting her way through calculus, spending huge amounts of time studying, and not getting to many AA meetings.

Someone suggested that "a wonderful antidote" to her current stressful situation would be answering phone calls at the local AA office. "I signed up. One day when I had been working on the hot line for a month, I was driving down the freeway on the way to work, and I felt this incredible joy, and it was overwhelming, astonishing, an emotional epiphany." It was also, as she gradually realized, very familiar. She drove on to the office where she answered the calls and starting telling people there about the feelings that had come over her. "I knew it was connected to the work. All of a sudden it hit me that I had felt like this when I was a young girl, when I left my father's alcoholic home and went to boarding school. It was like being released from the most god-awful kind of prison and terror." It was at this boarding school that she felt the sudden shock of both connecting with other people and fitting into a group. "I was released to be who I was."

The rush of joy that overwhelmed her on the way to work the hot line was the same one she had experienced at school. "I realized it was exactly the same feeling, that

I had in fact rendezvoused with my very best self through service." What that "best self" meant to her was her most "joyous" self. "That's an essential component of my being, which is extraordinary when you think about it. I came from such darkness, but I am most at home in my own skin when I am joyous and buoyant and totally unself-conscious, and identified with something larger. I was at home, and it showed. People told me over and over that something happened when I came in there to the office. It spilled right over into the whole place."

In a sense, it is no surprise that helping others can help someone stop his or her own addictive behavior. Helping essentially relaxes the body and eases tension, which is one of the compelling reasons that people drink—to relax.

Useful as helping is for addictions, it is also in itself habit-forming, which is important, since one helping act won't make you feel good for life. The habit-forming nature of helping's feel-good sensation has been observed by many people, not just recovering alcoholics. A regular helper who participated in our survey said, "As soon as I finish up one project, I want to start right away on another, because the feeling I get is so great that I get 'addicted' to it, and I don't want to lose it." Her quote is typical.

In addition to helping's unique contributions to the personal health of the helper, it has one more advantage, which is surely the most obvious of all: Helping other people often goes beyond the health benefits that accrue to the helper. Those who are at one moment receiving are helping others. Sandy Hendrickson, who in 1990 received the nursing-practice award from the American Nurses Association, has felt in her own life the power of the "ripple effect" of helping.

Sandy, who works as a public health nurse helping AIDS patients, decided some time ago that she only wanted to be paid for twenty hours a week. The rest of her work week she donates to the cause of helping people with AIDS. "I feel if everybody gave a little bit, we wouldn't need so much money—money that we never seem able to get anyway." She takes care of patients and has also set up a case-management system for her county, as well as speaking frequently at AIDS education programs. At home she and her husband have a small child to take care of, a four-year-old.

For her the good feelings that come from helping are crucial to the motivation to keep going. "All my patients die," she said, "and they're all fairly young. If you didn't get more than you give, you couldn't do it very long."

Then last year the tables were turned. Sandy discovered that she had cancer. As the word spread throughout the local AIDS community, "suddenly I had patients helping me."

One has been particularly helpful, a man whom Sandy had helped through several crises. In the two years since his diagnosis with AIDS, she had stood by his bed in intensive care units on three separate occasions. Each time he recovered.

Now Sandy is going through her own chemotherapy, with the nausea and discomfort that that brings. And her friend has stood by her the way she stood by him. "He goes with me, he holds my hand, he takes care of me."

She has felt the generosity of his gift to her, though "I'm not a very good taker," she said. At the same time she knows how good the effect of helping is for his health too. Helping to get her through this is a job he has to stay strong to do. "He said, 'I have something to live for.'"

5

The Critical Steps to Healthy Helping

TO assure that our helping efforts work in our own lives as well as those of others, it is important to choose the right type of volunteering. It requires choosing an activity that meets certain basic requirements, and I, like many others who have done a lot of volunteering, have arrived at them through the trial-and-error of my own helping activities. Indeed, as the results of our national volunteer survey began to come in, I found that the type of helping that had helped me the most, given me the best feelings, also turned out to be best for many other people.

You should, of course, keep in mind that the following guidelines are not the only basis on which to choose your volunteer effort. They are simply the kinds of helping most conducive to producing health benefits according to my survey.

1. PERSONAL CONTACT

Meeting and spending time with the person one is helping usually produces a far more lasting impact on the volunteer than does a less personal task, such as collecting clothes and canned goods for the poor. Personal contact is a particularly important factor to consider in choosing how you want to be of service. Of the volunteers I surveyed, only 5 percent of those who had a one-to-one personal relationship with the person they helped did not report experiencing helper's high. Of the people who helped without personal contact, 14 percent did not experience this exhilaration—a three times' greater difference. In addition the volunteer survey showed that helpers with personal contact were also more likely to report increases in self-esteem and the physical signs of reduced stress—increased feelings of warmth and energy—from their volunteering. To be able to see or feel the reactions of the person receiving the help is vital to giving us the positive emotion conducive to experiencing the health benefits.

It is this need for personal contact that I have found most urgent in my own volunteer work. For me the difference between working *with* someone and helping without that contact is astonishing. The efforts I've made that have brought me public praise and attention but have not brought me into direct contact with those I am helping have rarely produced a lasting good feeling. This has happened even at times when the work I was doing was important and useful and I felt proud and happy about the outcome. When there was no person to connect with, the feeling of sheer euphoria never occurred, nor did I get the relaxed, calm feeling that follows the initial high.

Case in point: You may have seen those posters in bars and restaurants warning you that drinking alcohol during pregnancy can cause birth defects. I notice those posters probably more than most people, because I initiated and led the fight for the first law in the country that required them to be displayed. I was then the executive director of the Alcoholism Council of Greater New York, and public education was one of our missions. It took a long and difficult political struggle before New York City made those signs a legal requirement for establishments selling alcohol. I was present when Mayor Edward Koch signed the bill into law; in fact I was called to stand behind him as he signed. Gallup polls before and after the posters went up showed that this poster warning significantly helped to increase New Yorkers' awareness of the dangers of alcohol to pregnant women. Subsequently many major cities have adopted similar legislation. The posters spurred the development of the federal legislation that now requires a warning to be placed on wine and liquor bottles. So I can think about the possibility that because of work I've done, numbers of birth defects have been averted. Yet, with all of that, neither doing the work nor seeing the reminders up there on the wall has given me feelings that are as intense or as lasting as those I get when I work with one person and really feel a bond between us.

In the book *Healthy Pleasures*, physician David Sobel and psychologist Robert Ornstein cite a study of volunteers at a Pennsylvania college that showed that those involved in face-to-face helping acts benefited more than those students who helped in administration. "The greatest surprise of human evolution," the authors conclude, "may be that the highest form of selfishness is selflessness." Personal contact increases our understanding and sympathy for the other person's situation. "The more contact we have with others, the better for us," Sobel and Ornstein say. "We need to meet the people we help, see their lives, connect with them."[1]

To see and talk with these people can also add to the sense of achievement that results from efforts to help. A feeling of accomplishment is in itself a good way to combat stress. Ervin Staub, a psychologist at the University of Massachusetts who has done much research on altruism, recommends that helpers always be made aware of the importance of what they are doing and the consequences of their acts. Disabled volunteers, who often help over the phone, report the power of *feeling* a personal connection, even though they can't see the person. A forty-two-year-old volunteer from Royal Oak, Michigan, who suffers from heart problems due to rheumatic fever as a child, discussed working as a phone counselor at a crisis center involved with problems of drug and child and spouse abuse. "As the contact progresses, I often feel a warmth. This sensation is very good, very reassuring and powerful. After a contact, I am almost always tired and simultaneously relaxed."

Many people believe that a big splash of public attention and acclaim will make them feel good and raise their self-esteem, somehow make them feel more tied to other people, but it doesn't usually work the way they'd hoped. It certainly hasn't had that effect on me. Several times I've been on national TV shows—"Today," "Good Morning America," "20/20"—to talk about a particular social problem. Sitting there in the lights knowing I'm talking to millions of people is exciting and fun. I remember once when I was walking out of the studio, a receptionist came running up to me to double-check my phone number, saying that they were expecting calls to come in from all over the nation. That's heady stuff, and I enjoyed it. But when I washed off the makeup and went back out on the street, the good feeling was over. What was left was a sensation that I can only describe as nice, but quickly fading. I felt the aftereffects of the stress of the interview without the buoying strength of the physical and emotional sensations of healthy helping.

The kind of experience that does seem to bring on the helper's high and the well-being that follows, with all of the consequent health improvements, is simply the intense, sustained contact with the person I'm helping, another person I can look at eye to eye. I did have some of those kinds of experiences while working for the alcoholism council, although much of my work as executive director involved administration and public policy. I remember one man in particular who came in, very reluctantly, to see me. He had been referred by a mutual friend, and he had only come because his wife was threatening to leave him if he didn't. The man was angry at being in my office; he was convinced that he had no problem with alcohol. This was an educated man, who, when drinking, would beat up his wife. At first he didn't want to be in my office, but he stayed, and he came to talk with me several more times. Finally he began to talk about how he felt, that he was afraid of being alone, that he cared about his wife and feared losing her, that he couldn't control his aggression when he drank. While we sat and talked together, he made the connection: If he kept on drinking, he would wind up alone. He decided to start going to AA, to tackle the problem of his drinking. It was a moment of naked emotion for him. I felt almost honored to be with him in that moment and to have a part in such a change for the better in his life. When he left my office, I was euphoric, bursting with energy. Now, years later, when I think about it again, it still makes me feel good.

2. FREQUENCY

Making helping feel good to the helper depends, perhaps not surprisingly, on how often we do it. My study showed that the more frequently people helped, the more likely they were to have encounters in which they experienced the feel-good sensation and to report superior health. As discussed before, I found a ten times greater chance that volunteers who perceived themselves as healthier than others would be weekly rather than once-a-year helpers.

The ideal frequency for the helper, from my observations, is about the same weekly amount of time recommended for getting the best benefits from either meditation or exercise—about two hours a week. In addition, meditators say, one should do mini-meditations of a few minutes a day, especially during periods of particular stress. The same prescription works for volunteering.

At least two hours a week of one-to-one helping, whether done on your own or through an organization, is enough to begin to make changes in your life. This is due partly to the direct effects of that weekly experience and partly to an important side effect: Regular helping seems to lead naturally to a more helpful attitude toward others throughout the rest of the week. These small daily acts, which cost very little in time and effort, can provide a mini-dose of the relaxation that the longer experience provides.

A survey on the link between social integration and mortality in rural Tecumseh, Michigan, found that the largest reduction in the death rate was among those who at least once a week attended meetings of some kind of voluntary association. At the same time, involvement more than once a week did not increase the benefit to the helper. The federal government's review of the Retired Senior Volunteer Program revealed that participants who volunteered at least once a week experienced significant health benefits, although nearly half had in the recent past suffered serious stress, such as a spouse's death, job retirement, or health problems.

Finally, it is your own comfort with a particular schedule of helping that will be the deciding factor. The right amount of time for your health is when *you* feel the symptoms of stress give way to relaxation.

3. HELPING STRANGERS

Though helping family and friends is obviously important, assisting strangers as well leads to the greatest chance
of feeling helper's high. Those who only helped people
close to them were the least likely to report this arousal.
The reason for this is that in coming to the aid of a
stranger, we get to decide for ourselves whether to help
or not and how to proceed. That freedom is a great boost
to our sense of self-control, which is another factor that
determines how much stress we feel. In the helping of
relatives and friends there is often at least some sense of
obligation. "Have-to" helping runs the risk of diminishing feelings of personal control and increasing stress for
the helper, while the freely given act, the gesture no one
would expect us to make, can create within us a rush of
good feeling.

This story of a refuge in a snowstorm is a good example
of the pleasure and satisfaction that can come from kindness to strangers: Dorothy Anderson was, at the time of
this incident, a seventy-year-old widow living alone in
Cleveland, Wisconsin. A heavy snow had begun to fall in
that area, and people driving on the nearby interstate were
unable to see well enough to drive. "There were many
cars in the ditches. Since I belong to the newly organized
Lakeshore Disaster Support Group, I was called by the
secretary at 5:30 P.M. to see if I could accommodate
anyone for the night. I have two extra bedrooms. At 6:30
P.M. the fire chief led four persons to my home—a man
and his twenty-year-old son on leave from the navy, a
lady with a dog on her way up north to look for work,
and a college student on her way back to UW at Green
Bay. These strangers had met at the police chief's home
and didn't want to be separated, since they were all from
Milwaukee.

"Taking in these strangers for the night gave me a good feeling as if I were floating on air—euphoric. It was as if I were entertaining my best friends, offering food, use of the TV, lodging and breakfast. I didn't even mind the dog in the living room or in the bed—something I don't allow my daughter to do with her dog.

"The feeling lasted all evening and until the last ones left in the morning, and it kept recurring as I talked or wrote about the event during the days afterward.

"Being a nurse, I've helped a lot of people in my line of work, and I'm constantly helping out friends who have had a broken leg or cancer, but I never experienced a high as great as this one when I could help out these strangers in trouble."

Pitirim Sorokin, the man who founded Harvard University's center to study altruism, said that neither kin altruism, which is taking care of family, nor tribal altruism, taking care of your community, is the most beneficial to society. It does not affect the sense we have of "them" versus "us." Helping a stranger does begin to break down that barrier, to increase the sensations of bonding. And that is one of the keys to experiencing "helper's high."

4. A SHARED PROBLEM

When a volunteer has something in common with the person who is helped—for example the helper has had the same illness—the sense of achievement and the feeling of bonding become more pronounced. We experience more empathy. To empathize is to experience a feeling in ourselves through the medium of another person, as though the boundaries between us had disappeared and we were experiencing it directly. In sympathy, we feel for someone else's situation but do not have that self-arousal.

People who empathize feel even more of a high than those who don't. A laboratory demonstration illustrates this very nicely:

Two different groups of people were asked to watch a person who was waving his arms and legs. One of the groups was told that the man was receiving a painful shock, and the people in this group showed physiological changes, as measured by increased heart rates. Some of the observers in that group were told that they were *similar* in some way to the person they thought was receiving the shock, and they felt even greater arousal.[2]

5. A SUPPORTIVE ORGANIZATION

Working through a volunteer organization offers some advantages. By taking this approach, you are more likely to be helping strangers than friends and you're more likely to be helping with regularity, rather than the sporadic pattern characteristic of individual helping. People who help through an organization are also about twice as likely to go on to offer acts of assistance on their own as those who don't have such an affiliation, my survey found.

Moreover, the sense of teamwork and connection with one's fellow helpers can itself be very powerful. For example the two men who both volunteered at a public radio station found their spirits boosted by the kinship with their co-workers. Working in such a group can also be very good for people who, for whatever reason, find that direct contact with those helped does not give them good feelings. Some people may feel that they get inappropriately involved or depressed by the problems of the people they would like to serve. Others may doubt their abilities to be useful. Some simply feel that they are not "ready" for personal contact. For anyone who might otherwise hang back from becoming involved at all, there is the chance to benefit from helping through work behind the scenes.

6. THE USE OF SKILLS

It's important to feel that you're good at the kind of activities the work requires. If you are volunteering as a reading tutor and you actually have the skills and knowledge to teach someone to read, the experience is far more likely to be positive. The sense of achievement grows. When the skills and the challenge are well matched, the volunteer emerges with increased confidence, feelings of self-control, and real usefulness. When the Gallup organization asked people who were already volunteering why they continued, the most frequent reason given was that they were able to do something useful.

To get the feelings from helping that will encourage you to go back out and do it again, find a kind of service that uses the skill you have or that gives you the training you'll need.

7. MAKING AN EFFORT

Some form of exertion, of reaching out, on the part of the volunteer is a vital part of what makes helper's high happen. This is very similar to what happens in the case of exercise. We do it, often with some reluctance, and find that the dreaded effort leads to energy rather than fatigue, good feelings rather than bad. We discover that we are expanded rather than used up by the effort.

The same effect occurs with helping. Linking the arousals of helping and exercise in this way would not have surprised early stress researcher Hans Selye. When he developed his concept of altruistic egoism, of helping that also serves the self, he predicted that it would require an effortful act. "Man has to fight and work for some goal he considers worthwhile," he wrote. Unquestionably a situation calling for exertion is an easy one to find, since most volunteering requires some significant extension of ourselves, either physically or emotionally.

8. LETTING GO OF RESULTS

A warning: If you are determined that the recipient of your efforts will benefit from what you do, you will probably emerge from the experience frustrated and unhappy. You must simply enjoy the feeling of closeness to the person you're trying to assist. That's the only thing that works. The health-enhancing emotions received come from the bonding; the helping act is only the pathway to this human connection. So, forget any benefits you might expect to give or receive. If you focus only on whether your efforts will truly change someone or improve the community or larger society, then what will ensue will likely be frustration, and the related negative feelings will create something like a "helper's low," more stress, more wear and tear on the helper.

By not concentrating on the results, we may be able in some cases to get better results. Norman Cousins, who spent some time with Albert Schweitzer in Africa, pointed out to me that Schweitzer's small hospital was never able to improve the health of the people around it significantly, but it *did* spur the development of many other hospitals in poor countries. So, in the end there was an impact. Yet if Schweitzer had hesitated because he alone could not change the world, there would never have been any change for the better.

* * *

These, then, are the basic guidelines for the kinds of volunteering that are most likely to be personally satisfying, the kind that help your own health and well-being. If your helping gives you personal contact and feedback from the one who is helped, if it is weekly and directed at people outside your circle of family and friends, if the nature of the person or problem arouses your empathy, if your mastery of the work allows you to feel confident, if you can focus on your work and not on the outcome, then it is highly likely that you will get the kind of results—good health and high spirits—that we've been talking about.

THE HARDINESS FACTOR

The foregoing criteria for the healthiest helping of others have in common one important quality: They each foster the development of an attitude toward life that is referred to as hardiness, because of the links it appears to have with good health. The hardiness concept, as developed by psychologist Suzanne Kobasa and her colleagues, encompasses the qualities of commitment, challenge, and control. A person who ranks high on the hardiness scale possesses the following characteristics: She (a) has a sense of commitment to a purpose, (b) sees problems as challenges, and (c) believes in her ability to exert some control over the course of her own life, as well as of outside events.

Working at the University of Chicago in the mid-1970s, Kobasa and Salvatore Maddi studied the mental and physical health of executives at Illinois Bell, a company that was then in tremendous upheaval. After seven years of study they found that the managers who had characteristics of hardiness were less likely than others to become ill, sometimes by as much as half.[3]

In an interview in *Advances*, a journal of mind-body research, Kobasa told how she came to do this research. She had been reading the literature on stress in the early 1970s and felt that something was missing. That "something" was a positive emphasis, an exploration of how to live in a healthy way. "Most of the studies seemed to be concerned with how people become ill in the face of stressful life events. My question was 'What about those people who don't?' "[4]

In a paper written with a colleague in 1983, Kobasa defined this health factor. "Persons high in hardiness easily commit themselves to what they are doing (rather than feeling alienated), generally believe that they can at least partially control events (rather than feeling powerless), and regard change as a normal challenge or impetus to development (rather than a threat)." When stressful events occur, they find opportunities for making decisions, confirming priorities, setting new goals, and generally performing tasks they feel to be important. "Further, they are capable of evaluating any given event in the context of an overall life plan. Their basic sense of purpose and involvement in life mitigates the potential disruptiveness of any single occurrence. The coping styles of hardy persons reflect their belief in their own effectiveness as well as their ability to make good use of other human and environmental resources." Coping for such people becomes an exercise in turning events that might be considered problems into challenging possibilities.[5]

Kobasa and her colleagues found that hardiness could be used as a predictor of which executives would be most likely to fall ill in the future. The studies pointed to this quality as an even better predictor of health than other buffers against illness such as exercise or a network of social support.

The guidelines that have grown out of my volunteer research are my attempt to suggest ways in which people's helping efforts can be tailored to foster the development of the three hardiness qualities. Each of the suggestions in some way helps the helper to enhance feelings of commitment, self-control, or challenge. A quick summary of the list will show the correlation in every case. For example, when we help strangers, rather than those to whom we feel obligated, we are exercising choice and adding to feelings that we are in control of our own lives. Helping frequently and making personal contact with the one who is helped increase opportunities for a sense of commitment, rather than alienation. Using our skills to help someone enhances feelings of competence and the sense we have of self-determination. Feelings of challenge as well as commitment can be increased by joining the team of an organization, helping someone with a problem that you may have had once yourself, or by working to make some small dent in a problem that one person alone cannot solve.

HELPER'S HIGH IN THE WORKPLACE

While most of the helping we've been talking about is volunteer work or individual efforts, our survey reports showed it is also possible to get the same positive reactions while doing paid professional work to help other people. But again, there are guidelines that can be followed to make the helper's high and its benefits likelier to occur.

Three things are important in on-the-job helping: (a) Do something extra, make an effort on someone's behalf that goes a little beyond what the job strictly requires; (b) establish a true personal connection with someone in need; and (c) lower your expectations by enjoying the satisfaction that comes from each small achievement rather than postponing happiness until the day you've saved the entire world. If you can do any or all of these, you're far likelier to feel the high and its subsequent effects.

The helper's high can occur in situations that for the worker are far from ideal. Human services workers are often severely underpaid and overworked. Teachers, nurses, social workers, and health and community aides have to deal with never-ending demands, and they usually don't have adequate support staff. As a result they often have a low self-image and suffer burnout, the physical and emotional exhaustion that prevents them from working well and causes poor morale at service organizations.

By doing something extra for someone, the paid helper can at least partly counteract these bad effects. The "volunteered" effort is not merely one more requirement of the job—it is a genuine gift. The helper has taken control by offering the extra service.

In asking the overworked person to make additions to an already busy day, I can easily imagine the skeptical laughter of readers who feel sufficiently pushed to the wall by their existing job responsibilities. It is ironic, but true, that one way to relieve the pressure is to do something extra. Do something good for somebody that you don't *have* to do. This will not only give you an added sense of being in control of the job and of your own life, it will enhance the other person's trust in you. You'll feel empowered both by your own ability to make choices for yourself and by the relationship with the person you have helped.

Fortunately the extra effort need not always take extra time. A fifty-four-year-old assistant in the radiology department of a hospital in Aurora, Colorado, explained the small kinds of extras that can be done and the feelings that result. "All our patients have an inner fear that their exam will be positive for something. When I joke with them or explain a procedure and see them outwardly relax, I feel like a teacher must feel when she sees a student finally grasp a problem. This feeling is a 'rush,' not only of physical energy but of a positive mental energy as well."

An excellent example of a man who has found great satisfaction in a helping profession is Jerome Ruderman. He was the friend who came with my wife to the party in East Harlem where I was celebrating with the tenants of the newly repaired building, the person who took a look at the effect that my helping efforts had had on me and decided he wanted that to happen in his own life.

That party started the process, Jerome said recently. "It started me thinking about my life and what I was doing." At the time he was a lawyer for Columbia Pictures. He didn't make the decision to quit in an instant. "It wasn't as easy as all that." The process that began that night extended into two years of therapy. Finally he was ready to make the major change. He left his job, went back to school, then got a job teaching in an elementary school in East Harlem, the same desperately poor part of Manhattan where I had helped with the work on the building. He taught for twelve years in that school. In 1983 he became a guidance counselor for several schools, including the one where he had been teaching. His work has included dealing with children who are abused or neglected and with efforts such as AIDS prevention education.

Many years later he is still glad he made the move. "I have been extremely happy in my career. It was a very important change for me."

The situations he faced in his new job were tough ones, though. Some of the problems could easily lead a helper into disillusionment. Jerome saw a child in the school one day who had a big bruise under one eye. It turned out that the boy's stepfather had hit him. Then eight or nine years old, this child was already limited in his capabilities, a student in a special-education program. The injury was reported to the appropriate agency and was investigated.

The decision, Jerome said, was that the bruise was an isolated incident. Six months later the boy turned up in school with a swollen elbow. His arm was broken; he had been hit with a racket for not cleaning his room. "Where do you think he is now?" Jerome asked. "He's still living in that same home. That's difficult," he said, "discouraging."

Yet day after day Jerome has continued to find the work "rich and rewarding." In doing it he feels "self-fulfilled." One attitude that helped make this possible had to do with the way in which he defined the criteria he would apply to judging his own work. "I just say, 'If I can move one child from here to there, or stop one suicide, or keep one kid from becoming a drug addict, this is a big thing.' " From the outside, it seems obvious that to save one life is a tremendous thing. Yet for those who are daily surrounded with more troubled lives than they can possibly help, it is sometimes easy to forget what an accomplishment it is to "move one child from here to there." You have to keep in mind, Jerome said, that you can't expect to be "*the* one" to solve all the problems.

Jerome Ruderman has continued to make changes in his career. After four years of psychoanalytic training he has established a private psychotherapy practice in addition to his work in the schools. From the psychoanalytic point of view, he says, people who choose helping professions tend to be people who need nurturing. The good feelings that result from the work are "a reward for service" in that the person is being nurtured by the process of helping and comforting someone else. "You're getting something for giving," he said.

It is vital that those who have chosen to make careers out of helping others should not be driven away by exhaustion and disillusionment. When the helper gives up, everyone loses.

A CRUCIAL QUALITY: PERSISTENCE

The experience of helping enhances our abilities both to do good and to feel rewarded by the effort. My survey found that the more frequent helpers were the most likely to report experiencing helper's high. Volunteers having personal contact were the most likely to become regular helpers. Empathy grows within us the more we interact with and understand people who need help.

Whether you are a professional helper or a volunteer, you're likely to run into difficult and discouraging situations. Furthermore, as a beginning volunteer you may very well choose an activity that is not a good match for your abilities and interests. If you've persisted in the effort and still find it burdensome rather than satisfying, take a look at the list of guidelines you've just read. You may find, for example, that you need more contact with people or a more regular schedule. If such changes as these bring no better result, try another form of helping. There are so many different ways to help. If you keep trying and don't give up, you'll find a way that is satisfying to you as well as useful to someone else.

6

What to Do When It All Goes Wrong

BRING up the subject of volunteer work in a group and there are almost always people willing to tell you what's bad about it, what happened to them that made them decide never to do it again. The reasons can range from being tired of the smell of stale sweat and rotting socks, to exhaustion and disillusionment with the human race.

Not long ago I gave a talk on my findings about helping to a small group of retired people at a local Y, many of whom didn't want to hear anything good I had to say. Primarily widows in their seventies and eighties, they were coming to this Y for companionship. When I started talking about helping others, though several kept nodding when I mentioned the good feelings, the group practically shouted me down with the stories of their bad experiences. Here's what they said:

- Being with sick people makes you depressed.

- People who help for free are resented by the paid workers.

- The person I tried to help didn't want any help.

- It's not that easy to become a volunteer.

- They don't want us; they want the society ladies.

- I couldn't stand seeing those children in that condition.

- The place I volunteered didn't show any appreciation.

- I've had enough hardship myself—I don't want to be around suffering.

- At this stage in my life I want to do what *I* want to do.

Many people have had one or more of these reactions to a volunteer experience. Often they stem from a lost sense of autonomy, or self-determination, the sense of mastery over one's fate. Helpers sometimes feel overwhelmed by the emotional or physical involvement required of them. Or they can feel rejected when their well-intended offers of help are met with a rebuff or when an application form gets lost in the bureaucratic shuffle. As with the rest of life, helping others is going to have its rough moments. In the case of the people at the Y, they had, as a group, tried to volunteer with two local institutions, and for various reasons, neither effort had worked out well. They didn't persist. While less than 1 percent of those I surveyed reported increased stress and health damage as a result of their helping efforts, almost inevitably helpers do meet with the occasional difficult and disappointing encounter.

WHEN HELPERS LOSE CONTROL

Randee Russell, the woman who became a Hospice volunteer twenty years after her boyfriend's death in a racing accident, found that helping transformed her life. But it's also important to remember that the healing experience she had with Jane occurred *after* she'd had a very difficult time dealing with another patient. Two things about that earlier bad episode allowed the later powerful healing to take place. One was that Randee did not give up the effort of helping. Secondly she learned from the difficult experience how to help in a way that was useful, both to herself and to the other person.

Her bad experience illustrates one of the most important causes of the problems that can arise in helping efforts. When the helper loses her sense of control in a situation, when she feels that her own freedom of choice is gone, that is when the trouble begins. Help must be freely given, not demanded, or the helper will wind up feeling depleted and resentful.

"I really did have a horrible experience," Randee said as she recalled the first woman she'd tried to help through Hospice. The work of Hospice volunteers is to offer assistance to terminally ill people who want to die at home. But "Alice," though she had asked for a Hospice volunteer, was very angry and was at the same time in severe denial—she refused to admit that she was dying. "This woman didn't have much of a support system," Randee said. She had a few friends, whom "she was rapidly driving away."

Alice was dying of lung cancer but claimed that any trouble she might have in breathing was simply irritation from allergies and from the air quality in Los Angeles. She continued to smoke, turning off her oxygen so that she could have a cigarette—and she continued to be furious. "My mistake," Randee said, "was that I thought I could make things okay for her. I was looking for a project, I guess. I think I was kind of lonely. I was looking for something to be devoted to. And she zeroed in on that."

As a result Alice made tremendous demands on Randee's time. "She wasn't appreciative, and I couldn't do enough for her. She railed and fought and denied and was furious with anybody who came near her. Then she would relent and say I was the daughter she'd never had."

However, being set up to try to be this woman's daughter created as difficult a situation for Randee as the fury did. This was a case where the demands were far more than what the volunteer was finally willing to give.

After two months of this, Alice "fired" the Hospice organization. But Randee continued to visit and try to help the woman on her own. "She ran me ragged for three, four months. She would call in the middle of the night, wanting to be checked into a hospital." Randee would get up and get her to the hospital, then leave when Alice was settled. "Three hours later she would call a cab and check herself out and go home."

Randee continued to make extraordinary efforts, even though the Hospice personnel tried to get her to protect herself better. The relationship ended suddenly, when Alice once again wanted a ride to the hospital. "She called me on a really hot day. It was about 106 degrees, and I had this Fiat convertible. It's not a car for 106 degrees." Alice was uncomfortable in the car and was complaining about that, among other things. "She started complaining to me about not being able to get hold of me. I said, 'Why do I feel like such an asshole when I try to be nice to you?' " After a long silence Alice "started into the daughter routine." Randee drove on to the hospital, and Randee decided the Hospice had been right; neither she nor Alice ever called the other again. Alice died two months later.

Instead of deciding the whole thing had been a mistake, Randee tried again with another patient. She realized it was worth another effort. The second time she was assigned to a woman who both wanted and appreciated Randee's help. And this time Randee was careful to set limits on her own availability and to refrain from trying to be the answer to all of the problems in the other person's life. She was helping in a way that increased her feelings of personal capability and self-control rather than diminishing them.

Very often, a bad helping experience is one in which our sense of self-control has been lost. University of Pennsylvania psychologist Martin Seligman is a leader in the research on what happens to us when we feel helpless. His work explains why people may even die from feelings of helplessness.

In his book *Helplessness: On Depression, Development, and Death,* Seligman discusses the work of George Engel and others at the University of Rochester. It indicated that the sense of helplessness accompanying a loss may weaken resistance to pathogens that had previously been successfully resisted. Engel and his colleagues studied 170 cases of sudden death—usually from heart failure—during a time of psychological stress and then broke these down into the eight types of loss that had produced the stress. Significantly, of these eight, Seligman notes, the first five involve helplessness: the death or collapse of a loved one, extreme grief, threatened loss of a loved one, mourning or the anniversary of mourning, and loss of self-esteem or status. Thus, though most people assume that coronary distress is caused by extreme emotional agitation, from these cases it appears that feelings of loss of control may be an equally important factor.[1]

Feelings of helplessness are not limited to times of death in the family or other major loss. They can be part of a chronic condition. Researchers call this trait learned helplessness, because it develops over the years through the individual's repeated perception that his efforts and interactions with others are again and again fruitless, unsuccessful.

As happened with Randee and her first Hospice patient, the helper can feel overwhelmed by the needs of the other person. Another kind of situation that often produces a sense of helplessness is "have-to" helping, when the helper feels that the assistance is simply one more thing she has to do. This can easily occur in cases where the person helped is a family member or someone to whom a favor is owed. Family members caring for relatives with Alzheimer's disease were found to have immune system strengths 200 percent lower than people without this big responsibility. This often-cited study—by psychologist Janice Kiecolt-Glaser and immunologist Ronald Glaser of Ohio State University—showed that after a year the caring relatives were often in failing health themselves.[2]

Taking care of a sick family member is isolating and, in addition to increasing stress, it reduces the availability of natural emotional give-and-take with others. People who are doing this work need to be sure that they get as much support for themselves as possible, that they talk with friends about the difficulties and bad feelings. Very often people in this position find some relief through a support group for the families of those who are suffering from a particular disorder. It does help to know somebody else who is going through something similar. At the same time you are helping those other people deal with the problems you share, and that in itself can bring on the healthy helping effects.

It's important to add that helping a family member, even without assistance from any other relative, need not mean bad health. Just the opposite: Aiding a relative can produce some of the strongest sensations of bonding. A forty-two-year-old volunteer who lives in Syracuse, New York, wrote me about the continued help she gives her aging in-laws: "It gives me surges of flushed energy when I think a positive step has been taken. As other family members have washed their hands of this situation, I think I continue trying from the good energy I receive from it."

In my own survey the people who reported feelings of

helplessness because of an obligation to take care of a family member rarely had support from other relatives. The sense of being "caught" in a have-to helping situation also occurs in helpers who for reasons of temperament, training, or circumstances always feel that they must "put others' needs first."

Though the details vary, the pattern is familiar to many. "For over forty years I was a caretaker," said "Sally." "From infancy I learned to care for and help others. I did not learn to care for *me*.

"My mother had a nervous breakdown when I was four. From that time I was the 'mother' and she was the 'child.' After my father's death, five years ago, she became extremely dependent on me."

After Sally began to have health problems, a counselor directed her to an Adult Children of Alcoholics meeting. "Although alcohol was not the problem in my family, I have the same characteristics as adult children from an alcoholic home. For the first time in my life I understood my feeling of resentment when helping others. This resentment was followed by guilt because I was taught from a very early age in a parochial school: Jesus first, others second, and yourself third."

Now, she said, she and her husband realize that they have been the victims of "caretaker burnout" and are taking steps to change to a healthier way of life.

"Any time anyone needed help," she said, "we were the first to offer. Somewhere our own feelings and needs got lost in the shuffle. In my mother's case it was necessary to separate her needs from her wants. Needs are met, wants are taken care of at our convenience."

Now when someone from her church calls her for volunteer work, she is "very choosy." For example she may say that she will do a specific part of a project but will not attend any meetings. In essence she has asserted some control, both in her helping of her mother and in her volunteer activities. Her advice to other helpers is to set limits and "take care of yourself, not to give to the point that there's nothing left of yourself." That can be difficult when a family member is accustomed to your constant attentions. "In families it's expected of you," Sally said. She has learned to limit her giving to what she can give without damaging herself. "It's probably the hardest thing I've ever learned."

If a helper doesn't learn to set limits, he or she will almost surely, sooner or later, start feeling helpless in the face of the never-ending list of others' needs. We each have a ceiling for psychological demands, beyond which we feel out of control. When the demands mount, stress increases. Individual tolerance levels vary, but everyone has some limit to the amount of external pressure he or she can withstand without beginning to pay a price. That price is the effect of prolonged stressful arousal of the body. When the helping act is one that the helper cannot physically and psychologically afford to make, the body, instead of being relaxed and diverted from daily demands, is taxed even further. It is receiving the negative arousal messages of stress. The heart keeps pumping blood at an elevated rate, racing oxygen to muscle cells that are staying in a fight or flight mode.

The care of a family member is one of the most common and difficult kinds of have-to helping. But this feeling of obligation also occurs in other settings. A woman working in a caretaking occupation, with a longtime history of helping as well, reported similar physical responses to pressures that never seemed to abate. "I am twenty-five years old, married, and in good health. I have been helping others for nine years now and have come to a point where my husband and social life have come in second. I am no longer that fun and exciting person. I carry with me all the troubles and lives of the people I care for.

"It first started feeling great—everybody so appreciative—till the dependency started, and more responsibilities. I was at the point that it did not bother me and I would not bring it home. Now my life circles around my work, clients. I am trying to learn to say no!" She had begun to feel that she would like to see a therapist. With "nerves that twitch and twang," she had become a person she no longer knew. "I have days I dislike myself and would like to turn into a monster because of pressure." She felt that others were in control of her and that she had no time to simply enjoy being herself.

A second helper who wrote to me has recognized these same tendencies in herself and is learning to keep her balance. "Knowing that I have done something that makes life a bit easier or less lonely for someone else does bring pleasure, and I think it should. Doing things grimly for what seem like the right reasons doesn't make sense to me.

"It is when I am trying too hard to be all things to all people that I feel overloaded and have back and/or neck pain, and occasionally other symptoms. You have to be creative about how you serve and use the qualities in which you are strongest."

Helping others can indeed help keep you young and healthy. Yet this woman, like many others, has had to learn that every effort is not a success and that taking on too much is anything but healthy. Most helpers probably have a story or two of well-intended efforts that turned into a headache or worse.

I'm no different. An experience of my own went awry because I accepted a responsibility that required more time than I could give. My efforts to do too big a job in too little time resulted in my becoming tense and worried, preoccupied through much of each day, and unable to sleep well at night.

It was about five years ago, so I was already fairly experienced in volunteer work. Even so, I got in over my head. The project itself was excellent. I live in Brooklyn Heights, a community just across the bridge from Manhattan, and I was involved in our neighborhood association, a group that is the oldest one of its type in New York City. I was happy to take part. But my problems began when I was elected to the board and given one of the most highly charged assignments: crime prevention.

Our plan was to begin to operate a civilian observation patrol car, staffed by volunteers, which would cruise through the community keeping an eye out for trouble. The car, with a flashing light on the top and a Brooklyn Heights Association sign on each side, had radio contact with the organization's office. The job of the two volunteers on car duty was that when they saw any sign of criminal activity, they were to call in to the association office, where another volunteer was waiting by a phone to the police precinct. Studies had shown that the presence of this kind of car was a good deterrent to crime.

So I organized the establishment of our civilian patrol. A car was donated. We got a grant from the state of New York to pay for the auto's maintenance, garage, and insurance. And then the car was out on the streets. Our goal was to have it running every single night. Every hour that it was patrolling required the work of three volunteers. Many people assisted in this project. But I was the one responsible for making sure that three people were always on the job.

As it turned out, the project was a success. We got it into operation, and five years later there's still a car out patrolling the streets, with more shifts of volunteers than ever before. I know it makes some difference in the safety of the neighborhood. And at the time of my involvement there was much about the project to make me feel good. I would see the car riding past: clear evidence of the success of my efforts. And I got a lot of feedback too. People who had seen the publicity in the local paper about it would congratulate me. There was also terrific camaraderie among the group of people who worked together on the patrol. And of course there was the hope that we were actually stopping some crimes. But none of that sustained me.

After about three months I began to wear down. Within another month I knew that this kind of work was not for me. All day long at work I was sure that every phone call that came in was going to be from a volunteer who was sick and couldn't work. Often that was the case. I had the same worry at home. It became a twenty-four-hour-a-day problem. And when I went to bed, I couldn't relax. My mind would be racing. I might drop off to sleep, but then I'd wake up again.

It wasn't simply a matter of finding three people to do the job every day. There was also the problem of keeping the car going. Some of the calls were to say that the patrol car wouldn't start. There were many frustrating details, such as keeping the flashing light flashing. The stick-on signs, which were expensive, kept falling off the sides of the car and having to be replaced. When I think back on those Keystone Kop adventures, these mishaps seem funny. They didn't then.

Dropping out of that job was difficult for me to do. I wanted to wait until a replacement was found, but that person wasn't easy to find. And I didn't want to be a quitter, in my own eyes or anyone else's. It was also true that there was so much that was good about the work that it was painful to think of not being part of it: We were tackling the crime problem; I loved working with the group; the response from the community was great. Nonetheless I couldn't stop worrying, and I couldn't sleep. So after about a year I did quit, leaving the job in someone else's hands.

Since then I have been glad to see that the neighborhood patrol has done wonderfully well without me. An all-volunteer crew is still keeping watch over the neighborhood. I see a new car pass by. The effort didn't collapse without me. In fact the patrol has grown and improved greatly. Though that job was not right for me, it was a good choice for someone else. I have gone on to other efforts that fit better with my schedule, interests, and abilities.

FEELINGS OF DISILLUSIONMENT

Feelings of being overwhelmed and helpless are not the only cause of bad helping experiences. There is also the situation where the helper becomes disappointed, disillusioned. Continuing to volunteer in these circumstances brings on frustration, feelings of lost control—the unhealthy helplessness. When a helper goes to a lot of trouble for someone—and comes to care about that person—it can be a great letdown if the one who is helped behaves badly. And it does happen. Many a person can tell a story of someone they helped who let them down.

Sometimes the unhappy ending is dramatic. "Lisa," now thirty-four, still has poignant memories of an effort she made more than ten years ago. Just out of school and working at her first job as a reporter for an Arkansas radio station, Lisa went out one day to do an interview with a young woman in a local prison, a heroin addict who had been supporting her habit through prostitution.

This prisoner seemed to be the opposite of any preconception Lisa had ever had about addicts or hookers. Small and blond, "Cheryl" had an air of fragility and innocence that seemed impossible in one who had lived the life she had. She was seventeen, only a few years younger than Lisa. She could have passed for a high school cheerleader on that day.

"I was totally entranced with her story," Lisa said. A

high school dropout, Cheryl had developed her drug habit at fourteen. As a prostitute, she had been working a strip of sidewalk along the town's central square. The $250 to $300 she might make in a day was shared with a pimp.

Lisa saw the girl's potential for a different kind of life and couldn't stop with a radio interview. "I heard about the community volunteer program and decided to be her sponsor." That meant that Lisa often took Cheryl home to her apartment with her on weekends. The two of them went to concerts together. As much as the situation allowed, they became friends.

When Cheryl became eligible for work/study release, Lisa helped her get a job in a business run by a friend, answering the phone and filing. Cheryl quickly became a part of Lisa's group of friends. Other people liked her; she got along well. At the same time Cheryl got her high school equivalency diploma. Then she was accepted into a nearby college in another state, and was paroled into Lisa's custody. Cheryl's new life was under way.

From all reports, Lisa said later, that new life lasted about three months. Then the trouble began. At first Lisa didn't know the extent of the problems, but they quickly became impossible to hide. Cheryl was back on heroin.

Lisa drove down to the school and got her friend put into the infirmary. Cheryl, it was discovered, had syphilis as well as a recurrence of her drug problem. Lisa stayed in the infirmary with her while she went through the period of "drying out."

"Then a month later the stolen-goods thing happened," Lisa said. Cheryl was arrested for receiving stolen goods. She was put on probation and sent to a residential treatment center. She came to stay with Lisa for Christmas, and that was the last time Lisa ever saw her.

The effort to help lasted three years. Lisa, then twenty-six years old, knew that Cheryl's old life had won out. As for her own reaction, "I ended up in therapy," she said.

What happened to Cheryl she never found out. "I heard a couple of years later that she was back on the streets here. God knows what she's into, if she's even alive."

When Lisa looks back on those three years in her early twenties when she tried to help Cheryl, she concludes that she took too much responsibility. When Cheryl went back to heroin, "I thought it was all my fault. I hadn't done enough." As a result of what happened, "I had doubts about my judgment." What she kept thinking was, "Oh God, was I ever manipulated and used!"

Lisa did recover from this experience. She did help another prisoner, a girl who had had a child by her father and was now in prison for murdering him. Lisa helped her get a job, and this time the results were better. The girl went on to do well.

Yet Lisa has not forgotten her experience with Cheryl. "It definitely makes you more skeptical and hardens you. The thing that killed me the most was that she had so much potential."

Now Lisa feels that it's important to know ahead of time what the pitfalls of a helping activity may be. "Talk to people who have done it before," she said. She recommends "a little common sense and skepticism." For herself, she said, "I had grown up in a totally sheltered life. I had never been exposed to anything like this before."

In retrospect she has found that "the key is having realistic expectations." You have to "take satisfaction in the fact that you made the effort."

There is yet another kind of disillusionment. It comes when a helper begins to feel that the problems she's fighting are too much, that there's no hope, that the stream of wounded people is endless and the troubles will never stop. Hopelessness about the effort of helping and about the future of society is a great burden to carry. No one can stand it for very long.

Paddy Kennington, a longtime helper with the homeless, is one who had to step back and "take a sabbatical," then come back to her efforts in a new way. She is a Third Order Franciscan, a member of an Episcopal lay order, and a spiritual director. Though the members of the order can marry and are expected to work and carry on a life in the world, they also take vows. She has promised to live a life of simplicity, joy, and humility, in short to live as much as possible in the same spirit that Saint Francis of Assisi lived.

Her twelve years of work with the homeless at one point made it hard to maintain a feeling of joy. While she was working on her master's degree in counseling, she began her first work with these people. But before she had been involved long, her efforts began to spread out into many different areas. Eventually she started a food bank, helped organize a new homeless shelter, and worked at increasing public awareness of hunger and at getting health care for the homeless. At the same time she was involved in working in a soup kitchen and in trying to direct people through the labyrinth of agencies that might be able to help them. Though she had started out to be a counselor, she was also spending a lot of time on the phone begging for help for her causes or driving food to where it was needed.

It was the sight of so much suffering that made her try to do everything at once. "People on the street, people in poverty are crushed. Gandhi said that poverty is the worst form of violence." What she saw of the people coming off the streets convinced her that was true.

But her efforts did not stop the river of suffering people. They kept coming; the magnitude of the problem never seemed to diminish. And she saw particular efforts fail. She went to her work at the homeless shelter with good contacts among the helping agencies. She would tell people where to go for help with their particular problems.

"You tell them to go to an agency, then the agency doesn't help." The people she was working with weren't merely getting "lost in the cracks," she said, "they were lost in a chasm." Often the reason was that that person didn't precisely fit the description of those whom the agency was to serve.

"I had a gentleman who told me he couldn't read or write." He was alcoholic and he had psychological problems. He was homeless. The agency he went to gave him a weekly appointment at 2:00 P.M. on a given day for adult counseling. The man had no watch to know when it was 2:00 P.M. and no home to live in from one week to the next. His immediate needs were basic, and his ability to keep a weekly two o'clock appointment very limited. When the help he got was so far from what he needed, he "went off the deep end, took a bath in a local fountain," and was taken off to jail. When he was released, he wandered on to another town and repeated the whole process.

"In twelve years I've seen that hundreds and hundreds of times." Paddy had thrown herself into the effort with the intent of making a difference. "I wanted to change a whole society." She found that "a whole society is not going to change like that."

Her realization led to periods of bitterness and hostility. The pressure of so much continuing effort and disappointment also took its toll. Watching people suffer is terrible in itself. "You get wounded by being close to that much misery and that much grief."

"As long as I was thinking about solutions, I was being destroyed," she said, looking back at that time. "I had to give up success."

She has now begun to move toward the philosophy that "it's the little rivulets of water that crack the rock in ways we may never understand." She is still involved in the effort, but she has stopped trying to move the rock single-handedly.

Now she is teaching reading to adult homeless people through a community technical school. She has also turned back to her original interest of counseling and is planning to go back to school for a doctorate. Her special interest is in developing new strategies for counseling the homeless. She has also begun to write about these issues. Her efforts are more focused, and she is doing more one-to-one helping than she did in her earlier days. Her own approach is centered more on being with the person in his troubles than on a frantic and fruitless effort to solve every problem in sight.

But even these changes have not been a panacea for all her own difficulties with these issues. She is still struggling to find ways to help and to live with joy in the face of so much human trouble.

THE WOUNDED HELPER

The term *burnout,* now a familiar one in the popular press, was first used to describe a condition observed in the members of a helping profession. It was psychoanalyst Herbert Freudenberger who noticed symptoms of physical and mental exhaustion among the staff members of a free clinic and coined the phrase to describe what he saw. This chronic condition, brought on by pushing too hard for too long, is a cluster of symptoms and consequences that range from physical problems to depression, anger, weariness, hostility, or the tendency to give up and withdraw.

"People who fall prey to burnout," says a writer who

has summarized some of Freudenberger's work on the subject, "are usually decent individuals who have striven hard to reach a goal." People in the helping professions often imagine restoring their clients to higher levels of functioning than is realistic. "Disappointments mount up until the helpers build impenetrable walls. Since it hurts too much to care, they tend to anesthetize their feelings and go about their daily routines in a mechanical and cut-off way. The burnout is someone in a state of fatigue or frustration brought about by devotion to a cause, way of life, or relationship that failed to produce the expected reward."[3]

In articles written for *Public Welfare*, published by the American Public Welfare Association, M. Bramhall and S. Ezell suggest ways to recover. While aimed at a professional audience, these suggestions can be used by any exhausted helper. They begin with a look at what caused the situation. Was it exaggerated feelings of responsibility? Impossible demands? Too many hours of overwork?[4] The helper must step back from his or her responsibilities to get this perspective.

Because burnout is in part the effect of a loss of idealism, it is accompanied by a sense of mourning. So it is helpful to find a friend to talk with about your negative feelings. Letting people know what you're going through will ease the feelings of pressure and of being alone with responsibilities. Similarly, asking friends for small favors diminishes the sense the helper has that everything is up to him or her.[5]

Problems emerge when the helper begins to neglect basic self-care in an effort to do too much for others. But the problems don't begin here, according to Bob Dick, Ph.D., a clinical psychologist in Chapel Hill, North Carolina. They begin with a basic personality style that inclines the person not simply to help but to rescue. In working with a burned-out therapist, one of the first things he does is to remind his client of one of the theories of transactional analysis, the idea that one person begins to take on characteristics of a Rescuer, bent on saving the person who is cast into the role of the Victim. What happens in this scenario, Dick said, is that in trying to do too much, the Rescuer is preventing the other person from growing up and learning to do it himself. He is in effect devaluing the Victim's ability to think for and take care of himself.

Inevitably the Rescuer's efforts don't work—they can't. "You can't think for and take care of the needs of any other adult, because only he knows what he really wants and what's really right for him. When it doesn't work, the helper is drained dry—and often he is mad at the Victim for not shaping up after all he's done for him." At this point the Rescuer has actually become the Victim of the one he tried to help—or perhaps even the Persecutor of that person.

Dick's work with an overburdened helper often involves two strategies. First he assists the person to change his or her patterns of rescuing to a different approach that will actually better help the other to help himself. Second he encourages in the helper habits of self-care—good diet, regular exercise, adequate vacation time, and time for friendships, family, sex, solitude, and hobbies. "If you don't take care of yourself," Dick said, "you run out of gas. Anyone who wants to spend a lifetime helping others usually needs help himself."

When Helping You Is Hurting Me, by Carmen Renee Berry, describes the characteristic style of the person who helps others to the point of hurting himself. What Berry calls the Messiah Trap is based on two false assumptions: "If I don't do it, it won't get done" and "Everyone else's needs take priority over mine." Overworked helpers often act on these beliefs without having stopped to spell them out and think about them. As a code of behavior these beliefs do not stand up well under scrutiny, since

they are absolutely contradictory. The helper who oper-
ates on these principles believes himself or herself to be
both indispensable and unimportant.[6]

These assumptions lead to other predictable and damaging attitudes. This kind of overburdened helper is typically:

- Trying to "earn" a sense of self-worth

- Controlled by others' needs

- Driven to excessive achievement

- Drawn to helping people with problems like his own
  rather than dealing directly with his own pain

- Having difficulty establishing intimate relationships

- Isolated

- Endlessly active

- Driven to the point of exhaustion[7]

This helper is not only hurting himself, he is usually
hurting the one he tries to help. As a result of his own
problems, the helper is often encouraging feelings of
helplessness in the other person, blocking any honest
communication, putting up barriers between himself and
the other, and trying to control the other person through
the guise of giving. Not only is the helper exhausted and
angry, but the effort to help is likely to fail.[8]

THE HEALTHY HELPER

Any helper, from professional to beginning volunteer, can
learn to help without doing damage to the self or to the
other, without becoming a victim of burnout. The stories
of helpers' bad experiences contain the warnings and safe-
guards we need to remember:

1. Pace yourself. Don't keep doing more than is good for you. If you're rushing from one task to the next, all with a sense of weary obligation, you're either doing too much or you're doing a job that's not the best choice for you. You are at risk of losing the sense of self-control critical for good health. Because overdoing is so damaging, hospitals, for example, sometimes restrict how often a volunteer can be scheduled to help.

Also, be sure to start gradually. Just as you wouldn't go from never exercising to running marathons, so you shouldn't try to do the equivalent with helping. Helpers can be overwhelmed by starting with a taxing schedule or very emotionally draining tasks.

2. Get plenty of support, encouragement, and company for yourself. Many people prefer to help through organizations because of the sense of teamwork and camaraderie, as well as the opportunity for training. In her work with a difficult dying woman, Randee Russell found that the people she worked with at Hospice took great care to help her protect herself. "They help you keep some perspective," she said. There were times when she'd be at the hospital day and night with Alice, and her friends would start calling her "Saint Randee." The people at Hospice would say, " 'What do you think you're doing? How long can you keep that up?' " The organization stayed in regular contact with her; "they'll call me and ask me about everything in my life, not just the patient." The agency "reminds you that you're important," she said, "so that you don't neglect yourself."

Paddy Kennington, the Franciscan who works with the homeless, also thinks that working with others is far better than a more solitary course. "If you go out and wing it on your own, you're going to be in a lot of trouble."

3. It's not necessary to rescue the whole world; in fact don't kid yourself that you have the total re-

sponsibility for even one other person. It's too much to take on. And in truth it's more than anyone can actually control. Lisa could not have kept Cheryl from going back on heroin. When you begin to help someone with a problem as tough as that one, it's important to realize that there may be a disappointment in store. Don't blame yourself.

4. Explore what kind of helping is comfortable for you. Jimmie Holland, director of psychiatry at Memorial Sloan-Kettering Cancer Center, pointed out to me the importance of a helper understanding his own motivation, as well as his ability to handle the emotional difficulties of the job. For example, she said, for a cancer patient to come back later to help other people with cancer can work well, or it can be very hard on the helper. For some people the helping brings back memories of the emotional and physical upheavals of the illness and actually gets in the helper's way of going on with his life. Yet for other cancer patients the helping may be emotionally strengthening. These people often feel that they want to give something back. Helping provides this opportunity, and it adds to a sense of mastery. It can be a way of declaring, "I am safe." The difference lies purely with the individual. Find out what works for you by learning about the work, talking with other helpers, and then by giving it a try.

5. Go ahead and do what you comfortably can. For many would-be helpers, the most difficult helping experience is just getting started. A lot of us are reluctant at first. It can be difficult to knock on a door for the first time, particularly if you know that needy people are on the other side.

Most of us are "incipient altruists," says Christie Kiefer, a professor of anthropology at the University of California at San Francisco. We want to help others but need encouragement to get involved. A brochure of the Lake Area United Way in Indiana says, "Getting involved in new things and meeting new people can be very exciting and a little scary, too. That's perfectly normal. Once you get involved, those fears quickly go away." One way to ease that initial nervousness is simply to take a deep breath and plunge right in. Another, much more pleasant, way is to take a friend or family member with you as a fellow helper.

Starting to volunteer through an organization offers the advantage of training and the possibility of switching to a different helping activity if the first doesn't offer the sensations of helper's high and the sense of well-being that follows.

For today's time-oppressed, two-income families, the possibility of family members volunteering together may be a chance to strengthen family relationships as well. This can become still another example of how we personally gain in so many ways from aiding others.

Later, when you are an experienced helper, be sure to continue to maintain the philosophy of do-what-you-can. Nobody can do everything. Take pleasure and the benefits of improved health out of simply doing what you can.

6. Feel free to give up on a particular effort when you get into a situation that isn't right for you. It took me a few months to free myself from the responsibility of running our neighborhood's patrol service, but it was the right decision. I've since found other activities that satisfy me more. Other people have volunteered to do the work that I was having such trouble doing. Nobody is indispensable.

7. Don't quit helping because of one rejection or disappointment or bad experience. Dave Glass, pastor of a church in Ohio, estimates that for every ten times we reach out to someone to help, we'll be rejected two or three times. Expect some rejections and some efforts that turn out badly, not to mention the losses that life inevitably brings, and then keep going.

Recently I was talking with volunteers at Beth Israel Hospital, people who help boarder babies, the abandoned newborns whose parents are often drug addicts. Many of these babies have medical problems and are small and weak. The volunteers hold and hug and cuddle the babies, providing stimulation that is critical for early physical and emotional development.

One volunteer, "Miriam," who is retired, told me about a baby she had become very attached to. During the time she was involved with him, she would "especially look forward to going to the hospital. He was delicate and beautiful and so small. And the way he looked at me when I picked him up," she said, "and I looked back at him. One day I arrived at the hospital and everyone was quiet. They weren't calling to me. The nurses are usually always so friendly. Then I found out—the baby had died that night." Miriam pauses, staring straight ahead, and then explained that she still volunteers in the unit, sometimes five times a week. "Coming to the hospital, holding those babies—for me it's a new life."

8. Recognize that even when you see other volunteers around you having a wonderful experience—while you're not—it does not mean you are not suited for helping. It simply means that you need to find the helping effort that is right for you. We are all different, from what makes us laugh to what makes us cry. The differences show up in our volunteer efforts as well. Emotional demands affect us differently.

Consider the responses from two volunteers involved in the same work at the same organization, the Carillon Foundation, an agency in northwest Indiana that assists people with emotional problems. One, thirty-four years old, said that in spite of feelings of physical fatigue, "it's rewarding." In contrast the second volunteer, twenty-seven, complained, "Most of the time I'm just going through the motions when helping, sort of a learned behavior."

It's possible to do a lot of good and get a lot of good out of trying to help, whatever the apparent results. Though the effort might seem to be a complete failure, we may be helping the other person in ways that we don't know. When we're deeply involved in a situation, it may be difficult to know how valuable we are. There's a sense in which we have to let go of the results, judging the experience only in terms of its value for us.

Twenty-five years ago Hildegarde Bailey of Benton Harbor, Michigan, made an effort to help that was good for her own health, as well as for a family in need. Though the people she helped later behaved in a disappointing way, it was still clear that she had served herself and others well on the day she brought food to a house where people were hungry.

At the time it happened, she was about fifty years old, and she and her husband owned some rental property. "People knew me as the landlady. When I came out of the apartment house, they knew I had collected rent."

One cold, icy day "I rounded the corner of the house and someone grabbed my purse. In fright I became rigid, clenched my hands, and screamed and screamed." Trying to get her pocketbook off her shoulder, the mugger yanked at her arm, slamming her against a barrel at the edge of the walk. "I received a good pummeling. My shoulder hurt terribly."

For the next week her shoulder was so painful that she couldn't dress without help. The motion of her husband turning over in their bed at night hurt her so much that she had to move to the davenport.

Then one morning she got a call from a tenant who said, "You told me to call you if my check ever didn't come. I haven't received it," the woman said, "and my daughter and I haven't eaten for three days." Hildegarde, still in pain and having difficulty with motion, loaded up a tray with food from her own kitchen. She took the tray to the woman, then drove her to the nearest grocery store and gave her ten dollars for milk, meat, and other perishables. "I took her home," Hildegarde said, "and believe it or not, I didn't have any pain whatsoever." She suddenly realized that she had used her arms, had dressed alone, driven the car. "I don't know when the pain left," she wrote.

"My husband came home early, and he asked, 'How is your shoulder?' I answered, 'I got healed. Do you believe it?'"

Hildegarde added a postscript to her letter. "The finish of the story isn't so great," she wrote. "The lady moved owing me about six hundred dollars in back rent, just about left the place in a shambles."

In spite of that loss, Hildegarde recalls the long-ago episode with pleasure and excitement, not regret. She was anything but sorry to have taken food to the woman and her child that day.

7

The Spirit of Giving

FOR centuries, long before endorphins were ever imagined, brotherly love has been a central premise of the world's religions. A multitude of different faiths have urged people to save their own souls and honor their deities by extending themselves to serve others. Charity through gifts and service is a virtually universal tenet of religions. It is difficult to find a faith that does not urge some form of reaching out to one's fellows.

Many people today confuse this idea of charitable giving with another tenet of some religions—self-denial. It is important to remember that giving is *not* a denial of the self. A close reading of the texts of many faiths shows what many of us have learned for ourselves: that giving to others is the farthest thing from self-denial. It is an enhancement of the self. As we give to others, we give also to ourselves—physically, emotionally, and spiritually. The Book of Isaiah (58:7–8, 11) makes clear the Old Testament view of the kind of actions that are pleasing to God. It is not fasting as a way for "a man to afflict his soul" that God commends to us. Instead "Is not this the fast that I have chosen? . . . Is it not to deal thy bread to the hungry, and that thou bring the poor that are cast out to thy house? When thou seest the naked, that thou cover him. . . . Then shall thy light break forth as the morning, and thine health shall spring forth speedily; and thy righteousness shall go before thee. . . . And the Lord shall guide thee continually, and satisfy thy soul in drought, and make fat thy bones: and thou shalt be like a watered garden, and like a spring of water, whose waters fail not." This biblical prescription of giving for both good health and a satisfied soul is one that modern research and experience bear out.

In the hills of eastern Ohio there is a church that is guided by this teaching to an unusual degree. Since 1984 the Family Worship Center, a Free Methodist Church in the town of Woodsfield, has run its own school, the Free Methodist Academy of Excellence, with an all-volunteer faculty and staff. The church and school together have fourteen people working at least forty hours a week without pay, and many others are working several hours a week as volunteers while holding down regular jobs.

This remarkable donation of time and effort is taking place in an area that pastor Dave Glass describes as a rural ghetto. The closing of a coal mine has caused much unemployment; the jobless rate is three times the national average. Per capita measures for homicide, suicide, divorce, and school dropouts are also high. Yet, situated in one small town in the area, this church has a membership of 1,100 people and an average attendance at services of 700. People who had moved as much as two hours away in search of jobs are coming back to the church with some regularity. And every weekday at the school, teachers are teaching and women are running a lunchroom for eighty children and their teachers—all without pay.

On a recent afternoon, when the lunchtime rush was over and the children were back in their classes, one of the volunteer cooks came out of the church kitchen and told her story, sitting at a big round cafeteria table in the church basement. Jean Truax was one of the earliest members of the church. She and her husband were members seven years earlier when the congregation consisted of about fifteen people. Not only was the membership back then so low but the congregation had also lost their preacher. In the face of these difficulties that band of a dozen or so decided to build themselves a church building, not a small chapel but a good-sized church. "There were those who told us we'd never get it done," Jean said. But with almost entirely donated labor, they did build it. The Truaxs owned an excavation company, and they did the digging, Jean working twelve to fourteen hours a day on the construction. "We just stuck together and kept it a-going," she said.

Then they found themselves a preacher in a town an hour away, a man whose father Jean knew. Dave Glass came to Woodsfield bringing even more support for the spiritual and healing value of helping others. He came, he said, even though people he knew told him he was crazy to do so. Coming to Woodsfield would probably not appear to most people to be the best career move. Located in a region of cattle farms and little villages strung along winding narrow roads, it's quite remote.

Dave Glass began the job without any sort of pay, borrowing money to buy groceries the first year. In recent years he and his wife have received a "love offering" from the congregation every three months. From the first he saw it as his role "to lead by serving." So he joined the volunteers who built the building, and the group began to grow. Volunteering was necessary if anything was to be accomplished, since money was in short supply. One of Dave's efforts to encourage the volunteer work to continue was to make sure that it was appreciated. The desire for respect and appreciation is our deepest inner craving, he said, second only to the desire for eternal life. "The only thing I can offer to the volunteers is love and appreciation." He wrote enormous numbers of notes thanking people for their efforts. At the same time the volunteers were receiving the physical, emotional, and spiritual benefits of helping.

And then a few years ago a court decision involving another organization gave the church's volunteer concept an inadvertent boost. When a U.S. Supreme Court ruling required at least a minimum pay standard wherever any payment was being made, the school went all-volunteer. Now not only the teaching but all construction of new buildings, janitorial and maintenance work, cooking, coaching, and secretarial work is done by volunteers. Again and again these people talk of their daily efforts as a profound and sustaining religious experience, as well as a source of general well-being.

Jean Truax, with her husband and their excavation company, had helped to build the church. Years later, in addition to raising two of her grandchildren and taking care of her sick mother, she volunteered as a cook at the school cafeteria four days a week. "God gives me the strength to do it," she said. "God gives us the love to love other people."

Nicki Blackstone described her church's volunteer effort as "a ministry of helps. Alone and as a group we go wherever we see a need—either physical or emotional or financial, and we fix it."

Because of her helping, she describes her life as "the happiest, most fulfilling, exciting that I ever dreamed of. We're a church family of seven hundred–plus people, and our community doesn't know what to make of us. They tell us we are the happiest, healthiest, most excited people they have ever seen.

"I am not on staff in a ministry. I am a farm wife— sheep, beef cattle, hogs, chickens, tobacco, hay, oats, corn—with three boys (ages eight, five, three) and a staggering workload. We raise all our own beef, pork, chicken, milk, eggs, fruit, and vegetables. We work eighteen hours every day, and we give and give and give and are happy, successful, and healthy. We live on a constant natural high. Our happiness and health are directly related to our giving and doing for others.

"With my overweight, and we're talking a hundred pounds overweight, I have perfect blood pressure, perfect heart, and that's with a workload that would kill a teenage man.

"David and I are typical pioneer-stock farm people. We don't have a fancy lifestyle. We're not what you would call the beautiful people." Their operation is large: They have three hundred sheep and work international livestock sales. Her husband works construction as well. She is "hooked to the harness" twenty-four hours a day. It's "one of the most pressure-cooker lifestyles. And we go around and around because we don't see eye to eye here on a lot of things." But none of this is a problem for her.

"*Euphoria* is a strong word," she said, "but it is an appropriate word." When she has helped someone, "a spiritual, emotional thing is taking place."

The kind of helping she does is on her own, throughout her day. She often takes care of the children of people who are volunteering at the church and school. Sometimes she cooks dinner and leaves it in the cars of the teachers so that they will find it when they come out to go home. She does informal counseling with people who come to her with problems. She sends money anonymously to people she thinks might have a particular need. "Sometimes you're thinking, 'This person is going to think I'm so stupid, that I'm reaching out too frantically.' " And sometimes, she said, when you go ahead and do it anyway, you "find out later that that person was in a spot at that time, and what you did was the only thing that helped."

Often, when someone comes to her with a problem, feeling depressed, she tells them, "Go home, cook a meal for someone, take it to them. You will feel better. The less you want to, the more you need to do it." She told the story of a neighbor going through a difficult divorce who kept coming over to talk. Nicki offered her usual pre-scription for helping somebody: cook a meal to take to someone. At first the woman tried it and didn't feel bet-ter. "She kept saying, 'Nick, it's not working.' I'd say, 'Do it again.' " Finally the woman began to feel better, to "get a grip on herself and feel special."

It may not work overnight, Nicki said, but finally it works. "Put as much of you into other people's lives as you can. When you need a blessing, the Lord is right there.

"I can show you hundreds of people, from all walks of life, every income bracket, every educational bracket, every denomination who are doing what I'm doing and feel like I feel. You can't outgive God. The more you give, the more it comes back to you. The more you do for others, the better you feel and the happier you are."

On the other hand she also knows a few "that there's nobody going to get into their pocket or into their sched-ule." She quoted a prayer that describes that kind of life: "Dear Lord, bless me, my wife, our son Bill, his wife, us four, and no more." That's a limited and unhappy way to live, she thinks. "If you live for yourself, you're missing out on a great big thrill." To go for days without doing something special to help someone "doesn't feel right. It feels a little bit like a letdown, like 'ho-hum.' "

Dave Glass, or Pastor Dave, as his congregation calls him, has preached at least one sermon to his flock on the subject of endorphins, love, and feeling good—he has a strong interest in reading medical journals. "It always pleases me a lot when I find medicine or geology or archaeology that confirms God's word." While his statements to his congregation about endorphins may be more expansive than those I am prepared to make, he is preaching a message about helping and its effect on health that is well-supported by survey data, and that is working impressively well in his own community.

When Dave Glass looks out across the congregation, he can see at the back of the sanctuary a row of big clocks telling the times around the world, in locations including Seoul, San Diego, and Nairobi, as well as Woodsfield. These are to remind people to extend themselves to pray for others in other parts of the world. Most of you here, he said to the people in the sanctuary before him one recent Sunday, have experienced a second wind. "You've had a job to do, and you've pushed and you've pushed and you've pushed until you were ready to drop."

His style of preaching is also to push and push. His speech is fast, urgent; he paces up and down the aisles as he hammers his message home. "It was something really serious," he said, "and you had to keep pushing on. And the first thing you know, you are feeling good, you are feeling energy, you are feeling happy, you are feeling strong, and you can work all day and all night. Whatever needs to be done, you can do it, and you can handle it. Why? Because the endorphins started to flow.

"Now, the only thing is, to trigger endorphins by extreme physical exercise is tremendous for our mind and attitude, but the human body would break down under that in a very short time. On those extreme occasions when you and I have pushed ourselves to extreme limits of our physical endurance, producing the endorphins, it puts us in an almost incredible invincible state. And our bodies can't really take that all day every day."

In recent years, he tells the congregation, doctors have

begun to study what it is that healthy people are doing right. One thing they found, he said, is that these people have learned how to love.

"The research is mountainous. What American people need to do is just what God says: Love your neighbor as yourself."

He talked about the feelings of people newly fallen in love. When that happens, "you are higher than any alcoholic or dope addict has ever been high, and you know that's true." Like a second wind, falling in love improves your health and your attitude, "all because it makes the endorphins flow. That's what your heavenly Father wants for you every day. You have to learn to love. Tear that crusty exterior down and realize that the joy and the energy and the enthusiasm and the health and the immunity, all of those things are produced by our obeying this book right here," he says, indicating the Bible. "That's all God has asked us to do." There are people in the room, he says, with "aunts, husbands, and wives that'll make you bitter enough you want to strangle them. I'm not saying you don't have a right to. I'm saying it's not in *your* best interest."

In an interview Dave Glass talked some more about helping, his reading of scientific journals, and how he arrived at his personal observations. "Almost everybody who goes to the hospital spends a lot of time praying." If those who are sick will pray, not for themselves alone but for someone else as well, their condition can change in a way that helps their healing. It doesn't matter, he said, whether you're praying for starving people in Ethiopia or for the person in the next bed. If patients will extend themselves on behalf of another with "true emotion," they are likely to fare better. The same thing happens with a grandparent who has been sickly and is suddenly needed to raise a grandchild. Maybe that person couldn't get out of bed before, he said, but suddenly he's out in the yard playing ball. "When there's a cause that is bigger than we are, that motivates us in an altruistic way."

The majority of the helping done by the members of his congregation seems to involve one-to-one efforts, such as the cooking of a meal or participation in the running of the church and its school, activities that put helpers in direct contact with those they are helping and with each other.

After they finished the church, the members continued to do further construction. Behind the church is the building that contains the classrooms, the gym, and the weight room, which was built entirely by volunteers. Beside the door are two plaques, one listing people who gave more than three hundred hours of labor and one listing those who gave at least five hundred dollars for materials. Dave Palmer, for example, built the flight of stairs up through the center of the building. His full-time job is teaching carpentry in the local public schools. The minister pitched in as well, and so did the teenagers in the church. One member loaned a bulldozer and a backhoe to the volunteer crew.

Now the buildings are up, and the contributions of work and supplies continue to flow in. Gas is pumped from a well owned by a church member, through five thousand feet of pipe laid across another church member's land. One farmer routinely allocates the money he makes from an acre and a half of sweet corn and the sale of one steer each year to the church. Many people spend their vacations working in the ministry.

Helping and high endorphin levels are "what our ministry runs on," said Jo Palmer, Dave's wife, who is one of the associate pastors. She finds that her own helping efforts produce a "Christmas-type excitement." But she would not claim that this makes everything in life go smoothly. She was one of several who pointed out that the church and its members still have their problems. "It's not perfect," Jo said. "There are no free rides and white picket fences. The trials are there. The difference is in how you deal with them."

Naomi Driggs sometimes puts in as much as sixty hours a week as a volunteer doing office work for the church. "It has changed my whole life, learning to love people. If it were a job, I might put in my eight hours and go home." Before she started to help at the church, she used to sleep a lot. Maybe she was depressed, she said. Now she wakes up curious to see "what kind of adventure the day brings."

Leo Smithberger is a member of the church's paid staff, one of the associate pastors, but his efforts go far beyond those that the job usually requires. Certainly he puts in more hours than he once did as a rural mail carrier. "People are wanting more out of serving God," he said, "not just sitting in church on a Sunday morning." Among his own recent efforts were helping to build a field house for the Woodsfield High football team, visiting people in prison, and cutting firewood to give to the elderly and to sell for maintenance of the church. "We look for ways to serve our church and the community. We serve God by serving other people."

The good that comes to each of us from giving is spelled out in the Bible. "Give, and it will be given to you. A good measure, pressed down, shaken together and running over, will be poured into your lap. For with the measure you use, it will be measured to you" (Luke 6:38).

THE UNIVERSAL TEACHING

The experiences of these church members dramatize well the emotional and physical sensations and health benefits that result from regular helping. This one Christian church in a small Ohio town is a stitch in the immense tapestry of religious practice and teaching that relates to giving.

William James, one of the most elegant and insightful of writers on religion and its place in human psychology, observed in his *Varieties of Religious Experience* that "charity" is one of the qualities universally attributed to the highly spiritual person. "There is a certain composite photograph of universal saintliness, the same in all religions, of which the features can be easily traced." Among these features are "an immense elation and freedom, as the outlines of the confining selfhood melt down . . . , a shifting of the emotional centre towards loving and harmonious affections, toward 'yes, yes,' and away from 'no,' . . . ." One of the practical results of these feelings is charity toward others. This is true across a broad range of beliefs throughout history, from the Hindus to the Stoics.[1]

In Judaism helping is spelled out in the Torah as one of God's moral laws. These govern the way people should treat each other—and a right and just generosity toward other people is one of these laws. Since God created us in his own image, every person is of infinite worth and deserving of the greatest respect. First we are to treat others with decency, not using someone for our own gains, never injuring, oppressing, exploiting or humiliating another. Then we are to go beyond merely refraining from abuse of others; we are to give to those who are in need.[2]

In the practice of Buddhism the believer seeks to reduce the boundary lines between the self and other people, whether these are strangers, enemies, or loved ones. The believer is expected to work at being a friend toward all. "Even as a mother watches over and protects her only child," says the Metta Sutta, "so with a boundless mind should one cherish all living beings, radiating friendliness over the entire world, above, below, and all around without limit; so let him cultivate a boundless goodwill to-wards the entire world, uncramped, free from ill-will or enmity." This feeling of goodwill is then supposed to lead to compassion; the believer should concentrate on the sufferings of others, suffer with them, and wish to take away their troubles.[3]

Mahayana Buddhism teaches an all-embracing sympathy exemplified by the bodhisattva, which means heroic or enlightened being. This enlightenment consists, in great part, of sympathy for others. The bodhisattva should help others toward Nirvana before allowing himself to reach this ideal state. According to the Prajnaparamita, "Doers of what is hard are the Bodhisattvas, the great beings who have set out to win supreme enlighten-ment. . . . They have set out for the benefit of the world, for the ease of the world, out of pity for the world. They have resolved: 'We will become a shelter for the world, a refuge for the world, the world's place of rest.' "[4]

Followers of Islam also believe in generous giving. Two of the most frequently used titles for God in this faith are "Compassionate" and "Merciful." Stories of the life of the Prophet Muhammad often mention his concern for the dispossessed, especially widows and orphans. Among the main tenets of this religion is the obligation to tithe a portion of one's income to help others who are in need.[5]

While Hindus believe that people must remain "de-tached" from the outcome of their efforts, they must still take action and perform their duties in the physical world. The *Yoga Sutras* prescribe joy at the sight of goodness, and compassion for the troubled as well as *action to relieve their suffering*, and indifference to the wicked.[6]

The faithful Mormon is a regular volunteer for efforts that serve others. *Why I Am a Mormon*, by Wallace Ben-nett, argues that this church calls for an unusually high capacity for unselfish service in the believer. "Not only is he asked to give of his time and talents without pay—not once but over and over for a lifetime—but all around him there are scores and hundreds of other people doing the same thing. The attitude is in the air he breathes."⁷

"Whatever be the explanation of the charity," William James wrote, "it may efface all usual human barriers." He called this charitable cast of mind tenderness and found that such feeling is integral to the religious life. "There is thus an organic affinity between joyousness and tenderness, and their companionship in the saintly life need in no way occasion surprise. Along with the happiness," James wrote, "this increase of tenderness is often noted in narratives of conversion. 'I began to work for others';—'I had more tender feeling for my family and friends';— . . .'I felt for everyone, and loved my friends better';—'I felt every one to be my friend.' "⁸

Strong religious feeling seems to turn almost inevitably to some form of giving, or "tenderness" toward others. Whatever our beliefs, this feeling often leads to a strong sense of unity with others. This sensation of tenderness and togetherness is one of great joy. Remember Isaiah's advice about giving to others, and the results that will follow: "Then shall thy light break forth as the morning, and thine health shall spring forth speedily . . . and thou shalt be like a watered garden, and like a spring of water, whose waters fail not."

BODY AND SOUL

Medical research is now expanding its efforts to find a physical basis for the promise of health springing forth from a spiritual life. We already know that mind and body interact in ways that can greatly affect physical health. Recently the research in the mind-body field has begun to explore interactions between spiritual beliefs and health, with some very promising results. Kenneth Pelletier, Ph.D., of the University of California at San Francisco School of Medicine, and author of *Mind As Healer/ Mind As Slayer*, brought together many of these findings in a paper he presented at the conference on altruism and health that I organized in New York in 1988. "There is a substantial and growing body of research data and clinical evidence," Pelletier wrote, "that an individual's spiritual beliefs are intimately related to . . . personal health and professional achievement."[9]

Pelletier summarized several studies that point to a connection between beliefs and health. For example, work with Mormons and Seventh Day Adventists has indicated that they have significantly lower rates of heart disease and cancer, as well as a lower mortality rate, than comparable populations. The rate of incidence of coronary artery disease among male Seventh Day Adventists has been found to be half that of the general population of white males. The physical health practices of these groups, such as abstention from smoking and drinking, are certainly important to consider in these results. However, Pelletier argued, "It is clear that it is not just these activities which result in these outcomes. In fact, it is increasingly evident that the values, beliefs, and attitudes underlying these practices and social support networks per se are an independent and powerful influence upon health status in and of themselves. . . . It is evident," Pelletier wrote in the conference paper, "that the positive emotions of love, compassion, joy, altruism, and states of inner peace developed during prayer and meditation do have a positive influence at the biochemical level in the human mind-body system."[10]

Probably the best-known study regarding the importance to health of a spiritual lifestyle was reported by psychiatrist George Vaillant in his 1977 book *Adaptation to Life*, which was based on a thirty-year study of a group of Harvard graduates. Vaillant's chief finding is that "health is adaptation"—thus the title of his book. He set out to examine the specific ways in which these men altered themselves to meet situations in life that were often very stressful. In his study each participant was asked to confirm or deny the accuracy of thirty-two statements about relationships, career satisfaction, and physical and psychological health, as they related to his own life, for example: "I have little contact with my family; I have few close friends." Each time a respondent identified with a statement, he was assigned a point. A score of less than seven indicated the highest level of health. Observing which men were healthy or ill by the time they reached their fifties and comparing this with the attitudes they lived by, Vaillant concluded that adopting an altruistic lifestyle is a critical component of mental health. He found, in words evocative of Selye's altruistic egoism concept, that "altruism provides a protective filter for the most searing emotions."[11]

The examples he gives are illustrations of what I consider to be the essence of spirituality: the capacity to go beyond the self, to transcend the limits of the self through helping others. Vaillant discussed, for example, a physician in his thirties, Godfrey Camille, who because of stress suffered from abdominal pains, indigestion, and cold hands. His escape to health involved "altruism and the capacity to function as a giving adult." For Camille this meant giving up his practice in a military dispensary, where he felt overwhelmed by the demands of the army wives, to start up a Baltimore clinic for allergic disorders, and to begin research on the needs of asthmatic patients with deprived childhoods. Another man in Vaillant's study became addicted to alcohol and gambling and was caught stealing equipment from his employer, Bell Telephone Laboratories. For his recovery he cited the importance of no longer doing analysis on military matters for Bell and instead performing actuarial work for a foundation concerned with population control. This man's recovery, Vaillant concluded, involved adopting altruism as a daily lifestyle: he took an active role in his church and became especially involved in reaching beyond the concerns of his own life through his work in AA. "Within Alcoholics Anonymous, he was positively addicted to helping other people."

Certainly there are many who profess no religion yet who are indefatigable servants of the needs of others in their communities. Observers of American life have often seen volunteering in this country as a sort of civic religion. The nineteenth-century French statesman Alexis de Tocqueville noted this in his famous travels through America. So did Ernest Michel, a man who spent six years of his youth in Nazi terror being shipped between eleven different concentration camps. Michael rose to be one of the most powerful leaders of organized Jewish communal work, devoting his life to helping new immigrants and the needy. "In no other country is charity so developed as it is here in the United States," he said. "In no other country do people give as much money and time."[12]

Our presidents have also observed this phenomenon, this secular and spiritual urge to volunteer. Herbert Hoover called service to our fellow man a part of our national character. Franklin Roosevelt spoke of "the generosity of our American people"; Harry Truman said we are a "neighborly people at heart. We have the impulse to help each other." According to John Kennedy, "A sense of responsibility to others . . . has marked our country from its earliest beginnings, when the recognition of our obligation to God was stated in nearly every public document, down to the present day."[13]

Pitching in and helping others seems to be at least as deeply ingrained in our national frontier-born character as gun-slinging and lonesome cowboys. A full 45 percent of the adult population of this country now claims involvement in some kind of volunteer work (though not necessarily performed regularly or with personal contact), and 75 percent believe that they *should* be doing something to help others.[14] A study of what our values will be in the next century was commissioned by Seagram Industries to find out what workers throughout the nation will want in the future. *Working Americans: Emerging Values* found a sharp interest in public service and an overwhelming preference for giving time rather than money.[15]

It seems clear that as a people we want to help each other. This desire can come from the moral precepts of religion as well as from the simple urge of the spirit to enlarge itself by making a deeply felt connection with another.

In my own experience the feelings that come from helping are similar to those I feel sometimes in group prayer. When I feel myself joining with others in this call to God, I seem to forget myself. It's a good feeling, very relaxing and calming. Yet when I actually take some action toward a better life for one person and can see that person and feel our connection, then the sensation is so many times stronger. And this human connection produces the strongest feelings of transcendence, of spirituality.

People describing their experience of helping make many of these same observations: a sense of unity, an uplifted feeling, a feeling of reaching beyond the usual definition of self. Pitirim Sorokin, in his book *Altruistic Love*, says that most of the saints are "masters and creators of love-energy." And this seems to have good results for their own health, as demonstrated by their long lives. The life span of Catholic and Russian Orthodox saints tended to be amazingly long, greatly exceeding that of not only their contemporaries but of twentieth-century Americans. Since most of these people lived prior to 1700, when lives were typically short, and since most of them endured not only the hardships of their time but the asceticism, persecution, and even martyrdom that went along with their religious life, their life spans are particularly remarkable. Of the Russian Orthodox saints throughout history, for example, more than half died past the age of seventy.

"This extraordinary longevity strongly suggests," Sorokin wrote, "that not only is there a causal bond between sainthood and long life, but that probably the saintly way of life is a very important factor in longevity. Through the highest kind of self-control, through the deep peace of mind and complete integration of personality, altruistic love and saintliness become truly life-giving and life-invigorating powers."[16] These highly spiritual people, living in different centuries and different parts of the world, are an astonishing testimony to the healing power of going beyond self.

A SPARK THAT CATCHES FIRE

Though religion is by no means crucial to the fostering of altruism—in fact only 22 percent of the volunteers surveyed in a 1988 Gallup Poll cited religion as their motivation for volunteering—a person who feels in some way affiliated with an organized religion is likelier than others to be a volunteer. A recent survey found that slightly more than half the people who belong to congregations were doing some helping. Of nonmembers, only one-third were volunteers.[17]

At its best, religion can inspire, promote, and even institutionalize altruism. The story of a very remarkable small town in France shows how the influence of a religious belief can transform a community. The story of Le Chambon has been told again and again, in movies such as Pierre Sauvage's *Weapons of the Spirit* and books such as *The Courage to Care*, based on a film of the same title, but it is a story that is worth many recountings.

Le Chambon-sur-Lignon sits on a high plateau surrounded by higher mountains in the south-central part of France. It will be remembered for what happened there during the German occupation of France. Each of the five thousand people of this town refused to cooperate with the Nazis and the Vichy government. They not only refused to identify their resident Jews, but they turned the town into a haven for Jewish children and families from elsewhere. Not one refugee was ever turned in. Instead, five thousand Jews were rescued by this community, a number equal to the total population of the town.

A Protestant minister and his wife, André and Magda Trocmé, were at the center of what happened in Le Chambon. In the book *The Courage to Care*, Magda Trocmé tells how it began. "A poor woman came to my house one night, and she asked to come in. She said immediately that she was a German Jew, that she was running away, that she was hiding, that she wanted to have shelter. She thought that at the minister's house she would perhaps find someone who could understand her. And I said, 'Come in.' And so it started. I did not know that it would be dangerous. Nobody thought of that."

Magda Trocmé's husband was a pacifist. From the pulpit of the church he preached, even on the day after armistice with Nazi Germany, that one's responsibility was to resist violence with the weapons of the spirit. When he himself volunteered to go to a camp to take care of Jewish children, he was told that there were already people to do that. What was needed instead was a place to hide Jews. "Is your village prepared to do that?" he was asked.

Le Chambon-sur-Lignon did exactly that. The matter was presented to the council of the church, and within minutes they had agreed.

So, in Le Chambon, Jewish children went to school

with Gentiles. They played together, sometimes with a pig that they called Adolf. Jewish children slept in the barns and stables of farms all around the town. In the mornings they would walk into town to school. One Gentile boy was in charge of a warning system to let children who passed down his road know whether it was safe. If the shutters of his room were open, they could proceed. If not, the children hurried back into hiding.

Finally André Trocmé was told by a prefect of the government to list the names of the Jews in hiding. He refused, saying that the Jews were his brothers. As a result he was imprisoned. When the gendarmes came to take him away, Magda Trocmé asked them to sit down and eat while she packed her husband's suitcase. To offer them such a kindness was nothing extraordinary, according to her. "There we were, and it was time to eat. . . . It was nothing at all."[18]

Movie director Pierre Sauvage recently visited this town to interview the now-aging residents, to ask them why they did what they did. Sauvage has a particular interest in what happened in this town. "It was in Le Chambon that I was born, in March 1944, a Jewish baby, lucky to see the light of day in a place on earth singularly committed to his survival at the very time when much of my family was disappearing into the abyss." When he went back to the town to interview people who were adults at the time of his birth, he received almost identical responses: a slight shrug, a few words explaining simply that it was the right thing to do. Many of them knew that it was right because of their own religious history, because they were Huguenots, French Protestants whose ancestors had been persecuted by the Catholic kings of France. The stories they'd heard all their lives of what their forebears had been through constituted a sort of preparation. When it came time to do so, they were eager to help others who were being persecuted. Sauvage quotes a letter from André Trocmé to an American friend, written in 1934: "Here, the old Huguenot spirit is alive. The humblest peasant home has its Bible, and the father reads it every day. So these people, who do not read the papers but the Scriptures, do not stand on the moving soil of opinion but on the rock of the Word of God."[19] Though many other congregations across Europe were closing their eyes to what was occurring, the people of this church understood the word of God to mean that they should help their brothers, the Jews. Importantly, the example set by this one church was heroically accepted by the entire town, many of whom were not Huguenots.

8

Magnificent Obsession

IN 1929, a year of hard times, Lloyd C. Douglas published a novel that has since become a popular classic. It was about a secret formula that would bring unbounded good fortune to the one who acted on it. The main character, Bobby Merrick, finds this formula written in code in the papers of a man who has died. After breaking the code and deciphering the secret, he has begun to live by it. In this scene he reveals it to someone else:

> "Sit down," he said gently. "I'll try to explain. . . . It's not easy, though."
>
> She walked with some reluctance to the little divan and sat.
>
> "Perhaps you never had it called to your attention,"—Bobby was feeling his way with caution—"that there is sometimes a strange relation between the voluntary, secret bestowal of a gift, without expectation of any return or reward, and certain significant results that accrue from it in the experience of the giver."

The giving of the gift, the "magnificent obsession" that the hero was describing, was the need to do good for another person and the astonishing benefits that result in the life of the giver. The formula—treated in the novel as a grand mystery—makes it clear that the kind of helping involved cannot be done by simply giving money. The crucial element is the personal contact. Bobby, the man with the "obsession," again tries to pass this knowledge on to someone else. To his wealthy grandfather he says,

"You can't do this with a checkbook! . . . By the way—did you know that old Jed Turner, up the road here, had to kill seventeen of his Holstein cows last week? The State Vet condemned them as tuberculous. . . . Jed's all broken up about it."

"I wonder if he has a telephone."

"Oh, you can easily send for him to come over. . . . I noticed, the other day, that Jim Abbot's ten-year-old boy is dragging a leg in a brace that didn't look right to me. . . . Why don't you hop into your car tomorrow, and have Stephen drive you about through the district? *You'll be amazed what it does to you to make connections with people who need you!* . . . Oh, I know you've done a lot. It was big stuff when you contributed a hundred thousand to the hospital in Axion; but you couldn't do it without getting your name on a bronze tablet in the main hall. You drop in at Jim Abbot's and inquire all about the boy. If they ask you to stay for noon dinner—corned beef and cabbage—you stay! I know you can't eat boiled cabbage at home, because it isn't good for you; but you'll be able to eat it at Abbot's and it won't hurt you a bit. I'll guarantee that on my honor as a medic."

Much of what this old-fashioned romantic novel told people during the Depression and in all the years since has now been scientifically documented. The results of our survey show that helping in the form of personal contact does bring good fortune to the helper, in the form of better physical, emotional, and spiritual well-being. To reiterate, only 5 percent of the survey respondents who had a one-to-one personal relationship with those they helped did not identify a specific feel-good sensation, the beginning of the beneficial effect of helping on the body. (In contrast, 14 percent of volunteers with little or no personal contact said they had not experienced a good physical sensation—a nearly three-times difference.) Respondents also observed the habit-forming effect of working with people to improve their lives—a truly magnificent obsession.

THE HEART OF HEALTHY HELPING

The forming of a genuine bond with another person—however short-lived—is the basis for the good that comes to the helper. For at least a few moments the one who is helping has a vivid sense within himself of the other person's life. It's a real and potent feeling, referred to as bonding or empathy. The positive, healing effect on the patient of the healer's simple caring has long been sensed. Now we are beginning to learn that the healer at the same time heals himself through the same interaction. The healing or helping process is a mutual one.

The focus needs to be the relationship itself, the moments of connection. How much we accomplish for someone is not as important as whether we *feel* a connection, a vicarious experience of the other person's problems, a recognition of him or her as a fellow being. These feelings which are transmitted to our bodies produce the good, relaxing sensations that seem to lie at the heart of healthy helping.

Some of the most important scientific work in this area has been done by Boston University psychologist David McClelland, whose work with the Mother Teresa film we discussed earlier. McClelland has devoted a long and distinguished career to research on human motivation, on the goal to which a specific behavior is actually directed. In the 1970s he, like many others, became intrigued by the burst of new research on the link between the mind and health. The work he did on immunity grew out of that research. He began to look at the ways people could improve the functioning of their own immune system. His work with various kinds of healers and the reasons for their success led to a persistent finding. "The thing that kept coming through to me was the way they care for their patients," McClelland said in an interview with psychologist Joan Borysenko, then with Harvard Medical School, in the journal *Advances*. "Some kind of tender loving care seems to be a crucial ingredient in healing. So the idea was that this kind of care had a positive effect on the immune system."

This research led to the showing of the Mother Teresa film to students. "We decided to work with movies as healers, to see if a film could transmit the feeling of caring and loving and then see if that experience had positive effects on the immune system. And it did." McClelland verified this by his measurements of the amount of immunoglobulin A (part of the body's defense against cold viruses) in saliva, which did indeed increase in those watching the film.

After so many years of work on human motivation, McClelland's first idea about this was to expect that the people who had the strongest drive to affiliate with others would be the ones most affected by the movie and who would have the greatest immune-system response. This did not turn out to be the case. "High aroused affiliation motivation wasn't the key to immune improvement," he said, "and I spent one whole summer trying to prove it was true. But the data were very stubborn, they just clearly indicated it was not." To figure out what the key actually was, a grad student was given the job of examining the responses of students who saw the film. His analysis found that those with the beneficial immune-system response were not those who were motivated simply to connect with others but those who want to do something positive for, with, or involving another person *without regard for the outcome.* "The curious part of it is that the person is not invested in the outcome of the thing—the person is not fixated on the goal of the activity. There are no statements about anxiety, tension, and so forth, if it fails."

This is very much the type of behavior that Mother Teresa herself exhibits. When she was asked in this film why she expends so much energy and effort on the well-being of dying babies who cannot be saved, she says that whether they live or die is irrelevant to the act of love.

Another interesting aspect of this study is that the students who watched the film did not need to like Mother Teresa or admire her work to get a positive immune-system response. Asked after the showing how they reacted to her work, the students divided into two groups. About half thought the woman and her work were wonderful; the other half didn't like or trust her religiosity and didn't think her efforts were making any difference. "We found that salivary IgA increased even in people who disliked Mother Teresa. To me," McClelland said in the Borysenko interview, "the results mean that she was contacting these consciously disapproving people in a part of their brains that they were unaware of and that was still responding to the strength of her tender loving care."[1] McClelland's work argues for the healing power of affiliation with another person, regardless of who the person is and regardless of the outcome of the effort. We seem to respond to the example of this kind of caring even when only seeing it in a movie, even when our conscious minds tell us not to.

Further research by others, in the wake of McClelland's measurements of immunoglobulin A, has shown that those generally high in feelings of affiliative trust (the quality of caring and connection without regard to achieving a particular outcome) have higher helper-to-suppressor T-cell counts, another immune parameter that reflects resistance to disease. They also reported a lower frequency of illness, particularly if they were not subjected to many major life changes.[2]

In a recent visit McClelland discussed with me his view that a helper must want to serve simply to experience the affiliative connection. "Otherwise," he said, "you really have a power motive, increasing your power over someone. Then you are not connecting to others, but in a sense isolating yourself, which has negative health effects."

He talked about his visit with Mother Teresa in India and the freshness of her spirit. In spite of the fact that she was in her eighties and working with problems that seemed to grow rather than diminish, she was vigorous. She told McClelland that this was because "I speak to the heart and not to the mind." He contrasted her attitude with that of a close friend who had spent much of her life working with problems of the homeless and indigent. "She at first only wanted to help, but in the end she destroyed herself. She remained fixed on the outcome. It had to change—and of course, it usually didn't. She really wanted power for herself. She stayed self-involved and destroyed her physical and emotional health." People operating in this manner, he said, really do not see themselves as helping, but rather stopping the hurt caused by others. This increases anger rather than dissipating tension.

So much of the helping that needs to be done is assisting people whose basic plight can't really be changed. Sometimes the volunteer is helping to make someone's last months more comfortable; but no matter what help is given, that person is going to die. Sometimes the helper is taking meals to people who are never going to be in good health again or who will probably never break out of poverty. Yet the feeling of human warmth between helper and helped can transcend the facts, which don't change.

FORMING THE BONDS THAT HEAL

I think back to the time when I was working in East Harlem, trying to organize the people who lived in those decaying abandoned tenement buildings to get the heating and hot water systems into operation. I wasn't too sure that what we were trying to do would ever happen. Drug addicts would break into the buildings and steal our building supplies. The building super was shot in the leg. So much happened that it would have been easy to give up hope.

But I had an ally in that project, almost from the start. For the effort to work it was necessary for the tenants of the buildings to pull together into a community. They had to trust each other enough to pool some money to buy the building materials. Under the circumstances of their extreme poverty and the terrible violence of the neighborhood, a task like that could be impossible.

The man who became the resident leader within that community was "Jorge." He was not the one I first had my eye on for this role, because he was working two jobs. It seemed clear to me that he had no free time. Married, with three children, he was working days in a hospital laundry and nights for a janitorial service that cleaned banks and office buildings. He was a short, roly-poly-looking guy, who showed on his face the effect of his chronic overwork. He perpetually had black circles under his eyes. But it was Jorge who volunteered for the job of working with me to organize the tenants. It was Jorge who became, for a while, a brother to me.

I was at his apartment several days a week—either very early in the morning or very late at night, so that we could fit in our conversations around his jobs. Day after day I saw what it was like for his family to live in this building. The children were continuously sick with colds. Often the only heat in the apartment was from the oven, which was kept running with its door open. Broken windows were stuffed with rags.

In spite of the two jobs he worked and the circumstances in which he lived, Jorge never once missed a meeting with me. And he never let me sit down in his house without offering me a cup of coffee or a sandwich. These were very poor people, but their hospitality was unfailing.

My main fear was that the great difficulties of the undertaking would cause Jorge to give up. I was often very discouraged about the project myself.

As it worked out, he took on the role of encouraging me. He would say to me over and over, "We're going to make it, Allan. We're going to make it." He would always call me at home to give me any good news he could report. It might be late at night, and I would be watching the snow start to fall outside my own windows and begin thinking, "The patch we put on the boiler isn't going to hold." In no time the phone would ring and it would be Jorge calling to say, "Allan, it's working. We still have heat." As a relative or close friend can sometimes do, he began to anticipate my fears.

Sometimes he would even stop by the rough storefront office in East Harlem where I was headquartered. He would want to contribute cash to keeping the place going. He'd say, "Can't I give you a few dollars to help you?"

Almost twenty years have passed, and Jorge has long since moved away, yet I still think of him.

On the day of the winter holiday celebration party, he

was part of the group who gave me that immense over-night suitcase for carrying my papers to the office. I was touched by the gift and overwhelmed by the warmth of my ties to Jorge and to the others in the community. He and I, all of us together, actually did succeed in getting hot water and heat into that building. And I really wanted to make it happen. I can't claim that I was indifferent to the tangible results. After all that we'd been through, I wanted those buildings to be clean and warm. But that goal was not what kept me going. It was Jorge and the others who kept me going. I needed them. It was a truly mutual relationship. If it weren't for those people, for Jorge in particular, I would have become one more burned-out young lawyer.

Over the years since, in my many helping efforts, I have been involved in more than one helping relationship that, for the time it lasted, felt almost like "family." I also now have a family—my wife and I have two teenage children of our own—so I have thought a lot about the differences between helping family and forming the kind of friend-ship that Jorge and I had.

People who know of my interest in volunteer work sometimes ask me, "With all the time you spend helping, do you spend any time with your family?"—and the answer is definitely yes. In fact my wife's answer to that question is that as a father "Allan's overinvolved." The high that I get from being close with my son and daughter is far more intense than any emotion I have ever experi-enced with volunteer work. At times—in ordinary activi-ties such as throwing a ball with my son or helping my daughter with homework—I have felt overwhelmingly happy about the fact that the person before me is my child.

Yet the experiences of friendship I've enjoyed because of helping others offer me something different that I also need. Though these helping relationships are not as intense, not as profound, not as close to my heart, they also give me a lasting sense of calm—that second phase of helper's high—that nothing else produces in quite the same way. My family involvement does not produce this relaxation. It takes the bond with a stranger to produce that lingering sense of well-being and heightened self-esteem. I don't know why that is so. But it has been my experience as well as the experience of many other volunteers. Perhaps the heightened self-esteem is based on the fact that while one is expected to love and help one's own family, to help a stranger is "extra." It is a pure gift. In making that gift I, like so many others, feel especially good about who I am, which is one of the best measures of emotional health.

Recently I have taken a new job. Through my research it became clear to me that people are needed to promote this knowledge about helping and to help others get started. So, when the Institute for the Advancement of Health was scheduled to move its office from New York to San Francisco, I did not go. Instead I became director of Big Brothers/Big Sisters of New York, the founding chapter of this nearly five-hundred-chapter organization. I have been spending time with young men and women primarily in their twenties and early thirties who have volunteered to be Big Brothers and Big Sisters. This nearly ninety-year-old organization matches volunteers to young children from single-parent families who are disadvantaged, often feel unconnected to society, are floundering in school, are at risk to abuse drugs, and often get into trouble.

The volunteers not only see these youngsters at least every other week for four hours, they also call regularly by phone to check on how they're getting along, and the child will sometimes visit the volunteer's home. The tie that forms between volunteer and child becomes very clear when the Big Brothers and Big Sisters meet. They proudly display photographs of their "Littles," and talk with excitement about attending their child's school's PTA meeting or rushing to a ghetto home because they hadn't received a scheduled phone call and were worried about whether the child was ill or in trouble. It's as if they are speaking of their own family members, so great is the bonding, the empathy.

If you ask one of these "Bigs" how the relationship is changing the child, you'll always get a hedging answer. They're not sure, there are so many other forces at work—the parent, the school, the neighborhood. Yet they are clear about one thing that is happening: They themselves feel wonderful. Studies of Big Brothers and Big Sisters show that the most immediate benefit in these relationships is the increase in the volunteers' own sense of self-worth. This feeling is one that grows not out of measurable accomplishment but out of the bonding itself.

That the heart of helping lies in the relationship is stated clearly in the Bible. "If I speak in the tongues of men and of angels, but have not love, I am only a resounding gong or a clanging cymbal. . . . If I give all I possess to the poor and surrender my body to the flames, but have not love, I gain nothing" (I Corinthians 13:1, 3).

In the King James version, instead of the word *love*, the word *charity* is used. The love referred to here and in all the writing and talking about helping and giving is certainly not the consuming emotion that is often meant by the word *love*. Among the definitions of that old-fashioned King James word are: "love for one's fellow men," "goodwill toward others"; and "leniency in judging others or their actions." It is this charity, this kind of love, that must be at the base of a good helping relationship, the kind from which both people ultimately benefit.

"Relationship is a process (not a 'state') of building a supporting, reliable bridge between one and another," writes Helen Harris Perlman in *Relationship: The Heart of*

Helping People. She offers a summary of some of the qualities, behaviors, and styles of interaction that are conducive
to the creation of a helping relationship. The following
discussion of various aspects of this process is not intended
to make you self-conscious about what is essentially a
natural and spontaneous act—the process of forging a
genuine connection with another person. But it may
serve as a set of reminders and guidelines that are useful if
you find that you're having difficulties with these contacts
or that these relationships are not satisfying to you. The
effectiveness of the help you give, as well as the health
benefits you receive, is strongly determined by the quality
of this one-to-one relationship between two people.

The helper must begin by recognizing the other person
as an individual, not merely seeing him as a problem. I
remember once hearing a nurse who worked in a clinic
refer to the patients who came through in a day as ABs
and OBs—women who were giving birth (OB) and
women who were having abortions (AB). Obviously
some such shorthand is necessary to communicate with
others on the staff. But to the degree to which the helper
thinks of the other person by any such label—whether it
is alcoholic, multiple-sclerosis patient, incest survivor,
burn victim, psychiatric patient, or any other—to that
degree the helper will not see him or her as a person.
"The 'bureaucrat with a heart' is simply one who, by
responding to the feelings of a person, is affirming that
person's worth and individuality," Perlman wrote.[3] This
is true for volunteer helpers as well as those who work for
helping agencies.

One way of staying in touch with the person rather
than the problem is through attentiveness, to both the
facts of the situation and the feelings that the person brings
to it, to what he says and to how he presents himself in
the moment at hand. A woman who has multiple sclerosis
helps other people with the same disease. "It is after a

one-on-one experience that I have a physical sensation of 'feeling good,' " she wrote me. "For instance a week ago I went to the VA hospital to visit an MSer. For forty-five minutes I forgot about everything else and directed my attention on this man. He shared the pictures of his family, the joys of working in the woodshop, and the pains of loneliness with me. I in turn shared a little of myself with him. After leaving his room and while walking back to my car, I felt flushed and warm. I've often wondered why I should be so elated afterward, as my efforts have not changed anything. He's still in the hospital. He's still lonely. I can only hope that he feels as good as I do after my visit. With each repeated visit, he responds favorably, so something good must be happening."

Another helper described her whole purpose in one helping effort as devoting time to paying attention. "I have sat with a few kind souls who were near death. I felt blessed to be able to share their last moments, thoughts, and insights into what really counts when life is done. Most of the time I just held their hand and talked (or more rightly—listened)."

This attentiveness to the other will naturally lead the helper to want to offer some response. The most effective way a helper can respond is by showing that she knows something of what the other person is going through, that she can feel what the problem is doing to the other person's life. This need not be a verbal reaction; it might be only a meeting of eyes and a nod.

On the other hand, a pretense of feeling is usually equally obvious to the person you intend to help. And a too-quick response of "I understand" is likely to be taken as a sign that the helper is going through the motions rather than actually paying attention.[4]

The basis of a good helping relationship can lie in the helper's personal warmth. The spontaneous expression of good feeling toward the other—tempered though it may be for appropriateness—is still the simplest, surest route to a relationship that is helpful to both people. This does not necessarily connote total admiration of the other person, nor need it involve any tremendous outpouring of excess emotion. Simple genuine interest will usually work very well. A sixty-nine-year-old woman who works with older people in a nursing home describes it as "a kind of love."

With a friend, she wrote, "I go once a week to a nursing home . . . and ask those who live there to come sing with us. We let them choose the songs. They are all strangers to me and my friend. . . . It makes you feel good when you get them smiling at you and laughing at mistakes all of us make once in a while.

"There is a kind of love that goes out to them, from me. Makes me feel good to know for thirty to forty-five minutes they are thinking of something besides their aches and pains."

Sometimes people who genuinely want to help others have doubts about their personal warmth or about their ability to project what they do feel. Fortunately shy people can still make good helpers. And often becoming involved with helping another person can make the helper forget his self-consciousness. In the meantime Perlman suggests some attitudes and attributes that can be more easily cultivated than something as intangible as "warmth." One of these is developing a willingness to accept the other person as he is. This may be difficult for some helpers when the person is someone who, like the heroin addict and prostitute, has behaved in a destructive or otherwise unacceptable way. In such a situation acceptance does not require suspending all judgment of the person's actions or automatically lowering expectations for what he could accomplish in the future. The attitude that works best is acceptance of the person and of whatever he says his intentions are, even though his past behavior may make those intentions seem suspect to you. The message is "I accept you but not your acts."

The needy person who has committed no crime will also welcome your acceptance of him—as a fellow human being rather than as a victim. Whether the person is suffering from a disease, from lifelong poverty, or simply from unfair treatment that day at work, he or she is likely to appreciate being treated with respect and dignity.

The same holds true for all kinds of people who need help in reaching their full potential. We are better able to become something more in the future if who we are now is greeted with genuine respect and acceptance.[5]

A teacher at a community college demonstrates the effectiveness of this attitude of belief in another person's possibilities. "I remember a particular incident. I had a woman (about forty years old) who had worked at a factory in a rural community for many years. The factory relocated; she lost her job. She was able to participate in a funded program where she could go to the community college and learn some new skills. She totally lacked self-confidence, but she worked hard. I assigned a project, which they all dreaded. They had to visit an office, study the filing system, interview the people in charge of the filing system, prepare a written report and evaluation of their findings, and then present the report to the class. I had assigned enough of these projects to know the growth that can take place by completing all of the tasks involved. This particular lady, very quiet and soft-spoken, got up in front of the class and presented her report. For her project she had visited a legal office in a small city within driving distance of her rural home. She had studied their disorganized filing system and then interviewed one of the attorneys. He was so impressed with her knowledge of the filing process and with her as a person that he offered her a job on the spot. She was elated. She said, 'Imagine, me! All I thought I could ever do was operate a sewing machine! Now I'm a legal secretary, and I'm going to be the best one he's ever had, because he believes in me.'

"I drove home that night with goose bumps running up and down my limbs. I cried for joy for her, joy for me. It made me feel so good knowing that I had been instrumental in her getting this job. To me this is what teaching is all about. It is a gratifying profession, working with these adults who are trying to better themselves."

Whether or not the helper is naturally demonstrative and warm, he can train himself to feel empathy for the other person, simply by being close to and giving help to another. The more we *experience* another person's situation, the more likely we are to have this understanding become a feeling inside us. One definition of *empathy* is "mental entrance into the feeling or spirit of another person or thing."

To empathize requires both some careful observation and a leap of the imagination. The effect is not to emphasize your own feeling over the person's plight. That's sympathy. Empathy is discovering and experiencing inside yourself how these problems feel to the other person.[6] Once we feel empathy, we then feel personally uncomfortable if we aren't able to find time to aid this person. In his book *Empathy: Its Nature and Uses*, Robert Katz describes the cast of mind involved as very similar to that of the artist. In both art and empathy, the person must relax his usual ways of thinking, become emotionally involved in the process, and project himself into the situation of otherness. "Like the creative artist who feels himself into his material, the effective empathizer is capable of blending himself with his subject."[7]

A woman in Nevada who, like another volunteer mentioned earlier, both has multiple sclerosis and helps those with the disease, reports how the ability to empathize helps her as well as the other person. "During the experiences, I have the most wonderful feelings! First, no matter how terrible I may feel or how much pain I am in, it all seems to leave like magic almost immediately when that call for help comes. My mind sort of tunes out from my self and *I become that other person* and actually experience what he/she is feeling. From there on, relating is easy. I am sure this sounds very weird to you. This feeling of peace, uplifting, and (to some extent) lessening of pain or illness remains with me for most of the rest of the day. Should I get another call for help later in the day, I am good into the night."

Finally the helper must be genuine in any expression of sympathy and caring. Perlman sees this as more than an absence of artifice, but as a healthy sign of the helper's trust in herself, her sense that her own real feelings will be a useful guide in helping the other person.[8] This should not be interpreted to mean that the helper should blurt out whatever feelings she has. It means that the helper knows she can trust her own responses as a useful part of the helping process. Because of this trust, pretense is not necessary.

Yet the warmth, acceptance, and empathy of a good helping relationship do not mean going to extraordinary lengths for the person, sacrificing your own needs, or losing any objective sense of the other person. Caring for the person should not lead a helper to burnout or to bad judgment in the helping relationship. It means doing what you can comfortably do to help a person whom you wish well. Keeping a balance is important.

Harold Lief and Renee Fox, researchers into the psychological issues involved in the practice of medicine, came up with the phrase "detached concern" to describe the balance a physician needs to keep between rational, objective thinking, on one hand, and understanding and concern, on the other. In *Burnout*, Ayala Pines, research associate in the psychology department at the University of California, Berkeley, and her coauthors quote a psychologist on the dangers of leaning too far in the direction of total emotional oneness with the patient: " 'In order to help, you have to be able to see more and understand more than the person who seeks your help.' "⁹ The ideal situation is a shifting back and forth on the part of the helper, so that, like the doctor, he or she can alternate between the rational thinking that is needed and the empathy and solace that are equally important.

A helping act need not take a long time and it need not accomplish measurable goals to have a tremendous impact on both people. An experienced helper describes her contacts with a man who was very ill. "Knowing that he had no family to visit him, I went for fifteen minutes every other day. He was on machines and could not respond to me. I was so overwhelmed with emotion that I could not say a whole lot. So I would just gently stroke his arm. He eventually died. Yet I still experienced the sensation of 'feeling good.' It's quite strange to feel sad and good at the same time. But that 'good feeling' helps motivate me to continue to reach out to others, even though I experience sadness along the way."

A CULTURAL COMPARISON

Writing in *The Sciences*, the journal of the New York Academy of Sciences, Leonard Sagan, a California physician and epidemiologist, has noted that the United States spends far more per capita on health care but has much lower life expectancies than Greece, Spain, and Italy. Why? Our sanitation, nutrition, and medical services are certainly not inferior. Sagan believes this difference exists because of the decreasing level of natural family support in America. Many of us badly need an activity that boosts our sense of social support and our connections with other people.[10]

"Something is wrong, something is missing," Nobel Prize author Saul Bellow has said about life in America today. "There is ice in the heart—the ice of self-interest—which has to be thawed out by anyone who really wants anything human from himself or from others."[11]

Albert Einstein was also terribly concerned about a society in which people increasingly disregard each other. "Our talk," he said, "must be to free ourselves from this prison." Each time we make an effort to help another person, with the sense of empathy and kindred feeling that that involves, we begin to free ourselves from the prison.

Charles Darwin was among those who concluded that human beings are biologically inclined to help each other. His theory of evolution recognizes that helping acts are likely to be performed when they involve reciprocity, when they benefit the helper as well as the helped.[12] The new knowledge about healthy helping demonstrates that virtually all altruism is reciprocal altruism. As we help, we receive help. The two are inseparably intertwined.

The more we help, the more we care for others and want to continue to help—the better we feel ourselves. A seventy-year-old in Colorado Springs, Colorado, who, after retiring from a law firm, became a volunteer bereavement counselor, is one of the many examples of how the helping process works. "What this has done for me is unbelievable to everyone except those who are involved with Hospice. The wonder of being able to help someone through the grieving process by giving loving support has enhanced my life beyond anything I could have hoped for. I had always had good health, but I can truthfully say I have never felt better in my life—mentally, physically, and spiritually." The feeling of empathy, and the relief of one's own vicarious distress through helping, makes coming to the aid of another a self-perpetuating behavior. That is why the novelist Lloyd C. Douglas could correctly call it a magnificent obsession.

9

The Healing of Our Human Community

LYNCHBURG is a small city of about seventy thousand in the foothills of central Virginia. There are four colleges here, the home church of the well-known conservative preacher Jerry Falwell, and historic sites where Thomas Jefferson once spent time. It's a pretty town, with lots of trees and some beautiful homes. There are also poorer sections of town, blocks around the downtown district that are run-down. According to Dennis Roberts, dean of student affairs at Lynchburg College, it's "a good old conservative Southern town."

Sitting on one hilltop in this town is the campus of Lynchburg College, a private school with about 2,500 students. The trees are so thick around the campus at the turnoff from the main road that at first it seems you might be turning onto the drive of a private nature preserve.

But in more fundamental ways than geography this school is no enclave set apart from the rest of the town. The conventional image of "the private college on its hillside looking down on the community" doesn't work here, said President George Rainsford, sitting in his office on a recent afternoon. This is a school that has made a policy and a practice of sending its students into the community to do public service—for the good of both the community and the students.

As a panel member of the Governor's Commission on the University for the Twenty-first Century, Rainsford has made public service one of the five factors that, at his own campus, are guiding decisions on how to get students ready for the coming decades. The college's platform for the future is the preparation of students for a world that (a) is racially diverse; (b) involves international partnerships; (c) is highly technological; and (d) requires cooperation and collaboration to reach solutions to problems. None of these is more important than the fifth premise: that public service is in the best interest of the individual and of the community.

For Lynchburg students the discovery, through helping, that they have something of worth to give to others is a central part of their education. The students at this school, Rainsford said, are typically from quite affluent suburban families, and perhaps because of their academic records, often arrive with self-image problems. The average SAT score is around 950, which prevents many of them from competing for the most prestigious universities.

The emphasis of the college is not on past accomplishments the student can bring to the campus, but on how he or she can improve and develop to fullest capability in the time spent here. Institutions attracting students with extraordinary academic records can simply "take in bright freshmen and graduate bright seniors," Rainsford said. The role of Lynchburg is to "take mainstream young Americans and send them out to compete with the best and the brightest and see them do that successfully."

"Our students discover themselves," said Dean Roberts, "they discover they have a right to be more self-confident."

And they discover their own sense of connection with other people. They feel empathy with people who might have seemed alien to them before. Students who might previously have been seen by other students as "party animals" act with real compassion; students who had never thought of themselves as helpers become deeply involved.

Wendy Bishop is one of the many students who spend an occasional weekend volunteering as a counselor at Virginia Camp Jaycee in Blue Ridge, about an hour's drive from the school. Students serve as counselors here during weekend camp sessions for people who are retarded. Wendy, a senior from Essex Fells, New Jersey, became a volunteer when she arrived at the campus and heard a speaker at freshman orientation.

She had known that she wanted to work with children, so she started volunteering in the local public schools, helping two or three times a week in classes for the handicapped. She has worked with young students in wheelchairs, as well as mentally disabled children seven to nine years old. She helps them with activities, watches them on the playground, takes them to the bathroom, helps them wash their hands. "I was like a second set of hands," she said of her role in the schools.

Her first experience at Camp Jaycee was in the fall of her freshman year. "Girls on my hall older than me said, 'Oh, there's this great volunteer weekend.' "

It's a forty-eight-hour commitment, from Friday to Sunday, that makes an indelible impression on many of the students who participate. "It's rough," Wendy said, "but it's the best experience. You really feel like you made a difference."

"One year I had a camper, she was a woman from one of the institutions, she was severely handicapped, had a walker, couldn't really talk, couldn't express herself at all." The student counselors began to complain to each other that perhaps she was too handicapped to be at the camp. It was unpleasant to watch her eat, and she needed a lot of assistance handling basic bodily functions. This could easily be a large order for even the most seasoned volunteer. Wendy found herself, along with some of the other counselors, feeling put off by the woman's condition.

Then that night Wendy was the one to help this camper take a shower. With great difficulty the woman crawled onto the floor of the shower and crouched there, waiting, the water spraying down on her. Wendy looked at her, huddled under the spray. "She was so helpless." Wendy started to cry. "I was able to put myself in her position when I saw her on the floor." Still crying, she got into the shower with the woman and helped her as best she could.

That moment changed her feelings about the woman. "I can't believe I had such an attitude about her," Wendy said. Then her change of attitude seemed to spread to the other student counselors. Earlier than scheduled they gave this camper a "warm fuzzy," a yarn souvenir of the weekend. They watched her as she held the little yarn ball, rubbing it against her face and saying again and again, "Mine, mine."

Wendy looks back in wonder at this moment. At the beginning "I wasn't going to give this woman a chance. It was her opportunity for the best weekend, and we had almost wrecked it. We still talk about that."

Wendy has now narrowed her career interest to teaching handicapped children. She plans to continue in volunteer work after graduation. When she's a teacher, she'd like to move into a different area of community service in her volunteer efforts, perhaps something like "holding the crack babies."

When she started working on projects like the camp experience, she didn't feel at all sure of her ability to handle the various situations that might come up. "I was nervous, afraid I was going to do something wrong, or not do something right." But by dinnertime on the first night, she said, you're so busy and "wrapped up" in what you're doing that all of that nervousness goes away. "Everyone helps each other."

She has seen a lot of different kinds of students volunteering at the camp, education majors, business majors, athletes. "You see them at a party or you see them at a class. Suddenly you see them in a different way." The wide participation in volunteering has shown that community service "doesn't have to be left to one certain type of college student."

Because of the volunteer work through Lynchburg, "I think we're more aware. I mean, I knew people were homeless in New York City, but I didn't think that in a city like Lynchburg there were people close to me who didn't have homes."

Wendy has continued the service work that she began in the fall of her freshman year. "It was important to me even last year—you know, junior year is kind of rough. No matter how busy I was, I felt good about doing it. It seemed if I could help, I should do it. I wanted to do it. I got a lot out of it."

On another high hill in this city, a few winding miles from the college, is another campus, established as an orphanage in 1903. These big, airy brick "cottages" now house children ages five through seventeen whose parents are, at least temporarily, unable to take care of them. The Presbyterian Children's Home is a place where some Lynchburg College students volunteer. Mark Hawkins of Belmont, Massachusetts, is one of those students.

The initial spur for Mark's volunteer work was quite involuntary: "I got into trouble," he said. He played "college pranks." It resulted in a requirement to do community service, about 120 hours' worth. By now he's lost count of those hours, which he has long since completed. But he hasn't stopped volunteering. "Last year I didn't have to do anything and I still continued," he said.

"It's not really that much, two nights a week for two or three hours." And then on Sundays sometimes "I go over and toss a football or basketball with them. I have fun when I go over. I get some satisfaction." Some of the time there he spends tutoring, some simply talking. "Once for two weeks the kids all had the flu in the house I worked in, so I was fluffing up their pillows and feeding them chicken soup. I liked the kids a lot, I grew attached to some of them." But he's glad to see them get to go back home. The experience has been so good for him that he has suggested it to others. "I got a few other people to go over to the Presbyterian Home with me," he said, "and they seemed to enjoy themselves."

He thinks the volunteer work has an effect both on the school and on its place in the community. "The college has a bad reputation right around the school for being loud, causing problems." But the helping efforts in the community are a way of balancing that. "I love to go to parties and have a good time, but the school is not just that."

"You see people out on Friday night partying," said recent graduate Jennifer Wright. "At eight the next morning they're working at Habitat or the Wood Ministry." Lynchburg had one of the first Habitat for Humanity houses built by a college chapter in the country. Students raised half the cost of the house and supplied manpower to build it, creating a home that a low-income family could buy at an affordable price. The Wood Ministry is located in a big open yard in one of the town's poorer neighborhoods. Students who volunteer to work here cut and stack wood or help to deliver it to people who are in need.

Rosemary Urban, coordinator of the campus organization SERVE (Students Engaged in Responsible Volunteer Experiences), has the job of helping students to get involved. Except in disciplinary cases, students at Lynchburg College are not required to volunteer. But they are encouraged to take part. When interviewed for this book, Urban had just come to Lynchburg from a private school in the Northeast that gave "lip service," she said, rather than support to its community service program. She is deeply convinced of the value of teaching students about helping others. After twelve years' experience working with youth in community service, she says, "I *know* it enhances their self-esteem."

Introducing the students to community service in the first week is important, Urban explained, "because it says 'this is part of our college life.' It isn't something they're tacking on, it's built in."

It's important in recruiting beginners to help them find an activity that will suit their temperament well. For example, if the student is very "physical," constantly active, then a home for the elderly may not be the best choice. Instead Urban might recommend the Wood Ministry or helping to hoist pots in a soup kitchen or working in a recreation program, an activity "he could use his energy for." She doesn't want to put a student in a situation that will be another obstacle for him.

In attracting students, she said, "the key word is *need*," that is, giving them an opportunity to be needed. The typical experience of a teenager is "nobody needs your opinion and nobody asks your help." When they begin volunteering, "all of a sudden they feel needed, and they have something to offer."

Lynchburg College was founded in 1903 in an old resort hotel that was a health spa dedicated to restoring the wellness and wholeness of its patrons. The college itself, according to Dean Roberts, has a similar mission today, in addition to academic education. "Wholeness, wellness, purposefulness, service"—those are the goals.

THE PROBLEM AND THE SOLUTION

The "wellness" that is achieved through helping others is the solution to the growing, unprecedented level of fear and tension that now prevails among residents of most American cities—and is spreading from our cities to all areas of the country. This increasing violence among us may well be the most severe test ever of our strength and even of our ability to hold together as a nation.

At whatever age we begin, the practice of helping others teaches us about how good we can feel. And with each bond that is formed, the likelihood of our willingness to harm and disregard each other decreases slightly. As one person and then another takes up this way of life and health, the effect on the larger community is incalculable.

Today's violence is not limited to war zones in distant countries or incidents in poverty-stricken neighborhoods. Everywhere we look, the rate at which we are hurting each other is growing. Those who blame crack as the source for the epidemic of street brutality are blaming the symptom, not the underlying pathology: It is the fraying of our bonds to each other—from men in expensive suits arguing over parking spaces to bands of youths brutally assaulting innocent people.

And it is those bonds that helping can help to repair.

The job is not an easy one. In this country, with all of its many advantages, the level of fear, tension, and violence is disastrous—worse than in all of the other leading industrialized nations. This country, per capita, has more people in prison than any society in the world.

Not long ago I attended a meeting in Munich, Germany. I walked around that old city, which had experienced terrible physical destruction and social upheaval during World War II, and I was surprised to find how safe I felt in its night air.

As I strolled along the Isar River, an older Canadian friend who was with me told me that he had been one of the World War II pilots who had used this very river as a landmark for bombing the city. So the memories of the war were vivid that night as we walked past tall glass boxes that held large life preservers to be thrown to swimmers in trouble. The area was dark, with few streetlights. The glass boxes had no locks. Yet there was no sign of vandalism or theft. How long would such equipment last today in an American city? It would be a matter of hours before the glass was shattered and the life preserver was stolen. And not for any purpose or profit, just for the sheer pleasure of destruction and vandalism.

Later during that same trip I went to a beer hall with several young German academics who had attended similar conferences in American cities. In one unforgettable conversation they began talking about what it was that struck them most powerfully on first coming to America. I tried to guess what that might be: bigger buildings? faster pace of life? dirtier streets? the greater mix of people? All of my guesses were wrong. They had expected and been prepared for all those things.

The real surprise on the first visit was the tension they could see and feel between people on the streets, in stores, everywhere. I heard this from men whose parents had created perhaps the greatest fear the world has known.

Researchers have done tests in which a stranger comes to someone's door asking to use the telephone, or someone purposely dials a wrong phone number and pleads for assistance. Or someone leaves too much money on the counter for a restaurant bill, or drops a stamped, addressed postcard on a street to see whether anyone will pick it up and mail it. The citizens of many other nations do far better on these tests than Americans do.

Australia has a far less sophisticated, organized volunteer structure. Yet, in contrast to Americans, Australians are more likely to give directions late at night or to provide change to a stranger to use a phone.[1] Our urban congestion is often cited as a reason for our crime rates. But Hong Kong, far more densely populated than our cities, has far less crime.

How can America record the world's highest rate of volunteering and also the greatest rate among industrialized nations of violence between citizens? These two opposing forces share similar roots: The frontier tradition that seeded helping societies also had a culture of violence. The immigration waves that furthered the formation of volunteer helping groups also brought forth the developed world's most heterogeneous population and the problem of getting citizens to understand and care for people different from them. So today we witness a national conflict between the tradition of helping and the rising level of daily violence. It is a conflict whose winner is waiting to be decided.

The gap between the young urban poor, who are the focus of a disproportionate amount of the fear and tension, and the rest of society has widened. While we have made significant progress in racial integration, the division between the haves and the have-nots still closely follows racial lines. And the fear of violence is a wedge driving us even farther apart. We are losing our basic sense of connection with each other, and this is happening across the country at an alarming pace.

My family lives in an apartment building in New York City that has perhaps 40 percent minority occupancy. The black residents are middle-class teachers, lawyers, judges, businessmen. My sixteen-year-old son has more friends who are black than I ever had when I was growing up. But although he is far more racially aware and tolerant, and a member of his school's anti-bias coalition I fear he may lose the feeling I was taught to have to try to change the plight of the socially disadvantaged. And minority youth make up a major part of the urban poor. One day I saw him, as he was preparing to go to school just a few blocks away, shove his watch high under his shirtsleeve. I asked him why. He said that if the kids from the nearby projects saw he had a watch, they would come over and ask him for the time, and then as he paused to look at his watch, they would jump him. He said he hated those kids.

Young people have always had fights. But today the fight is more serious. Being "jumped" means being knifed, shot, killed. And today's middle-class youth—if the tension in our society does not change—may very well grow up with even less compassion for the poor than now exists.

"Yes, it was dangerous for children twenty-five years ago, but the level of menace has increased," said the Rev. Jay Gordon, rector of Saint Matthew's and Saint Timothy's Church in Manhattan. "The gangs in the fifties had whips and sticks, but now they have guns, even Uzis."[2]

Children who are raised to be compassionate have a tough time sustaining sympathy when they go out into the world and are routinely faced with physical danger. Today's middle-class children, said Ian Canino, a child psychiatrist in New York, "have nightmares. They get terribly anxious and they feel terribly impotent. They're exposed to things that adults have difficulty dealing with."[3]

America's fear and anger now go beyond the tension aroused by the poor youth of our cities. The violence has spread: into rural areas and small towns, into neighborhoods long considered to be safe. And it has led to a social withdrawal—in what may seem to be our own best interests—to keep ourselves safe by not getting involved. Consider one classic, and horrifying, example. International headlines broke in 1964 over the fatal stabbing of waitress Kitty Genovese in the moderate-income, working-class borough of Queens, New York. Neighbors heard her screams for help, yet no one even called the police. This famous case exhibits not just the violence but the disregard for each other that has grown greater rather than less in the last twenty-five years. Unless we can reverse this diminishing sense of other human beings, we have to expect a growing distrust of and a willingness to harm one another.

During my Peace Corps training for work in Latin America twenty years ago, I was told about the high rate of violence in those countries. University professors and government specialists lectured about the dangers. I learned that the sight of private guards in front of businesses, of high walls around homes, of citizens walking around armed, were all signs of a nation in disarray. The experts were talking about poor, undeveloped countries, and they stressed that economic growth would decrease this level of violence. We are one of the wealthiest nations in the world, yet we are now prey to our own violence. We cannot say that national wealth will be the answer to creating a sense of community. Moving out of the city is no answer either. Crime is increasing in the suburbs and smaller communities.

People will continue to argue that the problem is mainly in poor areas or that it's a problem of only parts of the nation, especially the New York area. Not true. We are all at risk. Though we think of the Northeast as the headquarters for crime, the 19 percent of northeastern homes that were victims in 1988 constituted the lowest incidence in the country, compared with 34 percent of all homes in the South, 25 percent in the Midwest, and

30 percent in the West. Furthermore, middle-income households were victimized at about the same rate as black homes, which are more often in poorer areas.

Movies show us how we see ourselves. Analyzing the great growth in films about police-turned-violent who defy legal as well as moral limits, Jeanine Basinger, a professor at Wesleyan University, says, "It's not the violence that's new, even though it surrounds us on an increasingly horrifying scale. It's the desperate sense that we can't escape it, even in the best of neighborhoods."[4]

This sense of danger and dissension is most often compared with the peacefulness of our main rival for world financial strength, Japan. That nation's population density far exceeds ours, yet its culture, so deeply rooted in family and extended community, makes violence between citizens a rarity.

Willard Gaylin, the physician who runs a New York–based think tank on health ethics, the Hastings Institute, suggests the underlying meaning of the lawlessness and violence that surround us: "Surely the kind of adolescent brutality that is evidenced in the newspapers every day, in which a street mugger hits a random woman over the head with a lead pipe as a convenient means of gaining the six dollars in her purse, implies more than just the need for six dollars. It suggests that the concept of identity has been destroyed, or never developed; that the person now feels so 'other' that he is no longer within the framework of identification necessary for introjection of a value system." To create in our youth a value system that rejects violence, we must act quickly, while we still can.

The basic test of a society is the strength of the bond between citizens, the extent to which we recognize ourselves in each other, help each other—or, at the most basic level, agree not to harm each other.

For all of our problems, we in the United States have a solid foundation for a shift in values. Helping each other is more intrinsic to our national frontier-born heritage than violence. If it had not been so, we would not have survived to build this nation, which is so ethnically, religiously, and racially diverse.

The United States already reports a high percentage of people involved in volunteer efforts compared with other nations: Forty-five percent of the 177 million adults over eighteen years old say they are doing some form of volunteering. Although the majority of the country reports no helping efforts, this figure far surpasses the amount of involvement reported by other nations.

So, why, if we are already helping each other, is the level of fear, tension, and violence among Americans so high? The fact is most people are not doing the kind of regular personal-contact helping that promotes both individual health and a sense of larger community. As we have said, that kind of helping is more likely to produce good feelings powerful enough to make people want to help more, both through involvement in organized programs and in the spontaneous performance of small daily acts of assistance to their fellow citizens. While there is no exact statistic to cite, different studies do suggest that most people who say they volunteer are involved in things such as stuffing envelopes for a political campaign or donating clothes or helping to make repairs at the local school or church building, activities that, though worthwhile, lack the needed personal contact. Nor are most people volunteering on a regular, weekly basis—the schedule that most encourages the strong feeling of empathy inside us to grow, pushing us to become ever more involved. However that, as our survey results showed, is what is needed—regular, close-contact helping of strangers. This is the kind of helping that will bring us together and widen our sense of community—while we help ourselves.

Pitirim Sorokin, founder of Harvard's center to study

altruism, has explained why it is the helping of strangers that is most beneficial to the creation of that sense of community. When we help family and friends, we are helping "our own." And these acts, as good and useful as they are, do not fundamentally alter our sense of separateness from each other, our sense of society being divided between "them" and "us." It is the reaching out to "them," to strangers, that brings us all closer. Sorokin called the goal of volunteer work creative altruism. These are the helping acts that make "us" and "them" become "we."

Warm connections between individuals diminish the distances between us; this is true whether the divisions between us are economic, racial, political, or geographic. Helping, in addition to any other good it does, creates the friendships that erode barriers.

How such a feat could ever be accomplished has long been studied. In the 1950s two of the best-known of our century's social critics, Aldous Huxley and Arthur Koestler, both explored the research then known about behaviors that could affect the level of tension and violence in society. Koestler argued that we are "holons," beings composed of opposing tendencies. For example we each have some desire to be part of a larger whole, and at the same time we fight to preserve our separate identities. Koestler saw helping behaviors as a natural way to unite these two forces. "Such admirably altruistic pursuits as caring for the sick or poor, serving on committees and joining protest marches, can serve as wonderful outlets for bossy self-assertions, even if unconscious." But he doubted that such helping acts could ever become widespread enough. In frustration he and Huxley separately concluded that violence would drop only in the unlikely event that masses of people would agree to take some kind of a relaxation chemical. "Medicine has found remedies for certain types of schizophrenic and manic-depressive psychoses; it is no longer utopian to believe that it will discover a combination of benevolent enzymes," Koestler wrote.[5]

Both men worried over such a drug's side effects, and of course the issue of whether people would ever be willing to take it. Yet they saw no other way of changing what they viewed as humanity's aggressive impulses. It now appears that the act of helping creates in the helper a brain chemistry that is the functional equivalent of Koestler's "benevolent enzymes."

More recently, Jonas Salk, developer of the polio vaccine and probably one of the world's best-known scientists, has observed our ability to come up with cures. Similarly he has said that as crises worsen, people manage to identify knowledge to help them choose "the most evolutionarily advantageous path."[6] The question becomes, Will people act on that knowledge?

Today we have the research that shows that cut off from others, we cannot achieve the most basic goal—for individuals as well as for society—of good health. Scientists now recognize that it is primarily the culture we have developed rather than inborn aggressive instincts that determines whether we help, ignore, or harm each other. Researchers from twelve nations met in Seville, Spain, in 1986 to discuss aggression. This meeting resulted in the Seville statement, which said, in part: "It is scientifically incorrect to say that humans have a 'violent brain.' While we do have the neural apparatus to act violently, there is nothing in our neurophysiology that compels us to do so. . . . Humanity can be freed from the bondage of biological pessimism. Violence is neither in our evolutionary legacy nor in our genes."[7]

A turn toward the helping of others on a large enough scale has the potential to create the kind of radical changes that have heretofore seemed impossible. Helping meets the two necessary conditions: First, it has the power to cut through the divisions between us that breed mistrust and violence. And now, with the new information about health, we have not only the mechanism for change but a powerful motivator to put it into action. That motivation is enlightened self-interest. Helping improves the health of the helper. Each helping act is an opportunity both to express our needs for self-assertion and to celebrate our ties to others.

THE CHALLENGE

Our awareness of the powerful benefits of helping can cause us at least to try to perform helping acts, which—if they produce the powerful good feelings in enough people—can grow and lead us to a new level of daily altruism. What makes this such a great challenge is our national culture, which is heterogeneous, fast-paced, and overly reliant on the pleasures of material possessions. Heterogeneity is a problem insofar as it diminishes our ability to identify readily with others. Recall the study that measured people's ability to empathize with others like themselves. Two groups of people were observed, both of them watching a person waving his arms and legs. Only one group was told that the person was receiving a painful shock; and only these showed physiological changes such as increase in heart rate. Some of these same observers were also told that they were in some way similar to the person apparently in pain. These were the people who experienced the greatest arousal.

We live in the most heterogeneous society in the world. Sixteen of our states have a million or more black residents; four states have at least a million Hispanics. We are no longer a Judaeo-Christian country; in fact in one state, Hawaii, the dominant religion is Buddhism. To be able to think of ourselves as a family, we have to stretch—

and expand our definitions of *family*. We have to be willing to look to our basic human kinship, without the benefit of a shared religious, ethnic, racial, or cultural background. Regular helping behavior is the only way we know of that can achieve this lowering of the barriers that separate us.

Yet the multiplicity of cultures and races that we think of as so endemic to our melting-pot society characterizes not just this country but gradually more and more of the rest of the world. Urban centers everywhere are becoming increasingly mixed, their heterogeneity spurred by modern transportation as well as by the massive economic, social, and political upheavals of this century. Because we are ever more intermingled, "helping one's own" is no longer enough. If this nation can establish among its diverse citizens a visible level of caring—rather than the too-visible violence, fear, and disregard for each other—it may be our most lasting contribution to history, far more than the assembly line, light bulb, or TV.

The new knowledge about helping's benefits appears at a time of crisis, as the economy slows down and creates fewer opportunities. It is at times like these throughout history that people have shown themselves most willing to pitch in and help. During the Depression, people with little to give gave what they could. All over the country people flocked to Community Chest organizations to offer food, clothing, and health care to people in greater need.

Certainly we must attend to our own needs. A nation of resentful, burned-out helpers is not in anyone's best interest. What is in fact in our best interest is to begin to follow the biblical injunction to love our neighbors as ourselves (which implies that we must indeed love ourselves as well). Through helping others we not only help others but we attend to our own health as well as that of the community where we live. It is a form of "selfishness" that serves us all well.

Oxford University zoologist Richard Dawkins, author of a highly praised work, *The Selfish Gene*, has argued that individual genes must be selfish to survive. For survival we need to think of ourselves, but we are not compelled to be dedicated only to our own interests in the narrowest sense. "Man is uniquely dominated by culture," Dawkins pointed out, "by influences learned and handed down." He coined a new word, *meme*, to show that a behavior made powerful if adopted by enough people can be passed from one generation to the next, like a gene.[8]

This is how altruism can spread today. A critical number of people practicing helping behaviors will turn the tide. One person will feel the strong positive effect of helping in his or her own life and then tell another person. And on and on.

Why has this not yet happened in large enough numbers? Perhaps it is because too many of us have kept the secret. So many helpers who wrote to me thought, as I had, that there was something peculiarly personal about getting a "selfish" kick, a physical high, a burst of health out of helping. Many of the letters I received included such disclaimers as "You won't believe this," or "I know this sounds weird but. . . ." But we can now say for sure that it's not a funny quirk of a few people, it's the way we're built—and we have the physiological evidence to prove it. The helping of others is at the heart of living in good health.

One could ask the same question about the timing of other cultural changes. Why did the health revolution only begin in the 1960s, when people had been praising the value of exercise since the days of ancient Greece? The answer: We needed the new research to explain that what we were sensing was real and could be replicated by others.

How many people—what percent of our population—will have to become helpers before our culture begins to sense a change, a move away from violence, the dissolving of its tensions? Probably not that large a percentage. Think of the medical information about smoking, diet, and exercise, which has so visibly affected our way of life. The changes did not come all at once. They occurred more gradually, because people who were strongly affected by the new information acted on it and encouraged others to enjoy the same benefits.

A receptive audience waits—the millions of Americans who now volunteer but have not tried the close-contact, personal acts that produce the most powerful response in the individual. The health concerned. The millions of people who have stated that they want to volunteer but have not found the right opportunity. As a national conversation about the importance of regular helping grows, it will be fed by the powerful American tradition of volunteering.

The spreading of the word will also be assisted by the hundreds of thousands of nonprofit agencies that need volunteers, especially as government sources of money tighten up in times of trillion-dollar budgets. Religious organizations searching for ways to bring back membership will recognize that they are natural volunteer recruiting centers. We also have the motivation and interest of health-conscious parents concerned about their children's well-being.

With so many different forces motivating us to seek this change, the odds are good that we can become a helping society. That means we as individuals need to keep discussing the meaning of this change for our personal health, in the same way we now receive continued knowledge, and thus conditioning, about the vital importance of dietary and exercise changes in our lives. William James, psychologist and philosopher, wrote in *The Varie-*

ties of Religious Experience about the enormous potential of such a change. His subject was the biblical instruction to "love your enemies," the sense of an emotional tie between people that transcends differences. Rarely, James noted, has the notion of loving your enemy ever been taken literally. "Can there in general be a level of emotion so unifying, so obliterative of differences between man and man, that even enmity may come to be an irrelevant circumstance and fail to inhibit the friendlier interests aroused? . . . There is no saying . . . what the effects might be: they might conceivably transform the world."[9]

THE SEEDS OF A SOCIETAL CHANGE

It is certainly true that early training helps a helper to get started: the volunteers surveyed who credited parental, social, or religious training and feelings with shaping their attitudes were likely to be more frequently involved and more willing to help strangers. But my survey has found that slightly larger numbers of helpers are motivated by their own feelings for the well-being of the community than by the teachings of religion or of their parents.

When describing the one or more motivations that led them to volunteer, societal feelings—caring about the future of the community—were cited most often (64 percent) by the survey respondents as an influence on their helping habits. In addition, about half mentioned religious teachings, and 54 percent mentioned parental influence. The impact of parental emphasis on service and family and church influences, while valuable, are not crucial. Actual experience as a helper can be just as powerful a motivator.

The critical factor in bringing about a change toward an active desire to help is the personal involvement, the moment of felt kinship with the other person. Intellectual concepts—because helping is "right" or is "one's duty"—are not a strong enough force. We saw this in the War on Poverty in the sixties and early seventies. Media reports showed important local changes; the condition of the poor was improving. But at the same time there was a huge growth in violent crime. The middle class found that while its taxes were paying for this fight against poverty, life was becoming far more tense and difficult for them.

What killed the War on Poverty was not a failure of belief in antipoverty actions but the lack of a personal, emotional conviction. The poverty-fighting efforts of that period were supported *from a distance*. Unlike the civil rights movement, which required personal action and relatively little funding, our effort to eradicate poverty was an effort to raise the standard of living of the poor to that of the middle-class majority, through schooling, housing, and welfare programs. But the people of the middle class were, for the most part, not part of this effort, except by paying their taxes. The movement came out of intellectual decisions, founded on important books such as Michael Harrington's *The Other America*, and out of the fear created by the great urban riots of the late 1960s. Neither ideas nor fear is enough to sustain a societal change. What is needed is the empathy of one person for another, the sense of connection that can only come when people interact peaceably with each other.

Critics debate how much of today's violence is triggered by a surge in drug use, a sharp drop in the parenting role of low-income fathers, the dwindling of religious involvement, the increase in unwed teenage pregnancies, the violence on TV and movies, or perhaps even the frustrated hopes unwittingly raised by civil rights and poverty programs for a level of social equality that society did not deliver. Whatever the combination of causes, we have entered a period marked by increasing tension between the urban poor and the rest of society.

We need a national movement of helping now. The feelings we still have for our communities and our society must be translated into the action of direct personal helping. This action is not a substitute for the vital and costly improvements in education, job training, and opportunities, housing, and social services. But these programs will not appear or be sustained by taxpayers without this personal helping base. We must make the change before those who are at this moment growing up in violence and poverty, angry at their own deprivation, become the critical mass that shapes this culture. For they would then be met by the hostility of a correspondingly large group—the middle-class youngsters whose predominant response to them consists of fear and anger. For our health as individuals and as a community, we must reach each other before it is too late.

HOW TO PROCEED

1. The immediate establishment of a national student volunteer program.

Because regular, direct helping of others is vital for individual health, our schools should set aside the same amount of time for volunteering that they now do for physical activity—no less than two hours a week.

If some type of helping were required of each student for two hours weekly, that would amount to thirteen school days per year. Is that too much time to take away from classroom teaching? In contrast gym classes—required about three hours a week—take up about 120 hours a year, or the equivalent of twenty school days.

At least one school district—Springfield, Massachusetts—did institute a volunteer curriculum for each grade of the forty schools in its system. Each school was free to design its own service-learning program based on the needs of its own community. For example, one school's students helped at a housing project for the elderly, another's worked at a shelter for homeless men. The elementary students could write letters or do artwork, which the elderly residents hung on their walls, or they could make placemats for the meals at the homeless center. These young students received feedback through letters, photographs, visits from the recipients, and they felt their own healthy pleasure at being able to help. At the same time older students visited these same locations and did close-contact helping. Teachers integrated the volunteer experiences into discussion in English, history, and even math classes.

"This learning by doing works tremendously in making students aware of others," said Carol Kinsley, who directed the district's effort. "And, yes, definitely the students' self-esteem grew strongly. The program connects kids to the world who don't feel connected and gives them a philosophy to live by. It helps them understand they are spiritual beings.

"When students achieve success in helping others," she said, "they believe in themselves. Their self-esteem is affected, and positive attitudes develop. The outcomes affect the total school, family, and environs, providing a climate and culture that become a learning community."

In addition to the overall supervision by Kinsley, each school assigned a regular teacher, with extra pay of $250 per semester for promoting the program. But students did not have to be involved in this purely voluntary effort; and an individual school could encourage the program as much or as little as it deemed appropriate.

Regrettably Springfield suffered a severe budget crunch, and the district and individual school coordinator positions were eliminated. Much of the program's drive has been lost, Kinsley said.

This experience points out the need for a program that *requires* students to perform services for others, backed by national and local leadership through Washington and the state capitals. Without mandatory participation by all youth, a program cannot involve enough students to bring about change. We need student after student to experience the power of helper's high, the rush of pleasure, the increase in self-esteem, and to become part of the rallying cry for the effort. It is clear that most students will not begin volunteering on their own. Getting involved with people who may be different is hard for anyone, especially a young person, who is so sensitive to being rejected. And if most of their friends are not involved, spending the hours in this way will put them at a disadvantage in athletic, academic, and social competition.

Many private and parochial schools do require community service, but far less than two hours weekly throughout each school year. Still, the benefits of a mandatory school initiative can be seen in the required forty community service hours per school year at Carmel High School in Mundelein, Illinois. Students in grades nine through twelve must perform these helping services after school, regardless of sports, work obligations, or studying.

The students work at hospitals, nursing homes, schools for the retarded, shelters for the abused, and soup kitchens. "A senior told me that his helping was what he'll always remember in life—and this is a typical comment," said Marian Bresnen, chairperson of the religious services department at this Catholic school. Many of the students volunteer more hours than are required and continue to help after graduation. One boy recently spent four hundred hours in one school year helping an elderly person in a nursing home.

"They become aware of societal needs," said Bresnen. "They develop less self-centeredness and a deeper awareness of how interdependent we all are, that we're all valuable and needy."

While there has been at least one lawsuit challenging a school system's authority to mandate volunteer work, the response from students and parents is generally positive. In 1990 in Philadelphia a group of twenty-one families sponsored a suit against required service, saying that the mandatory service was inconsistent with their values and possibly posed a safety risk for the students. But supporters of the requirement see it as a way to instill humane values and—with proper supervision for the students—to help improve the safety of our communities in the future. High school dropouts now cost the nation billions of dollars yearly in social service programs and lost production and are responsible for increased crime, drug, and other problems. Prevention programs show that one of the best ways to keep youngsters in school is to have them volunteer to help others on a regular, weekly basis.

For example, "Carla" is a sixteen year-old junior at John Dewey High School in Brooklyn, New York. She is now a motivated student, but there was a time when both she and school officials doubted that she would graduate.

Carla was a chronic class cutter who kept promising her family and the school guidance counselor that she was going to change. She didn't. "I cut just about all classes," she said. "Cutting school becomes a habit, like smoking. I failed them all." School was still a place to see people, if nothing else, however, so she kept going to school, hanging out around the lockers, but not going into the classrooms.

She failed ninth grade, and then the next year went back to the school again, a ninth-grader for the second time. This time, with a group of other problem students, she met with several guidance counselors and the principal. They encouraged her to become a volunteer.

"I finally said I'd try it, and in November I started going twice a week to an elementary school close by to tutor those kids in reading. I was still cutting classes, but I began to change quickly. Suddenly I was someone important, because of these kids I was helping. They needed me. If I didn't go, they were hurt. Also, I realized, if I could help these kids, I could help myself."

She left her friends who were still cutting classes and started attending school regularly. By the end of last year Carla had passed all classes and was promoted to eleventh grade through a special program in which she made up a year. "My guidance counselor, he was amazed, he said he never thought I'd graduate.

"I want to help children. Volunteering with them—if it wasn't for that I'd never have changed. It helped me more than it helped the kids. I learned that if you can help someone else, you can help yourself. If I can help change someone else's life, I can help change my own. And I have."

Tony Maravola, an eighteen-year-old senior at Carmel High School in Mundelein, Illinois, wakes up at 4:30 A.M. every Saturday to travel from his home in Gurnee to the Chicago docks. An hour later, and for the next five hours, he is unloading food off huge trucks and arranging it in piles. Vans from agencies that serve the poor arrive to pick up this food.

The high school he attends is one mentioned earlier that requires all its students to do community service. But Tony began volunteering at the docks in eighth grade as a confirmation requirement. He felt so good about this experience that he's never stopped.

Since he doesn't have personal contact with the poor, he enjoys hearing stories from the pickup drivers about the people who receive the food. This work has changed him, he says. "I was an army brat, and we were always moving. I'd go to a new school, and I'd be broke in comparison to most students. I was always jealous of them. But since I began helping, I have no more jealousy. I'm much calmer. I realize my personal situation isn't so bad.

"I also know I'm accomplishing something, and that's given me a whole lot more self-confidence. I remember one Saturday I was real angry at having to get up early to volunteer. I had been out late the night before. I wanted to just get it over with. But as our work started and we began talking with the men about what we were doing, what we were accomplishing together, all of that bad feeling passed away. I was accomplishing something."

Tony's experiences led him to suggest that community service need not be required throughout high school, but just in the freshman year. "The great feelings you get, that should sustain you. But some kids never get into it. They goof off and forge cards from the organizations they are supposed to be helping, just saying they were there so that they can get school credit. Why force them?"

The schools these students attend are exceptional in that they require or vigorously encourage community service. Only about three thousand of the nation's twenty thousand public high schools have any kind of community-service program, and most of these are on an elective basis through club projects and do not require that the students have personal involvement with those they help. Private schools more frequently have community-service requirements for their students. One study found that about a quarter of the 448 private schools surveyed had such a requirement.

In late 1990 Congress approved legislation for a national youth service program, with the funds awarded competitively to states that develop volunteer-service projects, involving schools, colleges, and adults. Minnesota's Board of Education has issued a regulation that each elementary, junior high, and high school must offer an opportunity for students to volunteer. Each school is free to decide how many and which grades to include and what type of service students will be encouraged to do. Furthermore the state's 1989 Youth Service legislation provides more than one million dollars to public schools, from kindergarten through high school and college, to support local efforts, such as the training and supervision of student volunteers. Similar programs are beginning or are under consideration in Maryland, Pennsylvania, and Washington State.

The Princeton Center for Leadership Training has worked with inner-city as well as private schools in Newark, New Jersey, and Atlanta, Georgia, training seniors to be volunteer tutors for freshmen. One result, in an evaluation by the Educational Testing Service, was a sharp decline for both groups in absenteeism and behavior problems.

In San Antonio, Texas, Hispanic students on the verge of dropping out of school were trained to tutor elementary school students. The student tutors reported a dramatic rise in self-esteem, and their dropout rate was 6 percent, rather than the expected 32 to 37 percent.

The Carnegie Foundation for the Advancement of Teaching has recommended that every high school student complete a community-service requirement. This would "suggest to young people that they are needed," said Ernest Boyer, foundation president.

The 1988 study of the W. T. Grant Foundation on Youth and America's Future recommended for all the nation's schools either a required number of community-service hours in order to graduate or the awarding of elective credits for volunteering, which would count toward the total number of credits needed to graduate. In addition all classes—from kindergarten through twelfth grade—were asked to hold discussions in which the students and teachers talked about volunteer experiences in the context of curricular studies.

These moves and endorsements are a beginning. They indicate a public sentiment that will be receptive to the new information about helping, which could grow and rally behind a required weekly school community-service effort. The potential is enormous. Senator Edward Kennedy, a backer of federal funding to promote student community-service programs, has noted the immensity of the human resource. "The sixty million students from kindergarten through college across America are a powerful national resource that is largely untapped." This is not a "liberal" call. Similar views were echoed by conservative thinker William F. Buckley, Jr., in his recent book *Gratitude: Reflections On What We Owe to Our Country*. In fact Buckley, though not calling for required volunteering, would link service to getting student loans, driver's licenses, and other quite basic needs.

To reach the largest number of students before they are of age to drop out of school, it is necessary to help the youngest students to begin helping. Currently we are losing large numbers of our youth to the streets. In the sixteen-to-twenty-four-year-old age bracket, 12 percent of white youth, 15 percent of black, and 28 percent of Hispanic are dropouts. These are the very students who are the greatest loss and pose the greatest threat to our society. A required personal helping program starting in the earliest grades might help reverse this by creating in these students a sense of belonging. If we start with the young, we can help to build the values that will keep them in school. And while they're young, we still know where we can find them: 95 percent of the nation's fourteen-to-seventeen-year-olds are still enrolled in the classroom.

Child-development research has established that programs can begin at the third- or fourth-grade level, when moral values are formed and helping's feel-good sensation can be recognized. In 1932 the Swiss developmental psychologist Jean Piaget published a book, *The Moral Judgment of the Child*, that found that empathy, which leads to cooperation with others, begins at around age seven (though today some researchers argue that these feelings occur even earlier). "By age seven or eight," said Martin Hoffman, a psychologist at New York University, "you can appreciate another person's overall life situation, not just his or her immediate circumstances." Research shows that students who made toys for poor hospitalized children or taught other children were later more helpful to all youths.

"We would never expect a kid to learn to read or write just from hearing a lecture," says Steven Brion-Meisels, a Cambridge, Massachusetts, educator who has worked with school programs to foster altruism. "And we shouldn't expect them to learn social skills that way either."

There are practical questions about how a school helping requirement can be accomplished:

• *Will students feel genuine empathy with those they help when their "volunteering" is in fact required?* I think so. Many of the quotes of students you have read here are from participants in required community-service programs. Consider the following reactions from students in a required program, who give time at Good Shepherd Hospital in Barrington, Illinois:

"It has made me feel better about myself that I can really make a difference. That I am really needed." (age fourteen)

"It has been the best experience of my life. I would

never give up this feeling for anything." (age seventeen)
"It has increased my awareness. It has given me an increased self-worth." (age eighteen)

The practical outcome of mandated programs is that students feel better about themselves. And we need a requirement to help people get started. Becoming a volunteer for the first time is difficult for adults to do; it is far harder for young people, who worry about seeming different from their peers. We need to hand them the opportunity to find out how helping can help them. Merely making a suggestion is not sufficient.

• *What about the school time required?* The two hours weekly will have to come out of the school schedule. To supervise a program adequately and to emphasize its importance, it should be scheduled during the school day. The nation is in an emergency over its citizens' relationships; teaching our children how to live together is as crucial to our future as any other educational task our schools face.

Midwood High School is one of Brooklyn's most sought-after schools because of its academic excellence. Located in the center of Flatbush, Brooklyn, New York, Midwood has had an increasing problem of students being beaten and robbed. New students are lectured about not wearing jewelry, expensive jackets, or anything that will make them a target. At the beginning of the 1989 school year, frustrated Midwood officials decided to end school a half hour early, at 2:30 P.M., so that students could get onto subways and buses well in advance of the students at nearby schools who had been responsible for the assaults. That shortened classes by two and a half hours weekly, a decrease of teaching time caused by societal tension and violence.

To cut back on learning time to avoid violence is to take a posture of exhaustion and defeat. Surely it would be better if the two and a half hours were devoted to supervised volunteer activities in which all of the city's students participated. I talked recently with Pierson Keating, a partner in one of New York's largest executive-search firms, which places corporate executives in top-paying positions. "It's not that hard to raise technicians," he said. "But in today's complicated world, everyone must cooperate. Perhaps the best-known change that the Japanese have brought to American business is the need to get along with each other—from executives eating with regular employees, to creating quality-of-life units for assembly lines, where people have to be part of a workplace family. Parents who want a very competitive, aggressive child are not the modern parents they think they are, as far as equipping their children to be able to compete in the future."

• *How do we organize a school program, and what are the costs?* The best and simplest way to begin healthy helping— helping that is personal, regular, and involves strangers— would be to link a class with a nursing home, hospital, or any other community institution that needs volunteers. Younger students can be transported to the site en masse. Then, as students get older, they can choose individual volunteer projects.

The California legislature has passed a bill that encourages the 400,000 students at the state's public universities to perform thirty hours of community service a year. The legislators estimated that about $8,500 a month was needed on each campus for the coordination of these activities. This is more than offset by the work done by the students. At each school students are performing 18,000 hours of work per month. At entry-level wages that's $72,000 worth of work every month. Beyond this there are the incalculable savings yielded by the decreases in social ills.

To build a culture that is founded on a cooperative spirit, it is crucial to begin in the schools. And, to be effective, I believe that we must have a requirement. We cannot expect more students to take part in helping efforts regularly if they believe that they are missing out on study time, work time, or social opportunities that are available to non-helping students. In fact that is exactly the reason that physical education time is mandated. A teenager needs to recognize that "everybody's doing it." If we don't require that they all give it a try, too many will never have a chance to know the benefits.

2. Appeals to self-interest

"You have to realize," said Norman Cousins, as we talked about the new information on healthy helping, "that this will not be the reason people continue helping, but it can be the *motivator* to get them started. When [Swiss psychiatrist Carl] Jung talked about our collective conscience, he meant that we as a people have a collective wisdom, which for a variety of reasons doesn't always manifest itself. In other words people can be taught what they really already know. To do this, to break collective wisdom free, we need a shock of recognition. People can say *Aha!* If many more people will be exposed to the powerful feel-good sensations of healthy helping and understand this new evidence about why helping others is such a natural behavior, and so naturally healthy for them—this could be one of those shocks."

In addition to the positive effect on health offered by volunteering, different population groups receive special psychological benefits as well. We need to spread the word through the appropriate vendors of information, from doctors and social workers to relevant community organizations and our employers.

Men, for example, have a special need to act on the knowledge about healthy helping. Compared with women, they are more prone to aggressive behavior and have fewer friends. In *The Tangled Wing*, Melvin Konner, an anthropologist and medical doctor, reviewed the research on sex differences, and found that "the strongest case for gender difference" is in aggressive behavior. He looked at fifty-seven studies and found that fifty-two showed boys to be more aggressive than girls. Thus, in the earlier years of life, there is a greater occurrence of homicides, suicides, and accidents among men. In the later years, they experience a greater incidence of heart disease. In all of these, hostility and aggression-related stress play an important role, and we have seen how regular helping reduces feelings of hostility and thereby alleviates stress.

Women are also vulnerable to stress, though the sources of their tensions may often be different from men's. The famed Framingham, Massachusetts, heart study found that females who were especially stressed were twice as likely to suffer a heart attack as women who were more relaxed. Heart disease in fact kills about a quarter of a million women a year.

Women are also three times more prone to depression than men. Regular helping has a recognized potential to lift the spirits in a lasting way. First Lady Barbara Bush is one case in point. She has said that she suffered a severe case of depression after she and her husband returned in 1976 from two years in China and overcame it through volunteer work. "I would feel like crying a lot and I really painfully hurt," she told reporters. Working at Washington Home, a health-care facility for people who are seriously ill, she found that her depression vanished permanently within six months.[10]

The newly lonely are a group of people who have much to gain from helping others. Studies show an increased death rate among widowers, with heart disease responsible for half these deaths. Starting in the second year after the death, there is also a slight increase in mortality among widows. We know that helping decreases feelings of isolation, helplessness, and lack of control—the stress triggers experienced by mourners.

Divorce causes similar negative emotions. A Swedish study that followed middle-age men for three years found that the divorced men had a mortality rate of 20 percent compared to 9 percent for married men. Researcher Janet Kiecolt-Glaser, of Ohio State University, has shown that both men and women who are separated or divorced tend to be distressed and lonely and have poor immune-system values. For the newly isolated and lonely, whether recovering from divorce or the death of a partner or some other loss of companionship, involvement in regular helping is especially recommended.

People who are living in poverty can better cope with the stress of their lives and with their feelings of helplessness by helping others. Usually people who are poor are less likely to be involved in any formal volunteer program—surviving is already taking too much of their time—though in fact, from my observations, they are more likely to be active in informal helping activities, such as block parties and other neighborhood activities. Still, it is important that low-income people have the advantages of doing some kind of regular community service with strangers, with the resultant health benefits.

Martin Seligman, the University of Pennsylvania psychologist who did basic research on helplessness and ill health, points out the usefulness of the poor volunteering in social-action projects, particularly those aimed at reducing poverty. "If poverty produces helplessness, then effective protest—changing one's own actions—should produce a sense of mastery. Poverty is not only a financial problem but, more significantly, a problem of individual mastery, dignity, and self-esteem."

At the 1989 meeting of the National Medical Association, an organization for black physicians, there was a discussion of the link between poor self-esteem and health problems. John Chissell, a family practitioner from Boston, noted that blacks acquire lower self-esteem because of the limited number of occasions in which they see positive images of themselves. We know that successful personal helping sharply boosts self-worth.

In addition to the unhealthy feeling of helplessness, there is the problem of chronic anger. Ernest Johnson, a psychologist at the University of Houston, has studied large numbers of black adults and found that those who were unemployed and expressed high levels of anger had the greatest number of health problems. Johnson noted that such unhealthy levels of anger may be either the consequence or the cause of increased stress. In either case regular helping of others will lower the stress.

The elderly are another group particularly well-served by the health benefits of helping. The isolation, poor health, and resulting stress that affect the elderly are well known. Nonetheless the federal RSVP (Retired Senior Volunteer Program) study pointed out health improvements among members that seem almost miraculous. The examiners found that the volunteers' physical and mental health had improved significantly at 98 percent of the facilities studied. As then national director of the RSVP program Alfred Larson noted, "Doctors always tell us that elderly people who engage in volunteer work are a lot better off, visit the doctor less often, and have fewer complaints."

People over eighty form the fastest-growing segment of the population, and we have heard many reactions from volunteers this age, explaining what helping does for them. As we become older, we have a smaller circle of friends and work contacts. Health professionals have suggested that the elderly need to expand their social networks. Regular helping activities are a way to do this.

Marion Cleeves Diamond has done laboratory research

for over thirty years as a professor of anatomy at the University of California at Berkeley. This work showed, in contradiction to popular belief, that the brain does not stop growing and lose cells with old age. Rather the cells stop being stimulated, and the dendrites—the important communicative connection between neurons—can wither away.

But Diamond found with laboratory animals that an older brain, when aroused, can breed new dendrites—though mature animals required more stimulation than younger ones to experience this growth.[11] Unfortunately the stimulating interaction with others that occurs at a workplace is not available to most older people. However, opportunities to help, and therefore interact with, other people *are* available, even though it may take some time and effort to get started.

Since the elderly have the most free time, the time involved shouldn't be so much of an obstacle for them. Even so, volunteerism is lower among people over sixty-five than it is among younger people. Twenty-three percent of the older group are volunteers, compared to 33 percent of younger people. According to a Louis Harris survey, people over sixty-five indicated less satisfaction with life than people between the ages of eighteen and sixty-five. These findings were based on questions that included whether they expected interesting and pleasant things to happen in the future, whether they were currently able to do interesting activities, and how happy they felt. By contrast the RSVP study was a sign of the effect of volunteer work on optimism, happiness, and a sense of personal control. The RSVP volunteers found in their helping important gains in their sense of usefulness (mentioned by 97 percent), companionship (91 percent), self-satisfaction (84 percent), and independence (52 percent).

Robert Coles, the Harvard Medical School psychiatrist, has said that as we get older, "we are likely . . . to seek our satisfactions in daily deeds rather than grand designs: the small gestures toward one another, the concreteness of an hour's involvement in the life of another person."[12]

3. Other voices to carry the message

What is true of students is true, as well, of older people—and of *all* of us: We require some kind of push to get going. Fifteen to 30 percent of all nonvolunteers tell pollsters that the reason they are not helping is that they've never been asked. Our government leaders and the private organizations that use volunteers must promote helping programs—for people of all ages.

The way to reach all these groups is by giving them the opportunity to try helping. The schools will reach our youngest. For spreading the word to the rest of the population assistance is needed. We need to enlist the help of doctors, businesses, the media, and parents.

For example, doctors who believe a patient is suffering from problems linked to anxiety, depression, stress, or isolation can act as a new referral resource. "Doctors recognize the importance of the field of mind-body interactions, but lack mechanisms to use it," said Hal Holman of Stanford University Medical School and former chairman of the Department of Medicine. This suggests the need for greater communication between doctors and the hundreds of thousands of volunteer agencies throughout the nation.

A diabetic woman in her late fifties told me she had monitored her own blood sugar and knew that when she was under stress, the level rose. In response her physician had always just said, "You should relax." This was meaningless—she would relax if she knew how. Now, however, there is a technique a doctor can recommend: Helping other people is a highly reliable relaxation technique that provides distraction from tensions and actual pain, demands at least some physical effort, and can become a challenge to the helper's creativity.

Businesses are another force that can both utilize and promote the benefits of helping. Many of the nation's large companies do encourage their employees to volunteer. Some match workers with community opportunities. A few even allow employees paid time away from the job to take part in community-service projects. But such committed efforts are exceptions.

One time-honored reason for businesses to support community service is that it is good public relations: It makes the company look good in the eyes of the community. With this reasoning, firms can explain to shareholders the few dollars spent on volunteer programs. But the information about healthy helping now reveals far more significant benefits for industry. Getting more employees involved in helping can reduce the critical stress level in the workplace, which is typically a great source of staff discontent and decreased productivity. The resulting improvements in employee health can contribute to reducing the tremendous problem of soaring health and other fringe-benefit costs for business, which now often consume 30 percent or more of every dollar earned.

Volunteers through the AT&T program comment on how their helping has reduced work-caused stress while also stirring health-enhancing emotions:

> "I am in a stressful job, and my volunteer work helps me withdraw from the job frustrations." (age fifty-two)
>
> "My job is very stressful and frustrating. Helping others makes me calm, happy, satisfied. I get a good feeling of self-worth and self-esteem." (age fifty-five)
>
> "Helping others relieves a lot of the stress I experience from home and job. It makes me feel good about myself." (age forty-one)
>
> "I get a great feeling of pride and accomplishment

when helping others, and physically I feel better after sitting so long at my job." (age fifty-eight)

Another voice to carry the message of healthy helping is one that now keeps us informed mainly about the violence in our world: the media. If personal helping of others is to become a visible part of our culture, it must begin to appear on TV, just as exercise programs and information on health and nutrition do now.

While TV dramas periodically highlight certain problem issues—child abuse, drugs, pregnancy, alcoholism—they are not yet an ongoing force for prosocial action. They do not provide the continuous, repeated images that people need to see and think about before considering changing their own attitudes and behaviors.

But suppose the habit of helping was given the same kind of visibility that has made exercise so recognizable and familiar a pattern of behavior. We now see many TV shows with actors dressed in their workout clothes on their way out for a run or a racquetball game. When the message begins to spread, we may begin to see actors, just as naturally, on their way out to spend some time helping someone in need. Programs could depict the facilities where helpers work, showing the often dramatic effect on both recipient and helper as the bonds between them form.

If that happens, the cause of helping will take a huge step forward. There can be little doubt of the effect of the media, particularly television, in forming the habits of the nation.

In one study of TV's underused prosocial power, several hundred children between the ages of six and nine were asked to look at a videotape of someone bowling. Some saw the bowler win gift certificates and then give them to a charity; others saw a version in which the bowler kept the prize for his personal use. After watching the tape the children were given gift certificates themselves. Those who had watched the actor donate his to charity were more likely than others to do the same.

A similar study asked children to watch tapes of "Lassie." Some saw the dog's young owner rescue Lassie's puppies; others watched a show that showed no such altruistic acts. Then, after watching these tapes, the children played a game that was interrupted by the sounds of puppies in distress. If they left the game, they would hurt their score. Those who had seen the altruistic "Lassie" tape were more likely to go help.

There have been many other reports. J. Philippe Rushton, psychologist at the University of Western Ontario, has concluded, "These studies demonstrate that television programming can modify viewers' social behavior in a prosocial direction. Generosity, helping, cooperation, friendliness, adhering to rules, delaying gratification, and a lack of fear can all be increased by television material."[13]

Finally, parents can pass on to their children the message that helping others is a part of good health. It's as important as getting them to eat vegetables, get enough sleep, and brush their teeth. T. Berry Brazelton, the pediatrician associated with Harvard who has done so much writing and study about children's health, believes that we are going to see an increase in youthful stress disorders. "Nine- and ten-year-olds are going through the same kinds of psychosomatic disorders that adolescents used to have." It's important that we succeed in reducing stress in our children's lives.

The patterns of behavior that tension causes tend to lead to an accumulation of problems. The hostile young Type A individual is generally rated by peers as less likable than others. These children are often left out of activities, and with the growing isolation, the tension increases. Alexander Thomas, a psychiatrist at New York University Medical School, along with his wife, Stella Chess, a psychiatrist, studied seventy-five children over a thirty-year-period beginning in 1956. Those who were aggressive between the ages of seven and twelve had the most difficulty adjusting later.[14]

Parents can teach their children the health practice of helping by their own involvement, and by petitioning their local schools to institute a weekly personal volunteering program for all grades.

4. Appeals to idealism and adventure

The call for community service as an expression of our highest ideals—and social health—is coming from leaders at both ends of the political spectrum: from Ted Kennedy to William F. Buckley, Jr. More than a decade ago England's Prince Charles gave his support to a type of service that treats the entire world as a community. The project that began then has now spread out to many countries and has sent young people from forty-six nations to work in areas that need help. Operation Raleigh, named for the soldier-statesman Sir Walter Raleigh and based on an idea of Prince Charles' attempts to create a way for young people to rise to the challenges of war in peacetime. The expeditions give adventurous young people a chance for heroism without having to go to war. By working to assist eye surgeons in a clinic set up in a village in Chile or Panama, by building a badly needed bridge in Papua New Guinea, by digging freshwater wells on a Sioux reservation in South Dakota, or working on one of the many other projects worldwide, young people are taking part in life-changing experiences in community service, much like my own years ago in the Peace Corps in the barrios of Venezuela.

The venturers, as they are called, each go out on a three-month expedition, said Mark Bensen, executive director of Operation Raleigh, U.S.A., which is based in Raleigh, North Carolina. They then return home with their "service-minded enthusiasm" to work in their own communities. About 15 to 18 percent of those who have participated have come from economically disadvantaged backgrounds. The rest have each raised the $5,500 required to sponsor one venturer's trip, with fund-raising efforts that range from bike-a-thons to bake sales.

In 1989 a reunion of venturers was held in London's Royal Albert Hall, and more than four thousand people attended from all over the world. This was to be the end of what was originally planned as a four-year project. But in many nations the project is now continuing. England, the United States, Japan, Canada, Australia, as well as Eastern European countries, are all still sending out venturers. A group has just returned, Bensen said, from Costa Rica, where they helped local people build a clinic/recreation center in an indigent village in the country's interior.

While the tangible accomplishments of these helping efforts are valuable, Bensen notices another very important result. "In a lot of ways the bottom line is the number of international friendships that have been formed and maintained. At some point in the future those friendships may end up being very valuable, a grass-roots diplomacy that develops between citizens." It will be hard for these venturers even to think of going to war against people they have helped.

The possibilities for organizations that promote helping range from world-scale projects such as Operation Raleigh to neighborhood associations. Helping efforts can foster idealism even in prisons, possibly the most intensely violent sites on the map of our culture. A program at the Vienna Correctional Center in rural Johnson County, Illinois, trains inmates as emergency medical-care volunteers and sends them out with community ambulances. The prisoners say that their work makes them feel connected with the people of the area, even though the region is almost entirely white and half of the prisoners are black.

"I've discovered that I like helping people," a young man, jailed for participating in a burglary, explained to a reporter. "It's just the feeling you get when you have an eighty-five-year-old woman hold your hand and look up and say, 'You're such a good man.'" Early studies of this program show that the inmates who volunteered were less likely to get into trouble after release from jail.[15]

In a Los Angeles probation program hardened juvenile offenders spend two hours each day with disabled children, teaching them and helping them to exercise. The purpose of this effort is to raise self-esteem and teach responsibility. One former gang member told of pushing a girl in a wheelchair and receiving the kind of message he was unlikely to hear on the streets. "I love you," she wrote on a blackboard in her lap, holding it up for him to see. Los Angeles County has announced plans to expand this program.

In New York City, Project Return, a transitional parole program for men leaving prison, has sent many former convicts out to distribute sandwiches and drinks to homeless people. Once again the result has been increased levels of self-esteem.

A GRASS-ROOTS MOVEMENT

Before the 1988 election a survey for the Times Mirror Company found 16 percent of Americans—about 40 million people—to be strongly characterized by caring behavior. Mark Satin, editor of the periodical *New Options* and a longtime chronicler of social issues, commented, "It is only a matter of time before a major national movement or competent third party begins to articulate a politics of the caring individual."[16]

It is up to individuals to make this change in our society. Our own history teaches that a call from a leader does not bring about a fundamental change in patterns of behavior. What we need is a national call for change, originating with one individual after another who has received the benefits and then introduced another person to the experience, and so forth.

Eventually the support of our government agencies and leaders will be important. John Kennedy's announcements about the need for exercise stimulated schools to offer more physical activity. But this call from Washington in the 1960s was only successful because enough people had already heard the news about the health benefits of fitness. Kennedy might not have issued his call without this visible sentiment. People had begun to exercise, and to be seen doing it, and that was part of the growing pressure for cultural change. That was the real source of leadership—the people themselves.

I was very lucky in the timing of my own entry into helping professions and activities. Each time I was faced with a new decision, there was a wave of popular support toward the kind of helping activity I was considering. If it weren't for the fact that society made it easy for me to begin helping others, I might not have taken that particular course. My first introduction to the pleasure of helping was through an experience in the burgeoning civil rights movement. Then, by the time I finished law school, it was the late 1960s and the decision to go into the Peace Corps was easy because a lot of other people were either doing it or thinking about it. When I came back and decided to practice law in East Harlem, the War on Poverty had begun. Once again I was in good company; I didn't have to suffer the isolation and increased risk that any pioneer faces.

In recent years people have continued to make it easy for me to help. People around me now know that I like to do this kind of work. So when neighborhood efforts to help the homeless began to develop, I was asked to join in. Knowing how good that kind of helping feels, it was easy for me to say yes.

Sometimes, while having dinner with friends, I'll happen to mention a recent experience I've had working with the homeless or engaged in some other helping effort. Often one or two people will say, "I wish I was doing something like that." So I give them a name to call. But most do not make the call. They don't have the support or the popular pressure. Teenagers aren't the only ones who want each other's company and approval; we all do. Without either a strong sense of societal support or a personal history of helping, few are likely to venture into strange territory and offer their time without being asked.

When I began this research, I was the executive director of an organization devoted to the study of mind-body interaction. I did not know what my survey might find. Now I know it has established that regular, direct helping of others is an important health factor, and this information has brought me back to personal helping once again—with the organization of Big Brothers/Big Sisters of New York, where I now work.

One-on-one helping is the basis of Big Brothers/Big Sisters—matching a needy child with an adult who will be a steadying, older friend for an average of about two hours a week. It's precisely the kind of helping my research found is best for health, both of the individual and of the community. New on the job, I began talking with the "Bigs," seeing what their work was doing for them. There were so many examples of bonds being formed and walls falling down: the Big Brother from an Irish neighborhood who takes his Little Brother, who is black, home with him; the Big who stuck by his Little, the way family would, when the Little Brother went on trial for a serious crime; the Big Sister who tracked down her missing Little

Sister in East Harlem when the child's family had to move because of housing problems. The Big Brothers and Big Sisters are so excited, so happy, about what they are doing. For me they are the living proof of what my research has found. And the outside studies have found that this one-on-one bond, which often lasts a lifetime, cuts the incidence of juvenile crime by 40 to 50 percent, as well as increasing school achievement in 60 percent of the youth. And more than 80 percent of the Bigs report increases in their own self-esteem, optimism, and overall well-being.

Washington has a new agency called the Office of National Service, which is responsible for providing federal leadership on the issue of community service. President George Bush has encouraged more volunteering, describing the efforts of one helper and another across the country as "a thousand points of light." This action, and similar initiatives in several states, are a beginning, a stirring of the kind of support we need. But these government calls to be a helping citizen are not enough.

I received a letter from the president about my research, and I was invited to come to the White House to talk about the relationship between health and helping and the idea of a community-service requirement in the schools. As it happened, the day of my appointment was the day that the United States invaded Panama. I walked through the huge corridors of the Old Executive Office Building alongside the White House and saw that, in every office, people were gathered around TVs watching the news.

I did have my meeting, with Gregg Petersmeyer, deputy assistant to the president and director of the new Office of National Service. He seemed very interested in the information about helping and invited staff in for a minilecture from me. At the same time I knew as I walked back down that hall, hearing from one doorway and the next the latest updates on our troops, not to expect immediate action. Our government that day had—and always has—hundreds of crises to handle. It does not have the resources or the single-mindedness or the mandate to engineer a fundamental change in the culture. The matter of a helping revolution will have to come from the public at large. It will begin to move through individuals and the actions of their local agencies. And it has begun. For example Robert Wagner, Jr., until recently president of the New York City Board of Education, has written the federal Office of National Service asking for a national initiative to support weekly community service in the nation's schools and citing my research. In this letter, Wagner wrote, "The New York City school system is ready to work with the White House in making this happen." Perhaps as expected, Wagner said he never heard from Washington; but on the local level, other schools, states, and neighborhoods are beginning to pick up the same theme.

Inevitably, when the support of people is strong enough—when enough people are enjoying helper's high and the well-being that follows—then our leaders and the agencies of government can take steps to make helping a decision that is easy for all parts of our population. And we can each with our individual helping efforts live healthier lives, contribute to the healing of our nation, and create a cultural export of unprecedented value.

Getting Started

WHEN I first began developing the idea for this book, I had dinner with Norman Cousins at his home in Los Angeles. Internationally known for his writings about subjects from health and mind-body interactions to world peace, Cousins became excited about the book, and he gave me a piece of advice: Let the book have a practical side. Give people the names of organizations where they can start to volunteer. Since most of us have some health issue that affects us, he said, provide as a starting place a list of health-organization volunteer opportunities. So, as a result of that conversation, what follows is a listing of seventy-five national health organizations, as well as a few local voluntary groups with national reputations.

But health is only one field among many where volunteers are needed. You may be more attracted to working in the fields of literacy, feeding and sheltering of the homeless, care of the elderly or disadvantaged children, poverty, or education. If one of these or any other issue attracts you, the first step is to simply look it up by searching for the key word in the white or yellow pages of your phone book. It's highly likely that you will find local community groups working in that field. Or you might try looking up the word *volunteer*. Under this listing you may find the local agencies that are clearinghouses for volunteer services.

If this approach doesn't produce results, you may want to contact the national coordinating group: Volunteer— The National Center, 1111 North 19th Street, Arlington, Virginia 22209 (telephone: 703-276-0542).

An organization can provide invaluable support for the helper. While one-on-one helping can be practiced throughout the day, my survey research has shown that doing some volunteer work through an organization makes helping easier to sustain and more rewarding.

In choosing a type of helping that will maximize your good feelings and health, *and* keep you coming back, remember to find an activity that offers the following:

- Personal contact with the person you help (especially a stranger), or at least a strong emotional connection, such as by phone on a telephone hot line

- The opportunity for frequent helping, with a rough goal of two hours weekly

- A task that you are already equipped, or will be trained, to do

- An opportunity that is especially relevant to your interests

Often people say, "Oh, I tried giving time at that place, but volunteering just isn't right for me." The truth is that *particular* experience wasn't right for them. The choice is important; and it's equally important to persist until you find the right kind of helping.

The following directory of health organizations will expose you to a wide variety of types of agencies, ranging in size from those that are looking for their first volunteers to those that already have more than two million helpers. The mission of each agency will be described, answering questions such as: What do the volunteers do? Is there personal contact? Are there any qualifications that must be met? Is training provided? What are the time requirements?

One category that is missing from the list is hospitals, which provide opportunities for personal helping in almost every community.

May your helping bring you the best of health.

Volunteer Health Opportunities

AIDS

Birth

Cancer

Disability

Hearing

Heart

AIDS

Gay Men's Health Crisis

Mission: To maintain and improve the quality of life for people with AIDS and persons with AIDS-Related Complex and their care-partners; advocate for fair and effective public policies and practices concerning HIV infection; and, through education, promote awareness, understanding, and prevention of HIV infection.

You Are Needed: Uses 2,000 volunteers and serves people with AIDS, AIDS-Related Complex (ARC), and their families.

Helper's High in Return: Volunteers do have a chance for personal contact with the individuals served, providing psychosocial assistance, recreation, and everyday-living-activities support. Special training is provided. Volunteers do not come from one group, though 55 percent are from the gay community. The average number of hours volunteered per week: 4–8. The minimum number is 4; there is no maximum number of hours.

Getting Started: This is a local health organization, serving

New York City's five boroughs. The best way to volunteer is to call the volunteer office:

>Gay Men's Health Crisis
>129 West 20th Street
>New York, New York 10011
>212-337-3583

People with AIDS Coalition

Mission: To foster and encourage the philosophy and practice of self-empowerment and provide information about education and services pertinent to persons with AIDS and AIDS-Related Complex (ARC).

You Are Needed: Uses 100 volunteers and serves people with AIDS, ARC, care providers, and concerned others.

Helper's High in Return: Volunteers have a chance for personal contact with the individuals served, facilitating meals and socializing at a drop-in center; also one-to-one contact via hot line. Special training is required: Good social skills are desired. Volunteers do not come from one group, except for the hot line which is staffed primarily by individuals with AIDS or ARC. Average number of hours volunteered per week: 4–12. There is no maximum or minimum number of hours.

Getting Started: This is a local health organization. The best way to volunteer is to contact:

>Coordinator of Volunteers
>People with AIDS Coalition
>31 West 26th Street, 5th Floor
>New York, New York 10010
>212-532-0290

BIRTH

March of Dimes Birth Defects Foundation

Mission: To prevent birth defects.

You Are Needed: Uses 2.5 million volunteers and serves women, the unborn, the general public, and the medical and professional sectors.

Helper's High in Return: Volunteers do have a chance for personal contact with the individuals served, working with families of children with birth defects in parent-support-type programs. Special training is required; volunteers are trained by professionals. Volunteers do not come from one group. Average number of hours volunteered per week: 1. There is no maximum or minimum number of hours.

Getting Started: This is a national health organization with 133 chapters in 50 states. The best way to volunteer is to call your local office (see your telephone book) or call the national office:

> March of Dimes Birth Defects Foundation
> 1275 Mamaroneck Avenue
> White Plains, New York 10605
> 914-997-4444

National Sudden Infant Death Syndrome Foundation

Mission: To serve families who have lost a child to SIDS; educate the general public and relevant professionals; and promote research for SIDS and related issues.

You Are Needed: Uses 5,000 volunteers and serves parents and extended families who have lost a child to SIDS.

Helper's High in Return: Volunteers do have a chance for personal contact with the individuals served: by telephone, personal visits and/or correspondence, support-group meetings continued for as long as the client wishes, invitation to chapter meetings and formal/informal gatherings. Special training is required. Volunteer skills desired include accommodation of personal grief, objectivity combined with sensitivity, discretion, and good judgment. Volunteers are primarily members of families who have lost a child to SIDS. Average number of hours volunteered per week: 2–6. There is no maximum or minimum number of hours.

Getting Started: This is a national health organization with 72 chapters in 35 states. The best way to volunteer is to contact the national referral service through the national office:

> National Sudden Infant Death Syndrome
>   Foundation, Inc.
> 8200 Professional Place, Suite 104
> Landover, Maryland 20785-2264
> 800-221-7437 (outside of Maryland)
> 301-459-3388 (in Maryland)

CANCER

American Cancer Society

Mission: To eliminate cancer as a major health problem by preventing cancer, saving lives, and diminishing suffering through research, education, and service.

You Are Needed: Uses 2.5 million volunteers and serves the general public, cancer patients, and health professionals.

Helper's High in Return: Volunteers do have a chance for personal contact with the individuals served by providing assistance and counseling to cancer patients and their families. Volunteers also coordinate and conduct educational programs for the public and health professionals. Special training is required: organizational skills, leadership, planning and speaking skills; personal development is offered through local chapters. Volunteers do not come from one group. Average number of hours volunteered per week: unknown. There is no maximum or minimum number of hours.

Getting Started: This is a national health organization with

3,500 chapters in all states. The best way to volunteer is to contact the local Cancer Society unit in your telephone book or write the national headquarters:

American Cancer Society
1599 Clifton Road, N.E.
Atlanta, Georgia 30329

Cancer Care

Mission: To help patients and their families cope with the impact of cancer.

You Are Needed: Uses 1,000 volunteers.

Helper's High in Return: Volunteers do have a chance for personal contact with the individuals served, doing friendly visiting to home-bound cancer patients and transportation/escort services to treatment. Special training is required and includes the psychosocial needs of cancer patients, the effects of chemotherapy, and dealing with death and dying. Training takes place in New York, New Jersey, and Connecticut. Volunteers do not come from one group. Average number of hours volunteered per week: 2. Maximum number of hours permitted: 4; minimum number: 2.

Getting Started: This is a local health organization, serving New York, New Jersey, and Connecticut. The best way to volunteer is to call:

Cancer Care
1180 Avenue of the Americas
New York, New York 10036
212-221-3300

Leukemia Society of America

Mission: To find the causes and cures of leukemia and related diseases, assist the patients, and educate the medical profession and the general public.

You Are Needed: Uses nearly 1 million volunteers and serves patients, patients' families, medical and paramedical professionals, and the public.

Helper's High in Return: Volunteers do have a chance for personal contact with the individuals served: as family-support-group leaders and through contacts with patients. Special training is not required, except for support-group facilitators and patient-aid administrators. Volunteers do not come from one group. Average number of hours volunteered per week: unknown. There is no maximum or minimum number of hours.

Getting Started: This is a national health organization with 70 chapters in 36 states. The best way to volunteer is to contact your local chapter listed in the telephone book or the national office:

> Leukemia Society of America
> 733 Third Avenue
> New York, New York 10017
> 1-800-955-4L5A

Spirit and Breath Rehabilitation and Support Network

Mission: To help people who have had lung cancer.

You Are Needed: Uses a very small number of volunteers and serves people who have or have had lung cancer, as well as their families.

Helper's High in Return: Volunteers do have a chance for personal contact with the individuals served, talking to them on the telephone with a positive approach, answering questions (nonmedical), and making hospital visits. Special training is required. Volunteer skills desired: being a good listener, not offering information on the illness unless asked, schooling on proper answers to questions, and so on. Volunteers are people who have had lung cancer. Average number of hours volunteered per week: 2–4. There is no maximum or minimum number of hours.

Getting Started: This is a national health organization. The best way to volunteer is to call the home office:

> Spirit and Breath Rehabilitation and
>   Support Network
> 8210 North Elmwood, Suite 209
> Skokie, Illinois 60077
> 312-673-1384

DISABILITY

National Easter Seal Society

Mission: To help people with disabilities achieve maximum independence by providing a wide range of direct services, advocacy, public education, government relations, and resource-development programs.

You Are Needed: Uses an unknown number of volunteers; serves people with any kind of disability.

Helper's High in Return: Volunteers do have a chance for personal contact with the individuals served, doing work at direct-service centers and summer camps. Special training is not required. Volunteers do not come from one group. Average number of hours volunteered per week: open. There is no maximum or minimum number of hours.

Getting Started: This is a national health organization with 190 chapters in 50 states plus Puerto Rico. The best way to volunteer is to contact your local office or write to:

National Easter Seal Society
70 East Lake Street
Chicago, Illinois 60601

National Rehabilitation Information Center (NARIC)

Mission: To gather, manage, and disseminate information about physical disabilities, mental retardation, and rehabilitation.

You Are Needed: Uses 10 volunteers and serves rehabilitation professionals and consumers with disabilities, families, and friends.

Helper's High in Return: Volunteers are not involved in personal contact with the individuals served. Average number of hours volunteered per week: 15. There is no maximum or minimum number of hours.

Getting Started: This is a national health organization. The best way to volunteer is to write or call:

National Rehabilitation Information Center
8455 Colesville Road, Suite 935
Silver Spring, Maryland 20910
301-588-9284

Rehabilitation Institute of Chicago (RCI)

Mission: To provide an individualized, comprehensive, state-of-the-art program of patient care, education of health care professionals, and clinical and scientific research in the field of disability rehabilitation.

You Are Needed: Uses 125–150 volunteers to serve severely physically disabled children and adults.

Helper's High in Return: Volunteers do have a chance for personal contact with the individuals served. They assist therapists in physical therapy, occupational therapy, and communicative disorders; become "Friendly Visitors," referred by social work and therapeutic recreation departments; assist vocational rehabilitation counselors in testing and evaluating patients; assist child-life specialist in pediatrics. Special training is required. Volunteers receive both on-the-job training and attend required orientation "hands-on" training before undertaking volunteer experience. Average number of hours volunteered per week: 2–30. There is a minimum of 2–3 hours (per session), but there is no maximum limit.

Getting Started: This is a local health organization serving the Chicago area. It is also the rehabilitative unit of the federally appointed Midwest Regional Spinal Cord Injury Care System (SCI). A significant number of patients come from throughout the nation and abroad. The best way to volunteer is to contact:

Director of Volunteer Services
Rehabilitation Institute of Chicago
345 East Superior Street
Chicago, Illinois 60611
312-908-6075

HEARING

American Society for Deaf Children

Mission: To help parents help each other in raising their deaf and hard-of-hearing children.

You Are Needed: An unknown number of volunteers.

Helper's High in Return: Volunteers do not have a chance for personal contact with the individuals served. There is no minimum number of hours that a volunteer must put in.

Getting Started: This is a local health organization. The best way to volunteer is to write or call:

> American Society for Deaf Children
> 814 Thayer Avenue
> Silver Spring, Maryland 20910
> 301-545-5400 (Voice or TDD)

National Association of the Deaf

Mission: To assure that a comprehensive system of services is accessible to all persons with hearing impairments.

You Are Needed: The number of volunteers varies. They advocate for hearing-impaired and deaf individuals.

Helper's High in Return: Volunteers provide information and promote better services. Volunteers are mostly deaf or hard-of-hearing. Average number of hours volunteered per week: varies. There is no maximum or minimum number of hours.

Getting Started: This is a national health organization with chapters in all 50 states. The best way to volunteer is to call or write:

> National Association of the Deaf
> 814 Thayer Avenue
> Silver Spring, Maryland 20910
> 301-587-1788 (Voice or TDD)

HEART

American Heart Association (AHA)

Mission: To reduce disability and death from cardiovascular diseases and strokes, through research, education, and community programs.

You Are Needed: Uses 2.4 million volunteers and serves the general public, health professionals, and research scientists.

Helper's High in Return: Volunteers have personal contact with the people being educated, for example by leading CPR and emergency cardiac care programs. Other opportunities include education programs in schools, doctor's offices, and the workplace. Special training is required: Emergency cardiac care courses are found at local offices of the AHA; volunteer training courses are offered at affiliate and national headquarters. Volunteers do not come from one group. Average number of hours volunteered per week: varies. There is no maximum or minimum number of hours.

Getting Started: This is a national health organization with 1,800 chapters in all states. The best way to volunteer is to call your local office, listed in the telephone book. Ask for the volunteer coordinator. The national address:

American Heart Association
7320 Greenville Avenue
Dallas, Texas 75231

Citizens for the Treatment of High Blood Pressure for Public Action of Cholesterol

Mission: To advocate and educate regarding public policy and funding of public health programs.

You Are Needed: Uses 200 volunteers and serves the general public, public officials, and medical and education professionals.

Helper's High in Return: Volunteers do direct advocacy concerning policies, budgets, legislation, and regulations. Special training is not required. Volunteers do not come from one group. Average number of hours volunteered per week: 3. There is no maximum or minimum number of hours.

Getting Started: This organization is especially looking for volunteers interested in public policy regarding heart disease. The best way to volunteer is to write:

> Citizens for the Treatment of High Blood Pressure
>   for Public Action of Cholesterol Inc.
> 888 Seventeenth Street, N.W., Suite 904
> Washington, D.C. 20006

INJURY AND STROKE

American Paralysis Association (APA)

Mission: To fund research to find a cure for paralysis caused by spinal cord injury and other central nervous system disorders and to educate the public about paralysis.

You Are Needed: Uses hundreds of volunteers and serves those who are paralyzed from spinal cord injury, head injury, stroke, or any other central nervous system disorder/trauma; professionals in the central nervous system field; researchers; medical institutions; and rehabilitation facilities. Maintains a 24-hour toll-free information/referral service.

Helper's High in Return: Volunteer chapters raise research funds and conduct grass-roots public-awareness/education activities. Many chapter members are those who are paralyzed, their family members, friends, and peers. Special training is not required. Average number of hours volunteered per week: varies. There is no maximum or minimum number of hours.

Getting Started: This is a national health organization with 18 chapters in 13 states. The best way to volunteer is to contact:

> American Paralysis Association
> 500 Morris Avenue
> Springfield, New Jersey 07081
> 800-225-0292
> (in New Jersey, 201-379-2690)

American Trauma Society

Mission: To lessen the incidence of violent-injury trauma through public education and awareness and to educate the public about the need for trauma centers.

You Are Needed: Uses 50–100 volunteers to educate the public (people through age 44 are primary target).

Helper's High in Return: Volunteers do have a chance for personal contact, sharing information with people in their community. Special training is not required. Volunteers are also involved in sorting, stuffing, and labeling for mailings. Average number of hours volunteered per week: 5–10. There is no maximum or minimum number of hours.

Getting Started: This is a national health organization with 10 chapters in 10 states. The best way to volunteer is to contact:

American Trauma Society
1400 Mercantile Lane, Suite 188
Landover, Maryland 20785
800-556-7890

National Head Injury Foundation (NHIF)

Mission: To improve the quality of life for persons with head injuries and their families.

You Are Needed: Uses 20,000 volunteers and serves people who have sustained a head injury, their families, professionals, and the general public.

Helper's High in Return: Volunteer activities range from stuffing envelopes and clerical duties to participation in conferences and representation on the board of directors and other governing bodies. Some specialized activities may require training. As activities are diverse, it is best to contact the foundation directly for specific information about a particular volunteer activity. Volunteers do not come from any one group. Average number of hours volunteered per week: 10. There is no maximum or minimum number of hours.

Getting Started: This is a national health organization with 44 chapters in 44 states. It urges people who are interested in volunteering their services to contact the Foundation for further information. Write or call:

> Director of Operations
> National Head Injury Foundation
> 333 Turnpike Road
> Southborough, Massachusetts 01772
> 508-485-9950

Stroke Clubs, International

Mission: To help stroke victims overcome the physical and psychological problems caused by a stroke.

You Are Needed: Uses an unknown number of volunteers and serves stroke victims, brain-damage victims, laypeople, and medical professionals. Volunteers are part of the self-help groups of people who have had strokes.

Helper's High in Return: Volunteers do have a chance for personal contact with the individuals served, encouraging people and advising them where to get help. Special training is required: must have an understanding of disabled persons. Average number of hours volunteered per week: unknown.

Getting Started: This is a national health organization with more than 800 clubs throughout the United States. The best way to volunteer is to contact:

> Stroke Clubs, International
> 805-12th Street
> Galveston, Texas 77550
> 409-762-1022

MENTAL HEALTH AND RETARDATION

National Down Syndrome Society

Mission: To support research, promote public awareness and education, and provide services for families and individuals affected by Down syndrome.

You Are Needed: Uses 200 volunteers and serves families and individuals with Down syndrome.

Helper's High in Return: Volunteers do not have a chance for personal contact with the individuals served. They do, however, provide support services; for example, fund-raising. Volunteers do not come from one group. There is no maximum or minimum number of hours.

Getting Started: This is a national health organization. The best way to volunteer is to call or write:

> National Down Syndrome Society
> 666 Broadway
> New York, New York 10012
> 212-460-9330

Project Overcome

Mission: To provide hope and support to individuals currently suffering from mental health problems and to decrease the stigma surrounding mental illness by speaking to the general public.

You Are Needed: Has 1 volunteer at present. The agency serves mental health clients, community groups, public school and college students, and church groups, as well as professionals.

Helper's High in Return: Volunteers would have a chance for personal contact. Special training is required; good phone skills and ability to relate to the mentally ill are desired. Volunteers would not have to come from one group. Average number of hours volunteered per week: 15. There is no maximum or minimum number of hours.

Getting Started: This is a local health organization serving Minnesota and surrounding areas. The best way to volunteer is to call or write:

> Project Overcome
> 2735 Blaisdell Avenue South, #202
> Minneapolis, Minnesota 55408
> 612-866-7464

NERVOUS AND MUSCULAR DISORDERS

The ALS Association

Mission: To find a cure for and the prevention of ALS (amyotrophic lateral sclerosis), through information dissemination, public awareness, and research funding. ALS, sometimes called Lou Gehrig's disease, is a progressive, fatal neuromuscular illness.

You Are Needed: Uses 3,000 volunteers and serves ALS patients and families, health care professionals, and researchers.

Helper's High in Return: Volunteers do have a chance for personal contact with the individuals served, running support groups for patients and families. Special training is not required. Volunteers do not come from one group. Average number of hours volunteered per week: 5–15. There is no maximum or minimum number of hours.

Getting Started: This is a national health organization with 26 chapters in 18 states. The best way to volunteer is to call 1-800-782-4747. National headquarters:

> The ALS Association
> 21021 Ventura Boulevard, Suite 321
> Woodland Hills, California 91364

American Parkinson Disease Association

Mission: To educate the public and support research on this progressive disorder of the central nervous system.

You Are Needed: Uses 500 volunteers and serves Parkinsonians and their families.

Helper's High in Return: Volunteers do have a chance for personal contact with the individuals served, doing referral work to medical and other facilities. Special training is not required. Volunteers are people afflicted by this disease. Average number of hours volunteered per week: 10. There is no maximum or minimum number of hours.

Getting Started: This is a national health organization with 50 chapters in 48 states. The best way to volunteer is to write:

American Parkinson Disease Association
116 John Street, Suite 417
New York, New York 10038
800-223-2732

Guillain-Barré Syndrome Support Group International

Mission: To help people who have this rare, paralyzing disorder that strikes the peripheral nerves.

You Are Needed: Uses 100 volunteers and serves Guillain-Barré syndrome victims, families, and the lay and medical community.

Helper's High in Return: Volunteers do have a chance for personal contact with the individuals served, through visits. Special training is somewhat necessary; should be able to provide emotional support for patients and their families. Volunteers are primarily people with this illness. Average number of hours volunteered per week: few. There is no maximum or minimum number of hours.

Getting Started: This is a national health organization with 105 chapters in most states. The best way to volunteer is to contact the national headquarters:

Guillain-Barré Syndrome
P.O. Box 262
Wynnewood, Pennsylvania 19096
215-896-6372 or 215-649-7837

International Joseph Disease Foundation (IJDF)

Mission: To locate people who are either affected or at risk for Joseph disease—a fatal genetic disorder of the nervous system that cripples and paralyzes—and refer them to appropriate physicians.

You Are Needed: Uses 50 volunteers and serves people with the symptoms, which most commonly begin between the ages of 15 and 35.

Helper's High in Return: Volunteers have personal contact

when interviewing an affected person. Average number of hours volunteered: varies. There is no maximum or minimum number of hours.

Getting Started: This is a national health organization. The best way to volunteer is to write:

International Joseph Disease Foundation (IJDF)
P.O. Box 2550
Livermore, California 94550

Muscular Dystrophy Association

Mission: To support scientific investigators seeking the causes of and effective treatments for muscular dystrophy and related neuromuscular disorders.

You Are Needed: Uses approximately 2 million volunteers and serves individuals with any one of 40 neuromuscular disorders.

Helper's High in Return: Volunteers do have a chance for personal contact with the individuals served, for example during patient outings and summer camp programs. Special training is required. Volunteers do not come from one group. Average number of hours volunteered per week: varies. There is no maximum or minimum number of hours.

Getting Started: This is a national health organization with 164 chapters in 50 states plus Puerto Rico. The best way to volunteer is to contact one of the 183 local field offices throughout the country, found in the telephone book. Or write:

Muscular Dystrophy Association
3561 East Sunrise Drive
Tucson, Arizona 85718

National Ataxia Foundation

Mission: To combat all types of hereditary ataxia—loss of coordination of the muscles—through service, education, and research programs.

You Are Needed: Uses 50 volunteers and serves those affected by hereditary ataxia and related disorders.

Helper's High in Return: Volunteers do have a chance for

personal contact with the individuals served at meetings and clinics. Special training is required and varies with the position. The foundation provides the training. Volunteers do not come from one group. Average number of hours volunteered per week: 2–3. There is no maximum or minimum number of hours.

Getting Started: This is a national health organization with 8 chapters in 7 states. The best way to volunteer is to call or write:

National Ataxia Foundation
600 Twelve Oaks Center
15500 Wayzata Boulevard
Wayzata, Minnesota 55391
612-473-7666

National Multiple Sclerosis Society

Mission: To seek the prevention, treatment, and cure of Multiple Sclerosis (MS) and to improve the quality of life of individuals with MS and their families.

You Are Needed: Uses 5 volunteers at the national office; each chapter manages its own volunteers.

Helper's High in Return: Volunteers do have a chance for personal contact with the individuals served. Special training is not required. Volunteers do not come from one group. Average number of hours volunteered per week at the national office: 5. There is no maximum or minimum number of hours.

Getting Started: This is a national health organization with 95 chapters in 49 states and Puerto Rico. The best way to volunteer is to contact the personnel department at the national headquarters:

National Multiple Sclerosis Society
205 East 42nd Street
New York, New York 10017

National Neurofibromatosis Foundation

Mission: To sponsor research into the cause and treatment of neurofibromatosis (NF)—a genetic neurological disorder in which tumors develop along nerves. The foundation promotes the development of clinics, public education, and support services for patients.

You Are Needed: Uses 1,000 volunteers and serves people with neurofibromatosis and their families.

Helper's High in Return: Volunteers have a chance for personal contact with the individuals served, providing information on neurofibromatosis and referrals to specialists. Special training is required. Volunteer skills desired: familiarity with the disease and the resources available to patients. Training is received from local chapters. Volunteers come primarily from families with NF. Average number of hours volunteered per week: 1–3. The minimum number of hours per week: 1; there is no maximum number of hours.

Getting Started: This is a national health organization with 22 chapters in 22 states. The best way to volunteer is to call the national organization:

> National Neurofibromatosis Foundation
> 141 Fifth Avenue, Suite 7-S
> New York, New York 10010
> 800-323-7938

National Spasmodic Torticollis Association

Mission: To support victims and their families and to educate the public about this neurological disorder that affects the muscles of the neck, causing the head to pull, turn, or look toward the shoulder.

You Are Needed: At present no volunteers. The association serves people in severe pain; many are unable to work, lonely, and do not understand what has happened to them.

Helper's High in Return: Wants to attract volunteers. Could use volunteer drivers and help organizing support groups. There will be opportunities to work with the individuals served and also to offer support services.

Getting Started: This is a national health organization with 12 chapters in 12 states. The best way to volunteer is to write:

> National Spasmodic Torticollis Association
> Box 873
> Royal Oak, Michigan 48068-0873

Tourette Syndrome Association

Mission: To help people with Tourette syndrome—a neurological disorder characterized by rapid tics—and to find the cause and cure of this illness.

You Are Needed: Uses 200 volunteers.

Helper's High in Return: Volunteers do have a chance for personal contact with the individuals served, doing hot-line and support-group work. Special training is not required. Volunteers are parents of people with Tourette syndrome. Average number of hours volunteered per week: 2. There is no maximum or minimum number of hours.

Getting Started: This is a national health organization with 50 chapters in 40 states. The best way to volunteer is to write:

> Tourette Syndrome Association
> 42-40 Bell Boulevard
> Bayside, New York 11361

OTHER DISORDERS

American Anorexia/Bulimia Association

Mission: To provide information, referral, education, prevention, and self-help groups for people with these eating disorders.

You Are Needed: Uses 30 volunteers and serves eating-disorder victims, their families and friends, schools, colleges, and the general public.

Helper's High in Return: Volunteers do have a chance for personal contact with the individuals served through phone contact and as group leaders. Some volunteers need special training in areas of counseling; group leaders have to be trained therapists. Telephone workers are trained by staff. Volunteers do not come from one group. Average number of hours volunteered per week: 1–10. There is no maximum or minimum number of hours.

Getting Started: This is a national health organization with 3

chapters in 3 states. The best way to volunteer is to call or write:

American Anorexia/Bulimia Association
133 Cedar Lane
Teaneck, New Jersey 07666
201-836-1800

American Narcolepsy Association

Mission: To improve the quality of life for those who have narcolepsy—the frequent and uncontrollable need for short periods of deep sleep.

You Are Needed: Uses 10 volunteers and serves those who have or suspect they may have narcolepsy or other sleep disorders.

Helper's High in Return: Volunteers do not have a chance for personal contact with the individuals served. Average number of hours volunteered per week: 1–5. There is no maximum or minimum number of hours.

Getting Started: The best way to volunteer is to call or write:

American Narcolepsy Association
P.O. Box 1187
San Carlos, California 94070
415-591-7979

Cooley's Anemia Foundation

Mission: To develop programs of patient care, research, and public information concerning this genetic blood disorder peculiar to people of Mediterranean heritage.

You Are Needed: Uses 5,000 volunteers and serves patients with Cooley's anemia (also known as thalassemia).

Helper's High in Return: Volunteers assist in blood drives, fund-raising, and educational activities. Many are parents of thalassemia patients; volunteers primarily are related to patients. Average number of hours volunteered per week: 5. There is no maximum or minimum number of hours.

Getting Started: This is a national health organization with 22

chapters in 29 states and an affiliate in Canada. The best way
to volunteer is to call or write:

> Cooley's Anemia Foundation
> 105 East 22nd Street, Suite 911
> New York, New York 10010
> 212-598-0911

Dystrophic Epidermolysis Bullosa Research Association of America (D.E.B.R.A.)

Mission: To fund and promote research, aid education and
advocacy, and provide support and services for people with
epidermolysis bullosa, an inherited disorder in which the skin
is so sensitive that the slightest touch may cause painful blisters.

You Are Needed: Uses 25 volunteers each year and serves
patients and families with epidermolysis bullosa.

Helper's High in Return: Volunteers do have a chance for
personal contact with the individuals served, doing peer counseling and telephone networking. Special training is not required. Volunteers do not come from one group. Average
number of hours volunteered per week: 1–2. There is no
maximum or minimum number of hours.

Getting Started: This is a national health organization. The
best way to volunteer is to call or write:

> Dystrophic Epidermolysis Bullosa Research
>   Association of America
> 141 Fifth Avenue, Suite 7S
> New York, New York 10010
> 212-995-2220

The Interstitial Cystitis Association (IC)

Mission: To assist patients with IC—an inflammation of the
bladder wall of unknown cause—and also encourage research
and better public awareness about the disease.

You Are Needed: Uses 300 volunteers and serves patients of
IC and their families, urologists, and urologic nurses.

Helper's High in Return: Volunteers do have a chance for

personal contact with the individuals served. They organize support-group meetings and run telephone support networks. Special training is not required. Volunteers have all had the illness. Average number of hours volunteered per week: 3. There is no maximum or minimum number of hours.

Getting Started: This is a national health organization with 30 chapters in 26 states. The best way to volunteer is to write:

> The Interstitial Cystitis Association
> P.O. Box 1553
> Madison Square Station
> New York, New York 10159

Lowe's Syndrome Association

Mission: To foster communication among families, as well as provide information and encourage and support research concerning this rare genetic condition that causes serious health problems in men, ranging from glaucoma to mental retardation.

You Are Needed: Uses 12 volunteers and serves families affected by Lowe's syndrome. Especially wants medical, educational, and social service professionals, as well as anyone interested in the condition.

Helper's High in Return: Volunteers do not have a chance for personal contact. Volunteers primarily are parents and other relatives of children with Lowe's syndrome. Average number of hours volunteered per week: 10. There is no maximum or minimum number of hours.

Getting Started: This is a national health organization. The best way to volunteer is to write or call the president at the national office:

> President, Lowe's Syndrome Association, Inc.
> 222 Lincoln Street
> West Lafayette, Indiana 47906
> 317-743-3634

National Association for Sickle Cell Disease

Mission: To create an awareness of the impact on individuals and families of sickle cell anemia, a blood disorder especially affecting blacks that produces unpredictable attacks of pain and other serious health problems.

You Are Needed: Uses 2,000 volunteers.

Helper's High in Return: Volunteers have a chance for personal contact with individuals served, through summer camp and recreational activities. Special training is not required. Volunteers do not come from one group. Average number of hours volunteered per week: 8. There is no maximum or minimum number of hours.

Getting Started: This is a national health organization with 80 chapters. The best way to volunteer is to call or write:

> National Association for Sickle Cell Disease
> 4221 Wilshire Boulevard, Suite 360
> Los Angeles, California 90010
> 213-936-7205 or 800-421-8453

National Gaucher Foundation

Mission: To assist in finding a remedy and viable treatment for Gaucher's disease, a rare genetic disorder in which fatty material accumulates uncontrollably in the body and leads to damage of the organs and nervous system.

You Are Needed: Uses 10 volunteers and serves people with Gaucher's disease, their families, and medical researchers.

Helper's High in Return: Volunteers do have a chance for personal contact with the individuals served through meetings with patients at major research centers. Special training is not required. Volunteers are people concerned with Gaucher's disease. Average number of hours volunteered per week: 20. There is no maximum or minimum number of hours.

Getting Started: This is an international health organization. It serves the United States, the Netherlands, Israel, England, Australia, and South Africa. The best way to volunteer is to contact:

> National Gaucher Foundation
> 1424 K Street, N.W., 4th floor
> Washington, D.C. 20005
> 202-393-2777

National Hydrocephalus Foundation

Mission: To inform parents and adults with hydrocephalus about this condition, which involves a buildup of fluid in the head.

You Are Needed: Uses 25 volunteers and serves parents and adults with hydrocephalus.

Helper's High in Return: Volunteers do not have a chance for personal contact with the individuals served, but do receive calls from people in their state concerning hydrocephalus and then send information to them. Volunteers are usually adults with hydrocephalus, as well as parents or other related family members. Average number of hours volunteered per week: 2–15. There is no maximum or minimum number of hours.

Getting Started: This is a national health organization. The best way to volunteer is to write:

> National Hydrocephalus Foundation
> 22427 South River Road
> Joliet, Illinois 60436

National Organization for Rare Disorders (NORD)

Mission: To identify, control, and find new treatments for rare, or "orphan," diseases.

You Are Needed: Uses 50–75 volunteers and serves people with more than 5,000 rare disorders.

Helper's High in Return: Volunteers do not have a chance for personal contact with the individuals served. NORD has office work: Volunteers help answer mail and, outside the office, distribute brochures to doctors, libraries, and schools; handle display booths at medical conventions; and attend meetings. Average number of hours volunteered per week: 4. There is no maximum or minimum number of hours.

Getting Started: This is a national health organization. The best way to volunteer is to write, visit, or call:

> National Organization for Rare Disorders (NORD)
> P.O. Box 8923
> New Fairfield, Connecticut 06812
> 203-746-6518

National Pediculosis Association

Mission: To prevent head-lice infestation among children, thereby minimizing their exposure to pesticides.

You Are Needed: Uses 10 volunteers and serves parents, school administrators, school nurses, physicians and pharmacists, camp directors, and day-care providers.

Helper's High in Return: Volunteers do have a chance for personal contact with the individuals served; one volunteer, for example, directs community Head Start programs, doing teaching and networking. Special training is required to know appropriate methods for screening children for lice and passing on accurate information. Volunteers do not come from one group. Average number of volunteers per week: 5. For some volunteers there is a minimum of hours (office staff, for example, serve 20 hours each). There is no maximum number of hours.

Getting Started: This is a national health organization. The best way to volunteer is to write or call:

National Pediculosis Association
P.O. Box 149
Newton, Massachusetts 02161
617-449-NITS

National Tay-Sachs and Allied Diseases Association

Mission: To prevent and research Tay-Sachs and other rare genetic disorders and to educate and provide outreach to affected families.

You Are Needed: An unknown number of volunteers helps families, doctors, nurses, genetic counselors, clergy, librarians, students, media, social workers, and occupational therapists.

Helper's High in Return: Volunteers have a chance for personal contact with the individuals served, helping to do community screening for prevention. Special training is required; the staff provides written (and video) material. They also hold special training sessions if desired. Volunteers are primarily affected families; this illness is found especially in Jewish families. Average number of hours volunteered per week: unknown. There is no maximum or minimum number of hours.

Getting Started: This is an international health organization, with 10 chapters in 8 states, England, and Canada. The best way to volunteer is to call or write:

National Tay-Sachs and Allied Diseases Association
385 Elliot Street
Newton, Massachusetts 02164
617-964-5508

National Tuberous Sclerosis Association

Mission: To support research into the cause and cure of tuberous sclerosis and to provide information, education, and emotional help to people and their families suffering from this genetic disease marked by seizures, mental retardation, tumors, and/or skin lesions.

You Are Needed: Uses 150–200 volunteers and serves people with tuberous sclerosis and their family members, neurologists, pediatricians, and other medical professionals.

Helper's High in Return: Volunteers do have a chance for personal contact with the individuals served, participating in support groups as well as telephone and in-person peer counseling. Special training is not required. Volunteers primarily are relatives or friends of persons with tuberous sclerosis. Average number of hours volunteered per week: 5. There is no maximum or minimum number of hours.

Getting Started: This is a national health organization. The best way to volunteer is to contact:

National Tuberous Sclerosis Association
4351 Garden City Drive, Suite 660
Landover, Maryland 20785
800-225-6872

Prader-Willi Syndrome Association

Mission: To serve as a center for communication and education about this syndrome, caused by a birth defect, which affects body control, intelligence, and behavior.

You Are Needed: Uses 50–100 volunteers and aids people with Prader-Willi syndrome.

Helper's High in Return: Volunteers do have a chance for

personal contact with the individuals served, doing support groups. Special training is required. Volunteer skills desired: knowledge of what the syndrome entails, through reading or personal contact. Most volunteers have a personal connection to the syndrome (a family member). Average number of hours volunteered per week: varies. There is no maximum or minimum number of hours.

Getting Started: This is a national health organization with 27 chapters in 27 states. The best way to volunteer is to contact:

> Prader-Willi Syndrome Association
> 6490 Excelsior Boulevard, E-102
> St. Louis Park, Minnesota 55426
> 612-926-1947

Sickle Cell Anemia Foundation of Greater New York

Mission: To provide information, advocacy, and education on this blood disorder, found primarily among blacks and Hispanics.

You Are Needed: Uses 25 volunteers and serves medical and health professionals as well as patients with sickle cell anemia.

Helper's High in Return: Volunteers help educate the public as well as patients directly in coping with medical bills, educational problems, and other questions. Volunteers do not come from one group. Average number of hours volunteered per week: 15–20. There is no maximum or minimum number of hours.

Getting Started: The foundation has 3 chapters in 2 states, plus Trinidad and Tobago. The best way to volunteer is to call or write:

> Sickle Cell Anemia Foundation of
>   Greater New York
> 1 West 125th Street, Suite 206
> New York, New York 10027
> 212-427-7762

United Scleroderma Foundation

Mission: To aid patients with scleroderma—a chronic disease that literally means *hard skin*—through literature, referrals, quarterly newsletters, chapters, and research grants.

You Are Needed: Uses 2,000-plus volunteers and serves scleroderma patients, families, and the interested public.

Helper's High in Return: Volunteers do have a chance for personal contact with the individuals served, conducting support-group meetings and making home visits. Special training is not required. Volunteers do not come from one group. Average number of hours volunteered per week: 10. There is no maximum or minimum number of hours.

Getting Started: This is a national health organization with 28 chapters in 19 states. The best way to volunteer is to call or write:

> United Scleroderma Foundation
> P.O. Box 350
> Watsonville, California 95077
> 800-722-HOPE (in California, 408-728-2202)

OTHER ILLNESSES

Alzheimer's Association

Mission: To support research for the prevention, cure, and treatment of Alzheimer's disease and related disorders, and to provide support and assistance to afflicted patients and their families.

You Are Needed: An unknown number of volunteers serve patients and families of victims of Alzheimer's disease and related disorders, as well as health professionals and the general public.

Helper's High in Return: Volunteers do have a chance for personal contact with the individuals served, doing support groups, respite-care programs, and information and referral through a helpline. Special training is required and varies with each task. Volunteers do not come from one group. Average number of hours volunteered per week: varies. There is a 2-hour minimum and no maximum number of hours.

Getting Started: This is a national health organization with

196 chapters in 48 states. The best way to volunteer is to contact your local chapter listed in the telephone book or call or write:

Alzheimer's Association
70 East Lake
Chicago, Illinois 60601
800-621-0379

American Diabetes Association

Mission: To prevent and cure diabetes and improve the lives of people affected by the disease.

You Are Needed: Uses 25,000-plus volunteers and serves people with diabetes and their families.

Helper's High in Return: Volunteers do have a chance for personal contact with the individuals served, doing high-risk screening, support groups, health fairs, and camps. Special training is required. Training classes are offered through local offices and national headquarters. Volunteers do not come from one group. Average number of hours volunteered per week: 3–5. There is no maximum or minimum number of hours.

Getting Started: This is a national health organization with 800-plus chapters in all states. The best way to volunteer is to contact your local office or write:

American Diabetes Association
1660 Duke Street
Alexandria, Virginia 22314

American Kidney Fund

Mission: To provide direct financial assistance, comprehensive educational programs, research grants, and community-service projects for the benefit of kidney patients.

You Are Needed: Uses 500–700 volunteers and serves individuals suffering from kidney disease, health care professionals, and the general public.

Helper's High in Return: Volunteers are involved in raising money, clerical help, and educational meetings. Special training is not required for some activities, whereas others require skills in health care, specifically in the renal field. Volunteers do not come from one group. Average number of hours volunteered per week: 2. There is no maximum or minimum number of hours.

Getting Started: This is a national health organization. The best way to volunteer is to call or write:

American Kidney Fund
6110 Executive Boulevard, Suite 1010
Rockville, Maryland 20852
800-638-8299

American Liver Foundation

Mission: To reduce the human suffering caused by liver disease, through research, education, patient-support groups, and donor awareness.

You Are Needed: Uses 2,000 volunteers and serves all ages and ethnic groups.

Helper's High in Return: Volunteers do have a chance for personal contact with the individuals served, doing self-help support-group work. Special training is not required. Volunteers do not come from one group. Average number of hours volunteered per week: varies. There is no maximum or minimum number of hours.

Getting Started: This is a national health organization with 27 chapters in 15 states. The best way to volunteer is through the national office or local chapters. Write:

American Liver Foundation
1425 Pompton Avenue
Cedar Grove, New Jersey 07009

American Lung Association

Mission: To conquer lung disease and promote the maintenance of healthy lungs.

You Are Needed: Uses 170,000 volunteers and serves the general public, patients and their families, and health professionals.

Helper's High in Return: Volunteers do have a chance for personal contact with the individuals served: to conduct stop-smoking clinics, clubs for chronic-lung-disease patients, self-help classes for children with asthma; and also to help staff camps for children with asthma. Special training is required. Many volunteers are professionals such as physical therapists. Local lung associations sponsor training programs. Volunteers do not come from one group. Average number of hours volunteered per week: varies. There is no maximum or minimum number of hours.

Getting Started: This is a national health organization with 134 chapters in 50 states and Puerto Rico. The best way to volunteer is to call your local office or write:

American Lung Association
1740 Broadway
New York, New York 10019-4374

The American Lupus Society

Mission: To determine the cause, cure, and remedies for lupus, a chronic inflammatory disease that is in the same family as rheumatoid arthritis.

You Are Needed: Uses 500 volunteers and serves lupus patients.

Helper's High in Return: Volunteers do have a chance for personal contact with the individuals served, doing monthly meetings, rap groups, and so on. Volunteer skills desired include ability to run discussion groups. Professional training is available for the volunteer. Volunteers are primarily lupus patients, family, and friends. Average number of hours volunteered per week: 4–6. There is no maximum or minimum number of hours.

Getting Started: This is a national health organization with 18 chapters in 14 states. The best way to volunteer is to call or write:

The American Lupus Society
23751 Madison Street
Torrance, California 90505
213-373-1335

American Social Health Association

Mission: To lead the fight against sexually transmitted diseases and their threat against life, health, and society.

You Are Needed: Uses 150 volunteers and serves any individual seeking information on sexually transmitted diseases.

Helper's High in Return: Volunteers do have a chance for personal contact with the individuals served, leading support groups for individuals affected by herpes and their spouses. Special training is required. Volunteers are sent a training video for herpes groups or participate in intense training to become information specialists on a national hot line. Volunteers do not come from one group. Average number of hours volunteered per week: varies There is no maximum or minimum number of hours.

Getting Started: This is a national health organization. The best way to volunteer is to call or write:

American Social Health Association
311 Massachusetts Avenue, N.E.
Washington, D.C. 20002
202-543-9129

Asthma and Allergy Foundation of America

Mission: To help find the cure for, and ultimately eradicate, asthma and other allergic diseases through support of research, education, and service programs.

You Are Needed: Uses 150 volunteers and serves individuals who suffer from asthma and/or allergies, their family/friends, and interested community.

Helper's High in Return: Volunteers do not have a chance for personal contact. They handle telephone requests, conduct telephone surveys, do mailings, and provide clerical and administrative services. Special training is not required. Volunteers do not come from one group. Average number of hours volunteered per week: 8. There is no maximum or minimum number of hours.

Getting Started: This is a national health organization with 12

chapters in 12 states. The best way to volunteer is to call your local chapter or the national office:

> Asthma and Allergy Foundation of America
> 1717 Massachusetts Ave., NW
> Washington, D.C. 20036
> 202-265-0265

Epilepsy Foundation of America

Mission: To seek the prevention, cure, and optimal management of epilepsy and to provide assistance to people affected by the condition and those who serve them.

You Are Needed: Uses approximately 3,000 volunteers and serves people with epilepsy, their families, epilepsy professionals, and anyone else seeking information about the condition.

Helper's High in Return: Volunteers do have a chance for personal contact with the individuals served, helping at summer camps, providing general information to persons with epilepsy, and speaking to groups where people with epilepsy are in attendance. Special training is required and is available at most local affiliates. Volunteers do not come from one group. Average number of hours volunteered per week: 2–5. There is no maximum or minimum number of hours.

Getting Started: This is a national health organization with 90 affiliates in 38 states. The best way to volunteer is to contact your local affiliate or to call or write:

> Epilepsy Foundation of America
> 4351 Garden City Drive
> Landover, Maryland 20785
> 800-EFA-1000

Huntington's Disease Society of America

Mission: To find a cure for Huntington's disease (HD)—a hereditary brain disorder—and to care for HD patients and families.

You Are Needed: Uses 5,000-plus volunteers and serves Huntington's patients and families.

Helper's High in Return: Volunteers do have a chance for personal contact with the individuals served: friendly visitors, information and referral, support groups. Special training is required. Chapters train volunteers for local needs and programs. Volunteers tend to be care givers or at risk for HD. Average number of hours volunteered per week: 3. There is no maximum or minimum number of hours.

Getting Started: This is a national health organization with 31 chapters in 25 states. The best way to volunteer is to call your local chapter or contact the national office:

> Huntington's Disease Society of America
> 140 West 22nd Street, 6th floor
> New York, New York 10011-2420
> 212-242-1968

Juvenile Diabetes Foundation International

Mission: To fund research involving the cause, cure, treatment, and prevention of diabetes.

You Are Needed: Uses over 100,000 volunteers and serves all those involved with diabetes: patients, family members, professionals, libraries, schools, and so on.

Helper's High in Return: Volunteers do have a chance for personal contact, becoming involved in support groups for parents, children, and adolescents. Special training is not required; the experience of having a child with diabetes or being a diabetic is enough background. Volunteers are primarily persons who have some connection to diabetes. Average number of hours volunteered per week: unknown. There is no maximum or minimum number of hours.

Getting Started: This is an international health organization with 150 chapters in 45 states and 9 affiliates worldwide, serving the United States and 9 foreign countries. Chapters are forming in 4 more foreign countries. The best way to volunteer is to contact the world headquarters (national office) and ask for the Public Information Department:

> Juvenile Diabetes Foundation International
> 432 Park Avenue South

New York, New York 10016
800-JDF-CURE

Lupus Foundation of America

Mission: To help eradicate lupus—a chronic inflammatory disease involving the body's immune system—and alleviate the human suffering and cost and burdens associated with the disease through support of research, education, and service programs.

You Are Needed: Uses 3,000 volunteers and serves lupus patients and their families, and medical professionals.

Helper's High in Return: Volunteers do not have personal contact with individuals served. They do participate in support services and raise money. Volunteers do not tend to come from one group. Average number of hours volunteered per week: 20–25. There is no maximum or minimum number of hours.

Getting Started: This is a national health organization with 102 chapters in 47 states. The best way to volunteer is to contact the national office:

Lupus Foundation of America, Inc.
1717 Massachusetts Avenue, N.W., Suite 203
Washington, D.C. 20036
202-328-4550

National Council on Alcoholism

Mission: To combat alcoholism and other drug addictions.

You Are Needed: Uses approximately 10,000 volunteers, who serve alcoholics and addicts and their families as well as the general public.

Helper's High in Return: Volunteers do have a chance for personal contact with the individuals served, especially answering hot lines as well as speaking at community events. Special training is required. Volunteer skills desired: understanding the council's mission and an ability to communicate. There is on-the-job training. Volunteers are primarily alcoholics/addicts and their families. Average number of hours volunteered per week: unknown. There is no maximum or minimum number of hours.

Getting Started: This is a national health organization with 191 chapters in 38 states plus Washington, D.C., and the Virgin Islands. The best way to volunteer is to write or call:

>National Council on Alcoholism
>12 West 21st Street
>New York, New York 10010
>212-206-6770

National Foundation for Asthma

Mission: To help asthmatic patients who cannot afford private care. Also provides education and research.

You Are Needed: Uses an unknown number of volunteers.

Helper's High in Return: Volunteers are involved in various services. Special training is not required. Average number of hours volunteered per week: varies. There is no maximum or minimum number of hours.

Getting Started: This is a local health organization that serves southern Arizona. The best way to volunteer is to contact:

>National Foundation for Asthma, Inc.
>P.O. Box 30069
>Tucson, Arizona 85751-0069
>602-323-6046

National Foundation for Ileitis and Colitis

Mission: To raise funds for research to find the cause and cure of ileitis and colitis, collectively known as inflammatory bowel disease (IBD).

You Are Needed: Uses 1,500 volunteers and serves patients, their families, physicians, and the general public.

Helper's High in Return: Volunteers have a chance for personal contact with the individuals served: to help organize and participate in educational programs on IBD, mutual support groups with other members afflicted with IBD, and professional medical forums. Special training is not required. Volunteers primarily are afflicted with IBD, or a member of their family has the disease or has died from it. Average number of hours volunteered per week: 15–20. There is no maximum or minimum number of hours.

Getting Started: This is a national health organization. It has 84 chapters and satellites in most major market areas in the United States. The best way to volunteer is to call or write national headquarters:

> The National Foundation for Ileitis and Colitis
> 444 Park Avenue South, 11th floor
> New York, New York 10016-7374
> 800-343-3637

The National Foundation for Infectious Diseases

Mission: To support research that will lead to a better understanding of the causes, cure, and prevention of a range of infectious diseases.

You Are Needed: Uses 200 volunteers and serves the general public and health care professionals.

Helper's High in Return: Volunteers lecture, for example, at meetings, health fairs, and AIDS workshops. Volunteers are doctors and nurses. There is no average number of hours.

Getting Started: This is a national health organization with 5 chapters in 5 states. The best way to volunteer is to call or write:

> The National Foundation for Infectious Diseases
> P.O. Box 42022
> Washington, D.C. 20015
> 301-656-0003

National Osteoporosis Foundation (NOF)

Mission: To reduce the widespread prevalence of osteoporosis, through programs of public and professional education, research, advocacy, and public policy.

You Are Needed: Uses 50–75 volunteers and serves young and teenage girls, adult women, and older persons.

Helper's High in Return: Volunteers do not have a chance for personal contact with the individuals served. However, plans call for establishing an 800 hot line—volunteers would be trained to provide information. Volunteers do not come from one group. Average number of hours volunteered per week: 10–20. There is no maximum or minimum number of hours.

Getting Started: This is a national health organization. The best way to volunteer is to contact:

> Administrative Assistant
> The National Osteoporosis Foundation
> 1625 Eye Street, N.W., Suite 822
> Washington, D.C. 20006
> 202-223-2226

United Ostomy Association

Mission: To provide mutual aid, moral support, and education for people with colostomy, ileostomy, or urostomy surgery.

You Are Needed: Uses 5,500 (visiting program) volunteers, and serves people who have had or will have colostomy, ileostomy, or urostomy surgery as well as their families.

Helper's High in Return: Volunteers have personal contact with the individuals served, visiting new ostomy patients in their homes or hospitals; ex-patients bring practical help and courage to new patients. Special training is required; training programs are offered during the year in various regions of the United States and Canada. Volunteers are ex-colostomy, -ileostomy, or -urostomy patients. Average number of hours volunteered per week: varies. There is no maximum or minimum number of hours.

Getting Started: This is a national health organization with 600 chapters and 70 satellites throughout the United States and Canada. The best way to volunteer is to contact your local chapter or the national office:

> United Ostomy Association
> 36 Executive Park, Suite 120
> Irvine, California 92714
> 714-660-8624

PATIENT HELP GENERALLY

American Red Cross

Mission: To help prevent and relieve human suffering, whenever and wherever it occurs.

You Are Needed: Uses 1.1 million volunteers and serves disaster victims, military families, veterans, health and safety educators, and blood recipients.

Helper's High in Return: Volunteers do have personal contact with individuals served; for example, doing health instruction, disaster relief, and programs for the homeless, handicapped children, the elderly, and veterans. Special training is required for some services. Many different kinds of skills are needed, and training is provided at local chapters. Volunteers do not come from one group. Average number of hours volunteered per week: 3. There is no maximum or minimum number of hours.

Getting Started: This is a national health organization with 2,817 chapters in 50 states. The best way to volunteer is to call or visit your local office or write the national headquarters:

American Red Cross
17th and D Streets, N.W.,
Washington, D.C. 20006
202-737-8300

The Holiday Project

Mission: To visit people confined to institutions on holidays.

You Are Needed: More than 22,500 volunteers visit patients in nursing homes and hospitals on Christmas, Chanukah, and other holidays in cities throughout the country.

Helper's High in Return: Volunteers do have a chance for personal contact with the individuals served, bringing gifts and spending time for personal conversation. Special training is required, such as learning personal-contact techniques through in-house training. Volunteers do not come from one group. Average number of hours per week: 1–20. There is no maximum or minimum number of hours.

Getting Started: This is a national health organization with 30 chapters in 35 states serving the United States. The best way to volunteer is to write:

> The Holiday Project
> P.O. Box 6829
> FDR Station
> New York, New York 10150-1906
> 212-532-6158.

VISION

Associated Services for the Blind

Mission: To teach newly blinded individuals to live independently again.

You Are Needed: Uses 500 volunteers and serves elderly persons who are losing their eyesight through advancing age or illness.

Helper's High in Return: Volunteers do have a chance for personal contact with the individuals served, reading to a blind person, accompanying clients on field trips, and working as sales assistants in agency stores called Sense-Sations. Special training is not required. Volunteers do not come from one group. Average number of hours volunteered per week: 3. There is no maximum or minimum number of hours.

Getting Started: This organization serves the residents of the Delaware Valley, Pennsylvania. The best way to volunteer is to call:

> Volunteer Coordinator
> Associated Services for the Blind
> 919 Walnut Street
> Philadelphia, Pennsylvania 19107
> 215-627-0600

Blind Children's Fund

Mission: To provide information, support, and educational programs to parents and blind children (birth to age 7) and to the teachers who work with blind children.

You Are Needed: Uses 20 volunteers and serves parents, professionals, and blind/visually impaired and multihandicapped children.

Helper's High in Return: Volunteers do have a chance for personal contact with the individuals served, assisting in educational activities, for example a music group for blind toddlers, or a movement class for mothers and infants/toddlers, or engaging in stimulating free play with the children while the parents meet. Special training is required. The organization will train volunteers. Previous experience in childhood education and special-needs training would be beneficial for the volunteer. Volunteers are also needed to stuff envelopes, handle computers, and do typing. Average number of hours volunteered per week: 4–6 hours. There is no maximum or minimum number of hours.

Getting Started: This organization is located in Massachusetts and serves the New England states. It *nationally* responds to requests for information. The best way to volunteer is to write or call:

> Parent Coordinator
> Blind Children's Fund
> 230 Central Street
> Auburndale, Massachusetts 02166
> 617-332-4014

National Association for Parents of the Visually Impaired (NAPVI)

Mission: To provide support, information, and service to parents of the visually impaired.

You Are Needed: Uses 50 volunteers.

Helper's High in Return: Volunteers have a chance for personal contact, through workshops and conferences. Special training is required; skills can be obtained from seminars. Volunteers tend to be people involved in the field of visual impairment. Average number of hours volunteered: 5. There is no maximum or minimum number of hours.

Getting Started: The best way to volunteer is to join the

organization and become involved with committees and so on. Write:

> National Association for Parents
>   of the Visually Impaired, Inc. (NAPVI)
> 19 Main Street,
> Camden, New York 13316
> 800-562-6265

National Association for Visually Handicapped

Mission: To aid the partially seeing (not totally blind) by providing a large-print loan library, visual aids, information and referral, counsel and guidance, and education for the general public, professionals and paraprofessionals, and the business community working with the partially seeing.

You Are Needed: Uses 10 volunteers (3 in San Francisco, 7 in New York) and serves persons who have visual impairments but are not totally blind (do not need canes, guide dogs, or Braille).

Helper's High in Return: Volunteers do not have personal contact with the individuals served. Volunteers do not come from one group. Average number of hours volunteered per week: 10. There is no maximum or minimum number of hours.

Getting Started: This is a national health organization and does not have local chapters. The best way to volunteer is to write or call:

> National Association for Visually Handicapped
> 22 West 21st Street
> New York, New York 10010
> 212-889-3141

National Braille Association

Mission: To unite volunteers and professional workers in the production and distribution of reading materials into Braille, large type, and recording.

You Are Needed: Uses more than 100 volunteers, who assist

Braille readers, transcribers, and narrators.

Helper's High in Return: Volunteers do not have a chance for personal contact with the individuals served. Special training is not required. Volunteers do not come from one group. Average number of hours volunteered per week: 3–40. There is no maximum or minimum number of hours.

Getting Started: The best way to volunteer is to contact:

> National Braille Association, Inc.
> 1290 University Avenue
> Rochester, New York 14607
> 716-473-0900.

National Federation of the Blind

Mission: To promote equal opportunities in all aspects of daily life for the blind.

You Are Needed: Uses 50,000 volunteers and serves to integrate the blind into society on the basis of full equality.

Helper's High in Return: Volunteers do have a chance for personal contact with the individuals served, talking with newly blinded persons. Special training is required. Volunteers need an understanding of the agency's philosophy. Volunteers are primarily but not completely blinded individuals. Average number of hours volunteered per week: 10. There is no maximum or minimum number of hours.

Getting Started: This is a national health organization with 500 chapters in 50 states plus Washington, D.C. The best way to volunteer is to call or write the national headquarters:

> National Federation of the Blind
> 1800 Johnson Street
> Baltimore, Maryland 21230
> 301-659-9314

National Society to Prevent Blindness

Mission: To preserve sight and prevent blindness.

You Are Needed: Uses 30,000 volunteers and serves the public, professionals, and the community at large.

Helper's High in Return: Volunteers do have a chance for personal contact with the individuals served, doing vision screening as well as information and referral. Special training is required, which the organization provides. Volunteers do not come from one group. Average number of hours volunteered per week: 2. There is no maximum or minimum number of hours.

Getting Started: This is a national health organization with 26 chapters in 26 states. The best way to volunteer is to contact a local affiliate or the national office:

> National Society to Prevent Blindness
> 500 East Remington Road
> Schaumburg, Illinois 60173
> 708-843-2020

Recording for the Blind (RFB)

Mission: To provide taped educational texts to anyone who cannot read standard printed material because of a visual, physical, or perceptual disability.

You Are Needed: Uses approximately 4,000 volunteers and serves the blind as well as the visually, physically, and perceptually impaired who cannot read standard print or hold a book.

Helper's High in Return: Volunteers have occasional contact, but not on a regular basis, with the individuals served; in some cases volunteers are readers. They also provide clerical support. RFB volunteers are trained in the subject matter in which they record texts (readers are required to have some college education or equivalent). Volunteers do not come from one group; however, most are business and professional people who have experience in a particular area of study. Average number of hours volunteered per week: 2. There is no maximum or minimum number of hours. Recording for the Blind is currently recruiting volunteers who can read advanced or scientific books, as requests from borrowers are increasing in the areas of mathematics, computer science, engineering, natural sciences, law, medicine, and the social sciences.

Getting Started: This is an international health organization with 31 chapters in 17 states and 40 other countries. The best way to volunteer is to call or write national headquarters for referral to a local studio:

> Recording for the Blind
> 20 Roszel Road
> Princeton, New Jersey 08540
> 609-452-0606

Chapter Notes

CHAPTER ONE

1. Hans Selye, *The Stress of Life*, rev. ed. (New York: McGraw-Hill Book Co., 1976), pp. 21–28.

2. Martin E. P. Seligman, *Helplessness, On Depression, Development, and Death* (San Francisco: W. H. Freeman and Company, 1975), pp. 187–88.

3. Herbert Benson, M.D., with Miriam Z. Klipper, *The Relaxation Response* (New York: Avon, 1976), pp. 77–97.

4. James House, et al., "Social Relationships and Health," *Science*, July 29, 1988, p. 541.

5. Meredith Minkler, "People Need People: Social Support and Health," in *The Healing Brain: A Scientific Reader*, edited by Robert Ornstein and Charles Swencionis (New York: The Guilford Press, 1990), pp. 88–97.

6. Ibid.

7. Keith Sedlacek, *The Sedlacek Technique: Finding the Calm Within You* (New York: McGraw-Hill Book Co., 1989), pp. 18–19.

8. Suzanne Kobasa and Mark Puccetti, "Personality and Social Resources in Stress Resistance," *Journal of Personality and Social Psychology*, vol. 45 no. 4, 1983, p. 839.

CHAPTER TWO

1. Keith Sedlacek, *The Sedlacek Technique: Finding the Calm Within You* (New York: McGraw-Hill Book Co., 1989), pp. 140–41.

2. Joel Davis, *Endorphins: New Waves in Brain Chemistry* (New York: Dial Press, 1984), pp. 98–105.

3. Jaak Panksepp, "Altruism, Neurobiology," *Yearbook of Neuroscience* (Boston: Birkhauser, 1989), pp. 7–10.

CHAPTER THREE

1. Pitirim Sorokin, ed., *Forms and Techniques of Altruistic and Spiritual Growth* (Boston: The Beacon Press, 1971), p. vi.

2. Ibid., p. i.

3. Steven Waldman, "Credit For Good Deeds," *Newsweek*, January, 15, 1990, p. 61.

4. Carl Fellner and John Marshall, "Kidney Donors Revisited," *Altruism and Helping Behavior*, J. Philippe Rushton and Richard Sorrentino, eds. (Hillsdale, NJ: Lawrence Erlbaum Associates, 1981), p. 359.

CHAPTER FOUR

1. Steven Locke, M.D., and James Gorman, "Behavioral Immunity," *Comprehensive Textbook of Psychiatry*, fifth ed., edited by Harold Kaplan, M.D., and Benjamin Sadock, M.D. (Baltimore: Williams & Wilkins, 1976), pp. 172–87.

2. David Gelman with Mary Hager, "Body and Soul," *Newsweek*, November 7, 1988, pp. 88–97.

3. Clive Wood, "Optimism and Health: Expecting the Best," *Mind-Body-Health Digest*, 1987, vol. 1, no. 3, p. 3.

4. Neal Miller, Ph.D., "Biomedical Foundations for Biofeedback as a Part of Behavioral Medicine," in *Biofeedback: Principles and Practice for Clinicians*, ed. John Basmajian, M.D. (Baltimore: Williams & Wilkins, 1989), pp. 5–15.

5. John Barber, "Worried Sick," *Equinox*, September–October 1988, no. 108, pp. 91–93.

6. Ibid., p. 104.

7. *Journal of the American Medical Association*, July 18, 1986, vol. 256, no. 3, p. 313.

8. David McClelland and Carol Kirshnit, "The Effect of Motivational Arousal Through Films on Salivary Immunoglobulin A," *Psychology and Health* 2 (1988), pp. 31–52.

9. David McClelland, "Motivational Factors in Health and

Disease," August 1988 Distinguished Scientific Contribution Award Address to the American Psychological Association in Atlanta, Ga.

10. *Science News*, August 26, 1969, p. 141.

11. *Psychosomatic Medicine* 50 (1988), pp. 230–44.

12. David Gelman with Mary Hager, "Body and Soul," *Newsweek*, November 7, 1988, p. 89.

13. Locke and Gorman, "Behavioral Immunity," pp. 71–72.

14. Meyer Friedman and Ray Rosenman, *Type A Behavior and Your Heart* (New York: Alfred A Knopf, 1974), p. 10.

15. "Trusting Hearts Last Longer: Hostility May Be Type A Toxin," *Brain/Mind Bulletin*, March 1989.

16. Redford Williams, M.D., *The Trusting Heart* (New York: Springer Publishing Company, 1988), pp. 90–91.

17. Ibid., pp. 90–103.

18. Ibid., p. 11.

19. Clive Wood, "The Hostile Heart," *Psychology Today*, September 1986, pp. 10–12.

20. Larry Scherwitz, Lewis E. Graham II, and Dean Ornish, "Self-Involvement and the Risk Factors for Coronary Heart Disease," *Advances*, vol. 2, no. 2, Spring 1985, pp. 6–18.

21. Floyd Bloom and Arlyne Lazerson, *Brain, Mind, and Behavior*, 2nd ed. (New York: M. H. Freeman and Company, 1988), pp. 223–24.

22. Richard Restak, M.D., *The Mind* (New York: Bantam Books, 1988), pp. 145–46.

23. Irvin Yalom, *The Theory and Practice of Group Psychotherapy*, 3rd ed. (New York: Basic Books, 1985), pp. 13–15.

24. J. Mossey and E. Shapiro, "Self-related Health: A Predictor of Mortality Among the Elderly," *American Journal of Public Health* 72 (1982): 800–808.

25. Kenneth R. Pelletier, "Sound Mind—Sound Body . . . An Interim Report," presented to Altruist's Health conference, June 16–17, 1988.

CHAPTER FIVE

1. Robert Ornstein and David Sobel, *Healthy Pleasures* (Reading, Mass.: Addison-Wesley Publishing Co., 1989), pp. 235, 237.

2. Daniel Batson and Jay Coke, "Empathic Motivation of Helping Behavior," in *Social Psychophysiology*, edited by John Cacioppo and Richard Petty (New York: The Guilford Press, 1983), pp. 417–31.

3. Suzanne Kobasa and Mark Puccetti, "Personality and Social Resources in Stress Resistance," *Journal of Personality and Social Psychology*, vol. 45 no. 4, 1983, p. 839.

4. Clive Wood, "A Buffer of Hardiness: An Interview with Suzanne C. Ouellette Kobasa," *Advances*, vol. 4, no. 1, 1987, p. 37.

5. Kobasa and Puccetti, "Personality and Social Resources in Stress Resistance."

CHAPTER SIX

1. Martin Seligman, *Helplessness: On Depression, Development, and Death* (San Francisco: W. H. Freeman and Company, 1975), p. 184.

2. Janice Kiecolt-Glaser and Ronald Glaser, "Psychological Influences on Immunity," *American Psychologist*, November, 1988, p. 894.

3. David Gillespie, *Understanding and Combatting Burnout* (Monticello, Ill.: Vance Bibliographies, 1983), p. 18.

4. M. Bramhall and S. Ezell, "How Burned Out Are You?" *Public Welfare*, 39(1), 1981, pp. 23–27.

5. ———, "Working Your Way Out of Burnout," *Public Welfare*, 39(2), 1981, pp. 32–39.

6. Carmen Renee Berry, *When Helping You Is Hurting Me* (San Francisco: Harper & Row, 1988), pp. 6–7.

7. Ibid., p. 32.

8. Ibid., pp. 56–72.

CHAPTER SEVEN

1. William James, *The Varieties of Religious Experience* (New York: Longmans, Green, and Co., 1929), pp. 271–73.

2. Howard R. Greenstein, *Judaism—An Eternal Covenant* (Philadelphia: Fortress Press, 1983), p. 38.

3. Edward Conze, *Buddhism: Its Essence and Development* (New York: Harper Torchbooks, 1959), p. 102.

4. Ibid., pp. 127–28.

5. John A. Hutchinson and James Alfred Martin, Jr., *Ways of Faith: An Introduction to Religion* (New York: The Ronald Press, 1960), p. 301.

6. P. Spratt, *Hindu Culture and Personality: A Psycho-Analytic Study* (Bombay: Manaktalas, 1967), p. 47.

7. Wallace Bennett, *Why I Am a Mormon* (New York: Thomas Bennett & Sons, 1958), p. 238.

8. James, p. 280.

9. Kenneth R. Pelletier, "Sound Mind–Sound Body: Bridging Spiritual and Material Values," presented at the Altruist's Health conference, June 16–17, 1988, pp. 1–26.

10. Ibid.

11. George Vaillant, *Adaptation to Life* (Boston: Little Brown & Co., 1977), pp. 389–391.

12. Jonathan Mark, "People," *The Jewish Week*, May 12, 1989, p. 36.

13. David Adams, "The Imperative to Volunteer: Religious Themes in the Public Pronouncements of American Presidents: Hoover to Reagan," in *Working Papers of the 1989 Spring Research Forum, Philanthropy and the Religious Tradition* (Washington, D.C.: Independent Sector, 1989), pp. 291–304.

14. The Gallup Organization, *Giving and Volunteering in the United States*, survey conducted for the Independent Sector, 1988.

15. *Working Americans: Emerging Values for the 1990's*, The House of Seagram, 1989, pp. 1–150.

16. Pitirim Sorokin, *Altruistic Love: A Study of American "Good Neighbors" and Christian Saints* (Boston: The Beacon Press, 1950), pp. 197–99.

17. *Giving and Volunteering in the United States*, Table 4, "Percentage of Volunteers by Religious Membership."

18. Carol Rittner, R.S.M., and Sondra Myers, eds., *The Courage to Care: Rescuers of Jews During the Holocaust* (New York: New York University Press, 1986), pp. 100–107.

19. Ibid., p. 135.

CHAPTER EIGHT

1. Joan Borysenko, "Healing Motives: An Interview with David C. McClelland," *Advances*, vol. 2, no. 2, Spring 1985, pp. 35–37.

2. David McClelland, "Motivational Factors in Health and Disease," Distinguished Scientific Contribution Award Address to the American Psychological Association, August 1988, Atlanta, Ga. (Also in personal correspondence from McClelland, June 9, 1988.)

3. Helen Harris Perlman, *Relationship: The Heart of Helping People* (Chicago: University of Chicago Press, 1979), p. 53.

4. Ibid., p. 59.

5. Ibid., pp. 55–57.

6. Ibid., p. 57.

7. Robert L. Katz, *Empathy: Its Nature and Uses* (London: The Free Press of Glenco, Collier-Macmillan Ltd., 1963), p. 137.

8. Perlman, p. 62.

9. Ayala Pines and Elliot Aronson, with Ditsa Kafry, *Burnout* (New York: The Free Press, 1981), p. 54.

10. Leonard Sagan, "Family Ties," *The Sciences*, March/April, 1988, pp. 2-29

11. Susan Bell, "Thawing The Ice in The Heart: An Interview with Saul Bellow," *The Writer*, May 1988, p. 15.

12. Charles Darwin, *The Origin of Species*, 6th ed. (New York: Macmillan, 1927), pp. 197–98.

CHAPTER NINE

1. Robert Carbone, University of Maryland, from remarks made at the Independent Sector's 1989 Spring Resources Forum, "Philanthropy and the Religious Tradition," in Chicago, Illinois.

2. Glenn Collins, "The Fears of Children; Is the World Scarier?," *The New York Times*, June 19, 1989, p. 21.

3. Ian Canino, *Seven Days*, February 8, 1989, p. 19.

4. Jeanine Basinger, "Why Do We Cheer Vigilante Cops?," *The New York Times*, July 3, 1989, Op. Ed. page.

5. Arthur Koestler, *Janus: A Summing Up* (New York: Vintage Books, 1978), pp. 1–20.

6. Jonas Salk, *Anatomy of Reality* (New York: Praeger Publishers, 1985), pp. 3–4, 45–46.

7. Alfie Kohn, "Make Love, Not War," *Psychology Today*, June 1988, p. 37.

8. Richard Dawkins, *The Selfish Gene* (New York: Oxford University Press, 1976), pp. 206–15.

9. William James, *Varieties of Religious Experience* (New York: Longmans, Green & Co., 1929), p. 283.

10. "Chronicle," *The New York Times*, May 21, 1990.

11. Sandra Blakeslee, "The Return of the Mind," *American Health*, March 1989, pp. 94–96.

12. Robert Coles, "Our Time for Giving," *50 Plus*, May 1988, p. 88.

13. J. Philippe Rushton and Richard Sorrentino, eds., *Altruism and Helping Behavior* (Hillsdale, N.J.: Lawrence Erlbaum Associates, 1981), p. 105.

14. Daniel Goleman, "Aggression in Children Can Mean Problems Later," *The New York Times*, October 6, 1988, p. B25.

15. Michael Ryan, "When Prisoners Save Lives," *Parade Magazine*, July 2, 1989, p. 9.

16. Mark Satin, "The 1980's Were Better Than We Thought," *New Options*, no. 64, February, 26, 1990, p. 8.

Selected Bibliography

BOOKS

Anderson, Robert, M.D. *Wellness Medicine*. Lynwood, Wash.: American Health Press, 1987.

Barchas, Patricia, ed. *Social Hierarchies*. Westport, Conn.: Greenwood Press, 1984.

Bellah, Robert, et. al. *Habits of the Heart*. New York: Harper & Row, 1985.

Benson, Herbert, M.D., with Miriam Z. Klipper. *The Relaxation Response*. New York: Avon, 1976.

Benson, Herbert, M.D., with William Proctor. *Beyond the Relaxation Response*. New York: Times Books, 1984.

Bloom, Floyd, and Arlyne Lazerson. *Brain, Mind, and Behavior*, 2nd ed. New York: W. H. Freeman and Company, 1988.

Buckley, William F., Jr., *Gratitude: Reflections on What We Owe to Our Country*. New York: Random House, 1990.

Cacioppo, John, and Richard Petty, eds. *Social Psychophysiology*. New York: The Guilford Press, 1983.

Children's Defense Fund. *A Vision for America's Future*. Washington, D.C.: Children's Defense Fund, 1988.

Cooper, Cary, ed. *Stress Research, Issues for the Eighties*. New York: John Wiley & Sons, 1983.

Davis, Joel. *Endorphins: New Waves in Brain Chemistry*. New York: Dial Press, 1984.

Dawkins, Richard. *The Selfish Gene*. New York: Oxford University Press, 1976.

Doherty, William, and Thomas Campbell. *Families and Health*. Beverly Hills, Calif.: Sage Publications, 1988.

Duhl, Leonard, M.D. *Health Planning and Social Change*. New York: Human Sciences Press, 1986.

Fischer, Claude. *The Urban Experience*. Chicago: University of Chicago Press, 1982.

Flanagan, Owen, Jr. *The Science of the Mind*. Cambridge, Mass.: MIT Press, 1984.

Frank, Robert. *Passions Within Reason*. New York: W. W. Norton & Company, 1988.

Friedman, Meyer, M.D., and Diane Ulmer. *Treating Type A Behavior and Your Heart*. New York: Alfred A. Knopf, 1984.

————, and Ray Rosenman. *Type A Behavior and Your Health*. New York: Alfred A. Knopf, 1974.

The Gallup Organization. *Americans Volunteer, 1985*. Princeton, N.J.: The Gallup Organization, 1986.

Gaylin, Willard, et al. *Doing Good: The Limits of Benevolence*. New York: Pantheon, 1978.

Gibbs, Jack. *Social Control, Views From the Social Sciences*. Beverly Hills, Calif.: Sage Publications, 1982.

Goleman, Daniel. *Vital Lies, Simple Truths*. New York: Simon & Schuster, 1985.

Harris, Louis, and Associates. *A Survey on Aging*. New York: Louis Harris and Associates, 1974.

————. *Aging in the Eighties: America in Transition*. New York: Louis Harris and Associates, 1981.

————. *The Bristol-Myers Report: Medicine in the Next Century*. New York: Louis Harris and Associates, 1987.

Independent Sector. *Giving and Volunteering in the United States*. Washington, D.C.: Independent Sector, 1988.

————. *Philanthropy and the Religious Tradition, 1989 Spring Research Forum*. Washington, D.C.: Independent Sector, 1989.

James, William. *Varieties of Religious Experience*. New York: Longmans, Green & Co., 1924.

Justice, Blair. *Who Gets Sick*. Los Angeles: Jeremy P. Tarcher, 1988.

Katz, Robert L. *Empathy: Its Nature and Uses*. London: The Free Press of Glencoe/Collier-Macmillan Ltd., 1963.

Koestler, Arthur. *Janus: A Summing Up*. New York: Vintage, 1978.

Konner, Melvin. *The Tangled Wing—Biological Constraints on the Human Spirit*. New York: Holt, Rinehart and Winston, 1982.

SELECTED BIBLIOGRAPHY

309

Locke, Steven, M.D., and Douglas Colligan. *The Healer Within*. New York: E. P. Dutton, 1986.

Locke, Steven, M.D., and James Gorman. "Behavioral Immunity." In *Comprehensive Textbook of Psychiatry*, 5th ed. Edited by Harold Kaplan, M.D., and Benjamin Sadok, M.D. Baltimore: Williams & Wilkins, 1976. pp. 172–87.

Lorenz, Konrad. *The Waning of Humaneness*. Boston: Little, Brown and Company, 1987.

Lowe, Carl, and James Nechas, eds. *Whole Body Healing*. Emmaus, Pa.: Rodale Press, 1983.

Matarazzo, Joseph, et al., eds. *Behavioral Health*. New York: John Wiley & Sons, 1984.

Miller, Neal. "Biomedical Foundations for Biofeedback as a Part of Behavioral Medicine." In *Biofeedback: Principles and Practices for Clinicans*. Edited by John Basmajian, M.D. Baltimore: Williams & Wilkins, 1989.

———. "How the Brain Affects the Health of the Body." In *Prevention and Early Intervention: The Bio-Behavioral Perspective*. Edited by S. M. Weiss and K. D. Craig., New York: Springer, in press.

Nagler, Michael. *America Without Violence*. Covelo, Calif.: Island Press, 1982.

National Institute of Mental Health. *The Neuroscience of Mental Health*. Washington, D.C.: American Psychiatric Press, undated.

Oliner, Samuel, and Pearl Oliner. *The Altruistic Personality: Rescuers of Jews in Nazi Europe*. New York: The Free Press, 1988.

Ornish, Dean, M.D., *Dr. Dean Ornish's Program for Reversing Heart Disease*. New York: Random House, 1990.

Ornstein, Robert, and David Sobel. *The Healing Brain*. New York: Simon and Schuster, 1987.

———. *Healthy Pleasures*. Reading, Mass.: Addison-Wesley Publishing Company, 1989.

Ornstein, Robert, and Charles Swencionis, eds. *The Healing Brain: A Scientific Reader*. New York: The Guilford Press, 1990.

Padus, Emrika. *The Complete Guide to Your Emotions & Your Health*. Emmaus, Pa.: Rodale Press, 1986.

Panksepp, Jaak. "Altruism, Neurobiology." *Yearbook of Neuroscience*. Boston: Birkhauser, 1989. pp. 7–10.

Perlman, Helen Harris. *Relationship: The Heart of Helping People*. Chicago: University of Chicago Press, 1979.

Pines, Ayala, and Elliot Aronson, with Ditsa Kafry. *Burnout*. New York: The Free Press, 1981.

Raynolds, John, III, and Eleanor Raynolds. *Beyond Success*. New York: MasterMedia, 1988.

Restak, Richard, M.D. *The Mind*. New York: Bantam Books, 1988.

Rivlin, Robert, and Karen Gravelle. *Deciphering the Senses*. New York: Simon and Schuster, 1984.

Roskies, Ethel. *Stress Management for the Healthy Type A*. New York: The Guilford Press, 1987.

Rossi, Ernest. *The Psychobiology of Mind-Body Healing*. New York: W. W. Norton & Company, 1986.

Rushton, J. Philippe, and Richard Sorrentino, eds. *Altruism and Helping Behavior: Social, Personality, and Developmental Perspectives*. Hillsdale, N.J.: Lawrence Erlbaum Associates, 1981.

Sagan, Leonard. *The Health of Nations*. New York: Basic Books, 1987.

Salk, Jonas. *Anatomy of Reality*. New York: Praeger Publishers, 1985.

Schulman, Michael, and Eva Mekler. *Bringing Up a Moral Child*. Reading, Mass.: Addison-Wesley Publishing Company, 1985.

Sedlacek, Keith, M.D. *The Sedlacek Technique: Finding the Calm Within You*. New York: McGraw-Hill Book Company, 1989.

Seligman, Martin E. P. *Helplessness: On Depression, Development, and Death*. San Francisco: W. H. Freeman and Company, 1975.

Selye, Hans, M.D. *The Stress of Life*, revised edition. New York: McGraw-Hill Book Co., 1976.

Sorokin, Pitirim, ed. *Forms and Techniques of Altruistic and Spiritual Growth*. Boston: The Beacon Press, 1971.

Spacapan, Shirlynn, and Stuart Oskamp, eds. *The Social Psychology of Health*. Beverly Hills: Sage Publications, 1988.

Staub, Ervin. "A Conception of the Determinants and Development of Altruism and Aggression: Motives, the Self, and the Environment." In *Altruism and Aggression*. Edited by Carolyn Zahn-Waxler. New York: Cambridge University Press, 1986, pp. 135–63.

————. "To Rear a Prosocial Child: Reasoning, Learning by Doing, and Learning by Teaching Others." In *Moral Development: Current Theory and Research*. Edited by D. DePalma and J. Foley. Hillsdale, N.J.: Lawrence Erlbaum Associates, pp. 113–35.

Stein, Ben. *Hollywood Days, Hollywood Nights*. New York: Bantam Books, 1988.

Task Force on Psychosocial Aspects of Nuclear Developments of the American Psychiatric Association. *Psychosocial Aspects of Nuclear Developments*. Washington, D.C.: American Psychiatric Association, 1982.

Vaillant, George. *Adaptation to Life*. Boston: Little, Brown and Company, 1977.

Wasserman, Harry, and Holly Danforth. *The Human Bond, Support Groups and Mutual Aid*. New York: Springer Publishing Company, 1988.

Williams, Redford, M.D. *The Trusting Heart*. New York: Times Books, 1989.

Yalom, Irvin. *The Theory and Practice of Group Psychotherapy*, 3rd ed. New York: Basic Books, 1985.

Zahn-Waxler, Carolyn, et al., eds. *Altruism and Aggression*. New York: Cambridge University Press, 1986.

PERIODICALS

American Public Health Association. "1990 Exercise Objectives Likely Will Not Be Met." *The Nation's Health*, August 1989, p. 9.

American Red Cross. "Volunteer 2000 Study." *American Red Cross*, November 21, 1988, Sections 1–8.

Barber, John. "Worried Sick." *Equinox*, September–October 1988, no. 108, pp. 91–93.

Barry, Anne. "Doing Good to Feel Good." *New Woman*, December 1987, pp. 60–64.

Batson, C. Daniel, and Jay Coke. "Empathic Motivation of Helping Behavior." In *Social Psychophysiology*. Edited by John Cacioppo and Richard Petty. New York: The Guilford Press, 1983, pp. 417–431.

Bell, Susan. "An Interview with Saul Bellow." *The Writer*, May 1988. p. 15.

Berkman, Lisa, and Leonard Syme. "Social Networks, Host Resistance, and Mortality: A Nine-Year Follow-up Study of Alameda County Residents." *American Journal of Epidemiology*, vol. 109, no. 2 (1979), pp. 186–204.

Blakeslee, Sandra. "The Return of the Mind." *American Health*, March 1989, pp. 94–96.

Borysenko, Joan. "Healing Motives: An Interview with David C. McClelland." *Advances*, vol. 2, no. 2, Spring 1985, pp. 29–41.

Brody, Jane. "Emotions Found to Influence Nearly Every Human Ailment. *The New York Times*, May 24, 1983, pp. C1–C8.

"Can Mind Affect Body Defenses Against Disease?" *Journal of the American Medical Association*, July 16, 1986, p. 313.

Carnegie Council on Adolescent Development. "Turning Points, Preparing American Youth for the 21st Century." *Carnegie Corporation of New York*, June 1989, pp. 1–106.

Clary, E. Gil. "Socialization and Situational Influences on Sustained Altruism." *Child Development* 57 (1986), pp. 1,358–69.

Cohen, Sheldon. "Psychosocial Models of the Role of Social Support in the Etiology of Physical Disease." *Health Psychology*, vol. 7, no. 3 (1988), pp. 269–97.

Coles, Robert. "Our Time for Giving." *50 Plus*, May 1988, p. 88.

Collins, Glenn. "The Fears of Children; Is the World Scarier?" *The New York Times*, June 19, 1989, p. C1.

Dembroski, Theodore, et al. "Components of Type A, Hostility, and Anger-In: Relationship to Angiographic Findings." *Psychosomatic Medicine*, May–June 1985, pp. 219–233.

Emmet-Farnan, Nancy. "A Vote for Selfishness." *Longevity*, May 1989, p. 6.

Flannery, Raymond. "The Stress-Resistant Person." *Harvard Medical School Health Letter*, February 1989, pp. 5–6.

Fox, Bernard. "Depressive Symptoms and Risk of Cancer." *Journal of the American Medical Association*, September 1, 1989, p. 1,231.

Frank, Jerome. "Them and Us (Part I)." *Readings*, March 1987, pp. 4–6.

Franklin, Deborah. "Charm School for Bullies." *Hippocrates*, May–June, 1989, pp. 75–77.

Freudenberger, Herbert. "Today's Troubled Men." *Psychology Today*, December 1987, pp. 46–47.

Gelman, David, with Mary Hager. "Body and Soul." *Newsweek*, November 7, 1988, pp. 46–47.

Gergen, Kenneth, et al. "Individual Orientations to Prosocial Behavior." *Journal of Social Issues*, November 1972, pp. 105–130.

Goleman, Daniel. "Agreeableness vs. Anger." *The Good Health Magazine (The New York Times)*, April 16, 1989, pp. 20–43.

———. "Depressed People and Thought-Control Therapy." *The New York Times*, November 10, 1988, p. B21.

———. "Relaxation: Surprising Benefits." *The New York Times*, May 13, 1986, p. C1.

———. "The Roots of Empathy Are Traced to Infancy." *The New York Times*, March 28, 1989, p. C13.

Growald, Eileen, and Allan Luks. "Beyond Self." *American Health*, March 1988, pp. 51–54.

Harris, Louis. "Examine These Myths of the 80's." *The New York Times*, May 19, 1989, p. A35.

Hellerstein, David. "Plotting a Theory of the Brain." *The New York Times Magazine*, May 22, 1988, p. 15.

House, James, et al. "The Association of Social Relationships and Activities with Mortality: Prospective Evidence From the Tecumseh Community Health Study." *American Journal of Epidemiology*, vol. 116, no. 1 (1982), pp. 123–40.

———. "Social Relationships and Health." *Science*, July 29, 1988, pp. 540–45.

Hurley, Dan. "Getting Help From Helping." *Psychology Today*, January 1988, pp. 63–66.

Hurley, Thomas, III. "Altruism: Self and Other." *Institute of Noetic Sciences Newsletter*, Fall 1986, pp. 1–14.

Institute for the Advancement of Health. "The Health Benefits of Helping." *Institute for the Advancement of Health Report*, no. 102 (1989), pp. 1–9.

Johnson, Ernest, and Clifford Broman. "The Relationship of Anger Expression to Health Problems Among Black Americans in a National Survey." *Journal of Behavioral Medicine*, vol. 10, no. 2, pp. 103–16.

Kiecolt-Glaser, Janice. "Marital Discord and Immunity in Males." *Psychosomatic Medicine* 50 (1988): 213–29.

Kobasa, Suzanne, and Mark Puccetti. "Personality and Social Resources in Stress Resistance," *Journal of Personality and Social Psychology*, vol. 45 no. 4 (1983), p. 839.

Kohn, Alfie. "Beyond Selfishness." *Psychology Today*, October 1988, pp. 34–38.

Korpivaara, Ari. *New Choices*, August 1989, pp. 41–49.

Krebs, Dennis. "Empathy and Altruism." *Journal of Personality and Social Psychology*, vol. 32, no. 6 (1975), pp. 1,134–46.

Kutner, Lawrence. "Parent & Child." *The New York Times*, March 17, 1988, p. C8.

Lederer, Joseph. "Arthritis: The Mind-Body Connection." *Mind-Body-Health Digest*, vol. 2, no. 4, pp. 1–2.

Luck, Mary. "Kevin McCall: Work Is Love Made Visible." *Institute for Noetic Sciences Newsletter*, Spring 1989, p. 21.

Luks, Allan. "A New Youth Movement?" *The Humanist*, November–December 1984, pp. 5–31.

———. "Helper's High." *Psychology Today*, December 1988, pp. 39–42.

Mack, John. "On Being a Psychoanalyst in the Nuclear Age." *Journal of Humanistic Psychology*, Summer 1989, pp. 338–55.

———. "The Threat of Nuclear War in Clinical Work: Dynamic and Theoretical Considerations." Unpublished paper, pp. 1–47.

Madara, Edward. "A Comprehensive Systems Approach to Promoting Mutual Aid Self-Help Groups: The New Jersey Self-Help Clearinghouse Model." *Journal of Voluntary Action Research*, April–June 1986, pp. 57–63.

Mark, Jonathan. "People." *The Jewish Week*, May 12, 1989, p. 36.

McClelland, David. "Motivational Factors in Health and Disease." *Distinguished Scientific Contribution Award Address to the American Psychological Association*, August 1988, Atlanta, Ga. pp. 1–43.

McClelland, David, and Carol Kirshnit. "The Effect of Motivational Arousal Through Films on Salivary Immunoglobulin A." *Psychology and Health*, 1988, vol. 2, pp. 31–52.

Miller, Annetta, et al. "The New Volunteerism." *Newsweek*, February 8, 1988, pp. 42–43.

Minkler, Meredith. "The Social Component of Health." *American Journal of Health Promotion*, Fall 1986, pp. 33–37.

Morris, Gitta. "Pro Bono Work Is Good Business." *The New York Times*, November 29, 1988, Connecticut Section, p. 4.

Mossey, J., and E. Shapiro. "Self-Related Health: A Predictor of Mortality Among the Elderly." *American Journal of Public Health,* vol. 72, 1982, pp. 800–808.

Norman, Michael. "Volunteers in Dual Role on Campus." *The New York Times*, February 10, 1988, p. B9.

Ornstein, Robert, and David Sobel. "The Healing Brain." *Psychology Today*, March 1987, pp. 48–52.

Orth-Gomer, Kristina, and Jeffrey Johnson. "Social Network Interaction and Mortality." *Journal of Chronic Diseases*, vol. 40, no. 10 (1987), pp. 949–57.

Peacock, Mark. "Planning Ahead for Your Freedom Years." *Active Senior Lifestyles*, April 1988, p. 9.

Pelletier, Kenneth R. "Sound Mind-Sound Body . . . An Interim Report." Presented to Altruist's Health Conference, June 16–17, 1988.

Ratliff, Nancy. "Stress and Burnout in the Helping Professions." *Social Casework*, March 1988, pp. 147–54.

Rogers, Malcolm, and Peter Reich. "On the Health Consequences of Bereavement." *The New England Journal of Medicine*, August 25, 1988, pp. 510–11.

Rosenhan, David. "The Joy of Helping: Focus of Attention Mediates the Impact of Positive Affect on Altruism." *Journal of Personality and Social Psychology*, vol. 40, no. 5 (1981), pp. 899–905.

Ryan, Michael. "When Prisoners Save Lives." *Parade*, July 2, 1989, pp. 8–9.

Saccomandi, Patrick. "Can Self-Interest Volunteering Also Serve the Most Needy?" *Voluntary Action Leadership*, Summer 1988, p. 2.

Sagan, Leonard. "Family Ties." *The Sciences*, March–April 1988, pp. 21–29.

Satin, Mark. "Harman: Best & Worst of the New Age." *New Options*, December 28, 1987, p. 7.

Scherwitz, Larry, et al. "Self-Involvement and the Risk Factors for Coronary Heart Disease." *Advances*, vol. 2, no. 2, Spring 1985, pp. 6–18.

Schwebel, Milton. "Cause, Effect, and Nuclear Psychology." *Readings*, June 1987, pp. 19–20.

Science. "Meeting on the Mind." *Science*, January 8, 1988, p. 142.

Shell, Ellen. "Kids, Catfish and Cholesterol." *American Health*, January–February, 1988, pp. 52–57.

Smith, Eleanor. "The New Moral Classroom," *Psychology Today*, May 1989, pp. 32–36.

Smith, Susan, et al. "RSVP Project Evaluation Summary." *Office of Policy & Planning Division of Evaluation, Action*, October 1976, pp. 1–19.

Staub, Ervin, and Feinberg, Helene. "Regularities in Peer Interaction, Empathy, and Sensitivity to Others." Revised Presentation from the Symposium "Development of Prosocial Behavior and Cognitions," at the Meeting of the American Psychological Association, Montreal, 1980, pp. 1–11.

Stuart, Charles. "Nightmare in Princeton." *The New York Times*, May 26, 1989, p. A31.

Syme, Leonard. "People Need People." *American Health*, July–August 1982, pp. 49–51.

Tierney, John. "Wired for Stress," *The New York Times Magazine*, May 15, 1988, p. 81.

U.S. Department of Education. "Youth Indicators 1988." *Trends in the Well-Being of American Youth*, August 1988, pp. 1–135.

Vaux, Kenneth. "Religion and Health." *Preventive Medicine* 5 (1976), pp. 522–36.

Weidner, Gerdi, et al. "The Role of Type A Behavior and Hostility in an Elevation of Plasma Lipids in Adult Women and Men." *Psychosomatic Medicine*, vol. 49, no. 2 (1987), pp. 136–45.

Wilber, Ken. "On Being a Support Person." *The Journal of Transpersonal Psychology*, November 2, 1988, pp. 141–60.

Williamson, Gail, and Margaret Clark. "Providing Help and Desired Relationship Type as Determinants of Changes in Moods and Self-Evaluations." *Journal of Personality & Psychology*, in press.

Wood, Clive. "A Buffer of Hardiness: An Interview with Suzanne C. Ouellette Kobasa." *Advances*, vol. 4, no. 1 (1987), pp. 37–45.

———. "Optimism and Health: Expecting the Best." *Mind-Body-Health Digest*, vol. 1, no. 3, (1987), p. 3.

Index